Robin Shelton

THE INCOMPLETE ANGLER

One Man's Search for His Ultimate Fishing Experience

Sidgwick & Jackson

To Mum, for Mitten Pond

First published 2008 by Sidgwick & Jackson
an imprint of Pan Macmillan Ltd
Pan Macmillan, 20 New Wharf Road, London N1 9RR
Basingstoke and Oxford
Associated companies throughout the world
www.panmacmillan.com

ISBN 978-0-283-07053-2

A CIP catalogue record for this book is available from
the British Library.

Printed and bound in Great Britain by
Mackays of Chatham plc, Chatham, Kent

Contents

Preface

He who binds himself to a joy
Does the winged life destroy;
But he who kisses the joy as it flies
Lives in eternity's sun rise.

William Blake, *Eternity*

I am floating, along with the first spent, ochre foliage of autumn – as stealthy and noiseless as a puckered kiss on a sleeping baby's cheek – somewhere along the Helford river in west Cornwall. My precise location I cannot tell you. Primarily because my precise location is nearly as much of a mystery to me as the impulse that brought me here in the first place, and secondly because these grounds are guarded fiercely and jealously by those who have spent many long days in their discovery. All I know, and all I am prepared to divulge, is that I am somewhere between the imaginary line connecting Mawnan Shear with The Gew to the east and the upper, silted and brackish reaches of Bishop's Quay in the west. A glance at the Ordnance Survey Explorer map of the area will reveal that this does not narrow things down an awful lot, but broadly speaking I would rather be accused of ambiguity than come back to my car after a day's fishing to find four flat tyres.

All that lies between me and this most tranquil and benign of estuaries is around twenty-five kilograms of hollow plastic kayak – flat-bottomed, open-topped and hollow. Some use these craft for exploring, some for accessing places not available by any other means. Others use them simply to escape the land – to, in a physical as well as a practical sense, leave behind all that which pins them down on shore. I am sat atop this vessel – so clumsy on land, so poised on water – for all three of these reasons. And to engage some fish in a little dialogue. In front of me are two watertight hatches designed for storing the equipment required for a day's peaceful leisure but, apart from the necessary safety equipment, they are empty. All I need is either strapped securely in front of me in the form of a 9-foot long, sub-4-ounce single-handed fly rod and accompanying silent-retrieve large-arbour reel, or in the chest pocket of my waders in the form of a waterproof wallet snap-sealing a collection of my home-wrought, feather-bodied lures – Deceivers, Clouser Minnows, Whistlers, mackerel and shrimp patterns along with some more 'off-piste' concoctions of my own. Along with a flask, some food, 2 litres of water and a pair of clippers on a retractable leash for switching flies, this is all I need for a day of engagement in probably the least well-known, but possibly the most rapidly developing branch of angling – I am fly fishing in salt water.

This stretch of water, with its Huckleberry Finn panorama of spent, abandoned boats and hand-painted oyster-bed signs atop crooked poles, is one of thirty-seven protected bass nursery areas around the country. This vital measure, along with restrictions on mesh sizes for commercial fishermen and the implementation of a still shockingly small minimum landing size, has gone some way to restoring the population of this remarkable fish to its pre-trawler heyday. Here it is forbidden to target bass from any vessel, so instead I am on the prowl for mullet – canny, flirtatious, soft-lipped and indignantly hard fighting when hooked. I may also bump into the odd mackerel – vastly underrated in the fight on this gossamer gear and hugely undervalued when it comes to a meal. There is also the possibility (although not the probability) of a gilthead bream or two. I've heard tell of fifteen-pounders, but I'm not holding my breath – it is pretty much all I can hear, and without it the quiet would be too eerie.

The silty dregs and massive concentration of fish stocks of low tide are two hours away, and paddling against the ebb has sapped me, making my arms feel pumped with mercury, not blood. I decide to weigh anchor and sit for a while in a place where, if only for safety's sake, just one other person on this shrunken planet knows me to be, and fish. I free my 6/7-weight rod from its retaining bungee, pull the tapered leader through its twisted snake rings and fasten a size 2 Deceiver to the 6-pound, 3-foot tippet. A breeze as light as the day, barely a Force 2, swirls in plumey gusts across the surface of the water. Just enough to break the surface tension – glass-flat is no use as the fish will spook too easily. Sometimes the only time you know you've found a fish when paddling one of these vessels is just as you slide over the top of it and you recognize each other's presence in the same moment, each as startled as the other. In a breath like this, whatever is on the surface of the water is broken up. I am as good as invisible.

I tie my Deceiver – six white saddle-hackle feathers, white bucktail, peacock Angel Hair, hot pink Fluoro Fibre and a pair of stick-on holographic dome eyes – to the tippet using a knot invented by the same guy who came up with this pattern. The Lefty Kreh's Loop is similar to the usual blood knot, but allows the fly to move more naturally during the retrieve. It is also stronger. Before I tighten, I dab a small blob of saliva onto it in order to reduce the risk of friction burn and subsequent reduction in strength. The worst thing that can fail when you hook a fish is your knots. Finding an excuse for everything else is easy. As I tie and prepare for casting I notice how the boat, prey to the current, – has been swinging itself lazily around the anchor, which has found purchase in the black, viscous, oily bed. I am fixed around what I have decided is to be, for a few moments at least, the centre of my world.

I haul myself ninety degrees anticlockwise so that my wading boots are dangling over the side of the boat and pull out sufficient line against the reel's ratcheting drag. Just as there is nothing like casting a fly at sea to remind you how small most trout waters are, so there is no sound as deafening as a reel ratchet in a deserted, flat Force 1½. And nothing like a small amount of noise to raise a smile at just how peaceful your surroundings are. And how well you fit within them. A few more jet-roars of the rod tip swishing back and forth, whipping the throttled fly twenty yards or so in front of me, and the lure is sinking, beckoning, enticing. Deceiving? I pull the line in a steady figure-of-eight retrieve, but not this time. Not on the first cast of the day. I finish the retrieve, allowing the thick line to fall in lazy bright-green loops on the creased, glinting water until there is ten feet or so of it between the rod tip and the leader knot, then pull the fly violently from the water towards my backcast. Sometimes this sudden flash will fool a fish into snatching, but the lure hurtles empty past my emptying head and I repeat the cycle.

And a few more times. Each time to a different place – a fresh angle, a new hour around the clock-face. A few adjustments with the paddle or with the pulley system my anchor is attached to in order to allow me to cast to the early-evening big hand. At about seven o'clock, there is a nudge, followed immediately by a pull and a twitch. This is only a small fish, maybe not even a pound, but on equipment like this, size really is irrelevant. As it struggles, I breathe a sigh of relief that it isn't a bass. Not a mullet, either. Mullet are more tentative in the take, but fight harder when they know they've been had. They don't scrap like this though, swimming about in excited little circles like a demented puppy chasing its tail, darting here and there so quickly that it seems there is nowhere in between the two, away from you like a torpedo, then towards you as if torpidly resigning itself. But it's just trying to loosen the hook. Mackerel will do virtually everything bar say 'please' to get away. Eventually, I bring it alongside. It is still writhing the odds when it comes to hand. In a way I don't want it to end, but it is my responsibility to stay well behind the thick and immovable line between sport and cruelty. Just below the anus, the mackerel has a short, sharp spike. I have found out the painful way that this is best avoided – the salt for that cut is already waiting to be let in. With the rod tip high to retain tension and to take the pressure of the leader and spider-silk tippet, I grasp the fish by means of a finger in each gill. Placing my thumb on its 'neck' and pushing hard while at the same time drawing my two gill fingers towards me I snap its backbone mercifully before it has had a chance to realize it is in the thin air. I scoop some water into a recess in the boat and place this stiff missile in it to keep it fresh. Less than a pound he may be, but he is legal and enough for tomorrow's breakfast.

The thought of food has its usual effect, and I lug up the four collapsible spikes of the anchor and head for a nearby low-tide bay. I toy with the idea of mackerel sushi, but instead opt for the more substantial sandwiches I had prepared earlier, washed down with a couple of mugs of tea. As I prepare to paddle further upstream to the low-water flats, thick with thin-lipped mullet, I notice that the breeze has stiffened slightly, and backed a few degrees south-east. It is an hour or so before slack water, and the ebb has revealed the beginnings of a gravel bar protruding into the estuary. The combination of tide and wind has ensured that the seaward side of the bar is churned up nicely. Bass, skulking, predatory creatures, can be lazy in nature (especially the bigger ones) and will often lie in the refuge of just such a feature, waiting for any morsel that is swept their way by the tide. Wading along that bar, casting a lure and allowing it to drift over the drop before the retrieve will surely entice a take or two. Besides, I'd had enough of paddling against the tide before I'd even got onto the water. Sometimes the next step is to take no steps at all.

I snip the tippet just above the hook eye and replace my Deceiver with a small mackerel pattern that I made a couple of evenings ago. Blue bucktail, white bucktail, two matching grizzle hackles, some blue Krystal Flash, a couple of strands of peacock-eye herl and a pair of sinking dumb-bell eyes. Blue thread. If I may be allowed the immodesty, it's a beauty – the fish may not really give a damn whether or not the hackles are perfectly symmetrical, but I sure do. While I make flies, I try to imagine whether, if I were a fish, I would want to try to eat what I am tying. I think that this one is a bit tasty.

I walk out stiffly, carefully, feeling the ground for larger rocks or sudden drops. The water is compressing my waders into vacuum-packed folds around my legs and groin area. Cast one does not amount to much – either I am a little nervous or I am not hungry enough. I try to relax, before I realize that I am about as relaxed as I get, and simply excited – happy – at being where I am and doing what I am doing. I then remind myself that what I have to do is stop trying. Stop *trying* to cast. Stop *trying* to relax.

It may never happen on the first cast, but sometimes it does on the second. I let the 'mackerel' drop further this time before beginning the retrieve. This time a jerky 'injured fish' approach. On the fourth pull there is a definite 'hit'. No nudging, tickling or nuzzling – just a slam and a furious, screaming run. I allow the line to run through my fingers until all the slack is taken, then let the clickety drag on the reel take over. If this bass – for this is what it surely is – wants to swim, then swim it shall. This is a good fish for an estuary – probably around three pounds, and although the weakest part of my gear has a breaking strain of six pounds, if I try to pull against this kind of force something will, undoubtedly, give out. This is not about 'fighting', and concepts of 'winning' or 'losing' have become outmoded. By the nature of my tackle, and out of respect for this animal, I only desire to play. After taking about ten yards of line, my quarry decides to change tactics and swim back towards me. I am fishing with barbless hooks, which not only makes unhooking them far easier and less traumatizing (for the fish), but also makes it infinitely easier for the fish to throw the hook. Fishermen do not use 'tight lines' as a valediction for nothing, so I strip in line at a rate that I hope will ensure just that. Luckily, it does, and the fish is virtually at my feet in as much time as it has taken for me to regret not having brought my camera. Its initial run has tired this creature, so I stoop to bring it to hand. But as soon as it sees what I have in mind, it is off once more – upstream this time, then in an arc wide enough to strip sufficient line off my reel to partially expose the rarely seen backing. It weaves and jerks, sometimes seeming to reverse away from me, tugging and waggling from side to side. Eventually, though, I bring it in. It is one thing to allow a fish to have its say, but quite another to let it exhaust itself beyond the point of recovery. I cradle its belly as I slip the hook from its huge jaws, carefully avoiding its razor-edged and bony gill plates and monstrously sharp dorsal spines. It is easily a legal fish. Current legislation has increased the minimum landing size for bass from 36 to 40 centimetres. This is still too small. Bass do not spawn until they are at least 42 centimetres, and many people, myself included, do not feel comfortable killing a bass until 45 centimetres, if at all. This one seemed to look down at my lure before I unhooked it with an awareness that I had never seen before in a fish. I then realize that I do not need my camera. What has happened between me and that fish – what happens between any fisherman and his catch – is, or should be, essentially, private.

I hold this titanium-silver ingot with its head towards the current until I feel it is squirming strongly enough to be released. As it makes its first convulsions towards freedom, I gently run my fingertips against its scaly shank, and smile as it swims off, warier than it had been five minutes before, but still healthy. I watch it shimmer and flash, before disappearing back into a medium below the surface of which my barbless hooks have only just begun to sink.

Introduction

For most of us it's a question of priorities. Do we want to feed our family with real fresh food, including meat of traceable provenance and genuine quality? Everyone's instinct must surely be to answer 'yes' to this question. Yet we seem all too ready to save pennies on food so we can spend pounds on cars, clothes and computer games. This tendency has to be worth a rethink.

Hugh Fearnley-Whittingstall, *The River Cottage Meat Book*

Five thousand and forty.

This figure, I am fairly reliably informed by maths teacher and fellow allotment-holder Dennis, is the number of recipes it is possible to concoct using equal quantities of just seven vegetables. Just how accurate this information is I have not troubled myself to find out, as by the time we got to what felt like at least number seventy-three (carrot, onion and potato soup with peas as croutons) the boys and I had become of the same mind as the eponymous hero of *Withnail and I*. We wanted something's flesh.

There are two main methods of getting flesh: buying it from somebody else, or catching and/or killing it yourself. One of the benefits of growing my own vegetables was that it had instilled in me an increased awareness of certain quality and safety issues regarding the food I was eating. Because of this, there also developed a suspicion that if we did want something's flesh, then the animal that has sacrificed itself (an expression that perhaps suggests a level of volition with which the beast in question may take issue) should have been allowed a natural, unrestricted life and a dignified, rapid and painless death.

This heightened and more holistic awareness of welfare issues – both of consumer and consumed – made me look at these two methods of obtaining meat in somewhat different ways. Previously, my only real criteria for the meat that I bought were that I could afford it, that it wasn't riddled with maggots and that it wasn't still moving. Issues of animal welfare, of exactly what it was that I was eating and indeed of how it actually tasted (usually, and suspiciously, of whatever it was being cooked with) didn't really come into it.

Most supermarkets have a reasonable range of free-range and/ or organic meat products on offer, as do many butchers, even if sometimes you have to ask for it specifically. One of the most successful (and often enjoyable) means of tracking down really good-quality fish, game and other meat, though, is a trip to a local farmers' market. I am very lucky in that the twice-monthly event in Winchester is one of the country's very best, with a huge range of produce, from cakes to calves' liver, on offer. It is usually possible to chat with the people who either reared or killed the animals, to see photographs of them gambolling and frolicking happily with not a care in the worl— Hang on – I can feel a pang of vegetarianism coming on.

Just a pang. The problem, however, with buying any kind of welfare-conscious meat is the often prohibitive cost. Whether or not it is possible to place a value on tucking into a roast chicken knowing that it it did not spend its criminally short life in a space no brighter or larger than a shoebox and being injected with hormone and antibiotic cocktails is open to question. Suffice to say that compassion is not without its financial price – sometimes this is more than many people, myself included, can afford.

Before considering method number two of getting flesh, I could, of course, have toyed with the idea of going vegetarian. No chance. Not on your nelly. Now here I could drone on about how we're designed to be carnivores blah-de-blah because if we weren't we wouldn't have incisors in our array of teeth, and blather about how our glorious countryside, so beloved of all dietary persuasions tum-te-tum, would not actually look like it does, la-di-da, if we didn't eat meat (drystone walls and hedges aren't there to keep the crops from roaming about). I could witter on about the health of my children bingy-bangy-bong-bong and how their oh so rapidly growing frames might not be quite so robust were it not for the meat-exclusive vitamins and minerals they are getting. However, I'm not going to do any of that because it would be downright hypocritical because, compared with my primary reason for eating meat, I couldn't give a nut loaf about any of that. The real reason I do not wish to be a vegetarian is that I REALLY BLOODY LIKE MEAT! Sizzling, salty bacon; a thick, iron-rich slab of bloody, pink and blue steak; a delicate, fatty and sweet enough without the apples thank you little grilled pork chop and, of course, rosemary-roast, garlic-infused, heady, nostril-flaring and pungent lamb. Yep, little baby baa-lambs, Porky the pig, Ermintrude the cow and, of course, the eminently less cute and anthropomorphized but, to me, stomach-rumblingly, mouth-wateringly diverse array of seafood we have at our disposal. Love 'em all, and, to be frank, the bloodier the better.

I actually did forgo meat for just over four years in my early twenties in a misguided attempt at being healthy. This would have been just fine, and I may still be a carrot-cruncher now, if I actually enjoyed eating vegetables as opposed to tolerating them. As it transpired, though, a diet of peanut-butter sandwiches and a limited variety of recipes involving tomato and pasta is no way to put hairs on your chest, so a few years before she married me, Alex (now my ex-wife) cooked up a greasy, squelchy, juicy, melting and tender coq au vin. I was cured, and, in an attempt to catch up, the amount of dead things I have cooked on a regular basis since then is immense. The trouble is that, at farmers' market, butcher's or even supermarket prices, eating only free-range, organic arms and legs was going to cost, well, an arm and a leg. I came to the ineluctable conclusion that if we were going to get an environmentally friendly, guilt-free and tasty protein fix, I was going to have to get my hands dirty. Or, more precisely, bloody.

My initial intention was to tackle two ways of rendering animals ready for the oven: namely, shooting and fishing. However, in order to own a gun with sufficient power to kill an animal humanely (i.e. instantly and predictably) it is first necessary to obtain a licence that allows you to do so. Now, if this had simply been a question of popping down to the post office with a picture of the gun that I fancied and asking for a licence please, then I would have done it years ago and shot all the local cats. However, having done my research, it seemed that there was a little more to it than that. For a start, you need a proper gun safe bolted to at least five concrete surfaces, a six-month police surveillance operation to ensure your suitability and stability, a statement confirming your identity, written in blood, from your local MP, vicar *and* chosen patron saint (St Jude, in this case, would seem most appropriate) and finally, two 5,000-word eulogies written as testament to your moral fibre and upstanding character from a brace of people who have known you for at least five years longer than you have been alive. I may have exaggerated a little here and there, but I'm afraid that when I got to the bit about allowing a policeman to poke his nose around my house I switched off. It seemed to me to be a tedious if understandable ball-ache of a process to go through in order for me to legally own something that would probably end up quite literally costing me that arm and/or leg. Besides, I have a diagnosed history of relatively mild but nonetheless unpredictable mental illness behind me. Quite honestly, if I was a copper, I wouldn't let me get within a country mile of a shotgun. As my allotment buddy Stevie will testify to, I can even be a liability with a spade if I'm in the wrong mood.

It's true that I, along with anyone else over seventeen who is capable of operating a wax crayon without dribbling, am permitted to own an air rifle of not more than 12 foot-pounds of power. Indeed, I have two of them. The snag was that preliminary research with these devices had demonstrated that I could not hit the broad side of a barn with a blunderbuss at ten paces. The likelihood of me rapidly and painlessly curtailing the life of anything furry or feathery with any air rifle without being close enough to club it with the blunt end seemed remote indeed.

The *coup de grâce*, as far as the idea of shooting was concerned, was dealt by a passage in a book entitled *The Sporting Gun* by the splendidly bearded James Douglas. I picked this up in the Oxfam Books and Music shop in Winchester for what I thought was a fairly hefty £6.99. Hefty, until I remembered that the money was very likely to be going to help someone who perhaps didn't have the means, time or opportunity to consider the gathering of food in the same recreational light as I was. The passage in question described the wonderfully onomatopoeic process called 'the gralloch'. This, apparently, is the huntsman's term for what everyone else would call 'dragging the still-warm, shiny and pulsating guts out of a deer you've just shot in the head'. The word seems so appositely visceral somehow – perhaps sonically descriptive of the noise you might hear as an animal's insides fall onto the dry, shifting carpet of needles in a conifer forest. Or maybe (and perhaps even more likely in my case) 'gralloch' is representative of the noise made by the contents of my stomach being ejected shortly after the intestines of the deer. I reckoned it was probably a safer bet to get the mammals and birds from the farmers' market after all.

Fishing was different, however. I was an old hand. It was in my blood. I had been fishing for over thirty years. I first fished at the age of four, alongside my father perched awkwardly on a hot jetty while on holiday, blunting our penknives chopping bait on the concrete. Impressive statements indeed; if only they were all wholly true. They might *imply* that I had accrued over three decades' worth of know-how, guile, lore, local knowledge and enough stories of the Ones That Got Away to, erm, to fill a book, but I hadn't. A more truthful statement might read, 'I first went crab fishing off a jetty in south-west Scotland when I was four, since when I have, on the odd occasion, dangled a bit of bait in various bodies of water around the country. Even more infrequently I have pulled something edible out of them.'

'Crabbing', from that holiday jetty with my family, was an activity that at once both fascinated and repelled me. I was held transfixed by the delicacy and subtlety with which it was necessary to haul the catch, hand over smooth and rhythmic hand, from the water. I also remember being awed by the sheer determination displayed by the crabs as they clung and spun, sometimes single-pincered, to the bait, the other claw waving and snapping at the air. I could never understand, as a child, why they held on so desperately to the bait and to their fate. Why didn't they simply let go once they were removed from their safe saline security and brought into the sparse, unfamiliar and thin air? Maybe it takes an adult mind to grasp such things.

I think that my sense of repulsion also had its root in this transition. Quite apart from the horrifying resemblance that crabs bear to large, robotic, aquatic spiders (my only true phobia), I could not help feeling a sense of guilt – even if I did not vocalize it or even recognize it as such then – at the imposition of discomfort (sometimes, accidentally, even death) on these gurgling, bubbling, stiletto-legged animals purely for the sake of my own entertainment or amusement.

A natural development, then, morally speaking, was for me to progress on to fishing proper. To fishing for the sake of eating. Somehow, to my young mind, this was infinitely more justifiable than distressing or killing animals for the sake of sport. My now slightly older mind cannot help but concur. At least, having plucked this creature rudely and mercilessly from its home, I could pay it some perverse kind of respect by looking it in the eye before killing it. This progression from 'crabbing' to fishing really was, with the benefit of hindsight, only a development in a moral sense. In terms of technique, I didn't really move on at all for, well, let's think now – just over thirty years, I suppose. I had never made it beyond 'put bait on hook, which is attached to line, reel and rod. Throw bait in water. Wait. Jiggle bait about a bit. Wait. Wait a bit longer. Get bored of waiting and pull bait and/or fish from water.' When I began my journeys towards becoming a born-again angler, one of my purposes was to find out whether there was, in fact, any more to fishing than that anyway, and which form of fishing might convince me that this was indeed true.

Between these shimmering childhood holidays, I would attempt to get a fishing fix by trying my hand in fresh water. For all the success I had, I may as well have dispensed with the tackle and done just that and tickled trout. What's more, I just didn't have the enthusiasm for it – it was the smell, the taste, the sound of the sea that drew me. I spent fifty weeks of the year about as far from any salt water as it is possible to get in Britain, and my angling attempts there were nothing more than me trying, through muscle, memory and association, to recapture those clipped fortnights in August, when the smell of warm salt would permeate the cavity behind my nostrils and when everything dazzled with the scrape of scaled skin on concrete under mackerel skies.

Some thirty or so years later, the day after the longest of the year, I found myself sitting in my doctor's consulting room. The seasons had begun their steady but inexorable slide towards autumn and darkness, and the notion of tackling up and heading to some distant but familiar coastal spots to get into a spot of fishing as a means of providing food had been trickling into my psyche since just before the spring equinox. In addition to this impulse, I had reckoned that, if we really do get 'three score years and ten', my life had just turned a similar corner to the year – just past the half-way mark, and I felt an urge to take stock. After those Scottish holidays, most of my adult life has been spent within a few long casts of the sea, and in all of these places I have fished at least a little. I thought that it might be interesting to revisit them – perhaps also to get a glimpse of my previous selves in varying guises.

The room was warm enough to raise a bead of sweat merely by walking into it, and all the swivelling desktop fan could achieve was to rhythmically blow warm air back towards me, then let it hang around my body like a thick cloak while it completed its oscillation. I had just had a routine check-up, and everything, I was assured, was where it should have been and doing roughly what it was supposed to be doing. Out of surprise combined with a pang of schoolboy guilt that I felt that I'd got away with something, I asked a little too quickly and eagerly whether there was anything else I could do in terms of my lifestyle that might increase my chances of making sure it stayed that way. I told Dr Roberts that I was eating reasonably well and that I exercised daily. Scratching a sudden and mysterious itch on my nose, I asked him whether there was anything I should be including more of in my diet, perhaps, other than the obvious fruit, vegetables, lager, etc. He scrolled down my seemingly interminable medical records on his computer screen.

'You've got a history of mental health problems, yes?'

'That's right. Manic depression.'

'Uh-huh.' Dr Roberts turned his swivel chair towards me, tilted it back and laced his fingers. 'Omega-3 fatty acids.'

'Oh, right, er – what can I eat that's got plenty of those in it?'

'Well, you *can* buy tablets or capsules from health food shops, but a really good natural source of it is fish, especially oily ones like mackerel.'

I needed no further incentive. All I was lacking was some gear.

1 Gear, Gadgets, Gizmos and Geeks

> *The fisherman loves his tackle. It is an obsessive love and, like*
> *most obsessions, irrational. Golfers do not, after all, talk fondly*
> *about their three irons; footballers don't hurry home after a*
> *game to polish up the ball. Yet anglers will spend hours debat-*
> *ing the relative merits of rods, reels, lines, bits of metal, plastic,*
> *fur and feather which to any impartial passer-by look nearly*
> *identical.*
>
> Jeremy Paxman, *Fish, Fishing and the Meaning of Life*

Most men, if pushed, would grudgingly (or in my case quite
enthusiastically) acknowledge that they are gear freaks. What is
perhaps less well understood is that, by some strangely apposite
spooneristic quirk, the admission of this trait automatically con-
firms us as much freer geeks. I wish to inspect some of the reasons
for this predominantly masculine characteristic (the acquisition
and categorization of gadgets often seemingly for its own sake)
later on; however, I should like to pause for a moment here to consider the notion of the 'geek', with particular reference to its
largely derogatory overtones.

I don't think that a great deal of new ground is being broken
when I suggest that the post-feminist male has become confused,

emasculated and, well, a bit screwed up. Rightly or wrongly (overwhelmingly the latter – I am all for equality), until the mid twentieth century, men generally 'controlled' women and, since the advent of feminism, women have, rightly or wrongly (overwhelmingly the latter – I am all for *equality*) increasingly taken an upper hand. A friend of mine has a lovely phrase to follow 'As much use as a . . .' ('chocolate teapot', 'one-legged man in an arse-kicking contest', etc.). His is 'a man in an advert'. At times I think this is funny, but at others it makes me want to weep. At least it would do if I felt entirely comfortable about weeping. It strikes me that men have been shovelled into a corner where we are implored to show our feelings, but when we do we often get branded as weak, lily-livered and oversenstive. We get the sense that we should be 'real men', but haven't got any idea exactly what that is any more. We have, rightly, lost our previous 'control' over women; however, instead of the two sexes achieving some kind of mutually beneficial equilibrium, the pendulum seems to have swung the other way. When I was a teenager, it was deemed perfectly acceptable to bandy the phrase 'A woman needs a man like a fish needs a bicycle' around like some kind of whimsical charm. This sort of glibness may well have spelled liberation for a generation of women. For my generation of men it has spelled redundancy. Besides, it is a phrase that seems to desert women's mouths when they can't get the U-bend back on underneath the kitchen sink. So, men have not only – rightly – in one sense lost control, but have also – wrongly – been made to feel in some ways outcast, superfluous and belittled. If one more person remarks to Jackie, my girlfriend, on seeing me cooking, washing up or doing the laundry that she's got me 'well trained' I swear on my father's grave I shall clout them. Ladies, you wanted out of the kitchen.

Well, that's fine, but who did you think was going to fill the space – a fish on a bicycle?

Spleen vented, my point is this: there are precious few activities that a lot of men feel justified in being involved in right now without having a snort and a 'Huh – typical man!' fired at them. Drinking until they fall over, brawling, meaningless sex, swearing and having farting competitions spring to mind, but women are even catching up in these departments, it seems. Is it even a small wonder, then, that us blokes have an unquenchable urge to scuttle off to our sheds (literal or metaphorical) and fiddle with stuff – organize it, clean it, play with it, practise using it, talk about it with our similarly disenfranchised mates? And what do we get labelled as by women as well as by less enlightened men (those with the thumbprints on their foreheads) when we do? Geeks. Anoraks. Saddos. Losers. Not very well-trained ones at that.

So, to prove my manliness once and for all, I needed to do something dirty; something atavistically motivated; something primal – I was going to be needing some porn. Okay, so in the context of fishing I naturally don't mean the various mags that are usually ranked over the top shelves of newsagents, furtively hiding behind each other like the giggling, pointing schoolboys who are too timid to buy them, and that contain usually tawdry photographs of bored-looking women clutching and staring at a breast as if vaguely surprised at having just found it. No – when I say 'porn', I mean in the sense conjured up by my dear friend Jeremy: 'geek porn'. Jeremy should know. He's got mountains of it, and what he doesn't know about railways isn't worth a hump-shunter.

Geek porn is the paraphernalia – magazines, books, videos, DVDs and now, of course, the unfathomable depths of the Internet – that surrounds any given activity. It is the stuff with which the geek cossets himself (or, more rarely, herself) with in the absence of the real thing. It represents access to a vicarious experience of an unavailable activity. The similarities in format between the top-shelf flesh-fetish mags and those of less corporeal interest are staggering. Alongside graphic, well-lit studio shots of models, there appear less professional, but equally well-intentioned, grainy photographs of the readers' loved ones. In the text are to be found 'real-life stories', swapping opportunities and small-print advertisements intended only for the most hardcore and hard-to-satiate reader. However, enough of *Model Railway Journal,* or indeed the singling out of any one discipline or publication. For virtually any pastime, hobby or occupation there is a periodical that underpins and informs it. Teddy bears? Yup. Cross stitch? You bet. Investment banking? I'm afraid so. All these publications feature, in full detail and often in lurid colour, the techniques, tackle and terminology associated with the activity in question.

Fishing is no exception. I found myself one day browsing the shelves of WHSmith's in Winchester (it's more anonymous than the local shop), and found the array of publications devoted to fishing in general to be quite overwhelming. After considering buying *Total Carp* merely for the sheer genius of its title, and perhaps to ascertain whether there might be a market for a sister, sea-based journal entitled *Utter Pollacks*, I reminded myself that I was, at that time, interestedly solely (however much I try to avoid fish- and fishing-based puns, some are inevitable) in sea angling. Happily, this reduced the choice from approximately the twenty mark to exactly the two mark. There was a brace of mags that were dedicated to sea fishing, and I was tempted to snap them both up right there, but I remained daunted somehow. A glance at their covers suggested that their intended readership might have had a little more knowledge at their disposal than knowing what mackerel look like. I had a basic grasp of fishing techniques from boyhood, but felt that I may be wasting my time and money by buying a publication whose cover kindly promised to help me 'Understand Magnetic Brakes' when I didn't know what they were. Besides, I just didn't feel I was ready to have 'Pro Worm Digging Secrets' revealed to me. I left Smith's feeling horribly inadequate and uninformed – as if I was missing something that everyone else took for granted. I needed to have someone point out the very basics to me before I could buy with any degree of confidence a magazine that reviewed 'six stunning reels' without assuming that they would be discussing the relative merits of half a dozen devices that you throw at fish in an attempt to knock them out.

Bearing this in mind, one sunny, chilly and breezy half-term day, I told my two sons that we were going to trawl the charity shops for 'whatever we fancied'. I gave them a fiver each and proceeded to lay out the rest of the ground rules in an attempt to disguise the fact that this trip was, in fact, a way of bribing them into accompanying me on a hunt for fishing books. I explained that, with the exception of real porn and hard drugs (not likely finds in the average Cancer Relief shop), they could spend their money on pretty much anything they liked. The pay-off for this fiscal autonomy was that as soon as they had spent it they would then have to lurch from one famine/cancer/poverty/injustice-of-some-kind-or-another relief shop to another while watching their old man looking for books about fishing and reminiscing about his happy boyhood holidays and his two-piece fibreglass rod with a cork handle. If there is a better way of teaching your children the value and benefit of being cautious about how – and how quickly – you should spend your money, I should love to hear about it. I've found that it works even more effectively if you have previously spent a good deal of time with them standing ankle deep in mud on your allotment and spouting misty-eyed twaddle about your dead dad. Scares them stupid.

Gabriel, then eleven years old and teetering over an ever-lowering cusp between boyish enthusiasm and adult maturity, chose a rather fetching dark-grey and red hooded jacket that I had a suspicion Dylan was also eyeing up for future use after Gabriel had outgrown it. Gabe also found himself a 'so achingly dull we are giving them away with a magazine' edition of Bram Stoker's *Dracula*. He also bought, in a gesture that made my nose tingle and my eyes swell with proud tears, a mug for Dylan glazed with a cartoon of two aliens and the words 'Best Brother on the Planet'. Finally, I think he cheated and spent a pound on sweets but what the hell – I made sure that they were chewy ones, which would at least keep him quiet for a bit while I made grumbling noises about the lack of fishing books.

Dylan was also faring a lot better than me, largely because his criteria were as broad as the open ocean. Whereas I was targeting a definite species – fishing books and only fishing books – he was casting a great big net with tiny small holes in it with the sole intention of bagging himself some 'stuff', and when you are seven, a fiver can get you an awful lot of it. The stuff he got himself, like Gabriel's practical, educational and altruistic purchases, perhaps spoke more about him than some clunky words ever will. He bought himself a toy similar to a Rubik's Cube but with about twenty-three sides, much more fluorescently coloured stickers and, it turned out, far less stamina than its original inspiration. He then found himself a pair of hand-knitted red and light-grey fingerless gloves for 79p (I have a feeling that he was bearing Gabe's coat in mind as he did so – they'll go nicely together). Next was a

'100'-piece dinosaur jigsaw puzzle, which actually turned out to contain 96. I toyed with the idea of taking it back under trade description and fitness for purpose legislation, until I remembered that it had come from a shop that funds a children's hospice. I don't know, it just seemed kind of mean and churlish somehow. He also desperately wanted to find something for Gabriel in return for his mug. I tried to help him, but we couldn't really find anything that we thought he would really like. I reassured Dylan that there was no need to reciprocate immediately. I also put a gentle, paternal arm round him and whispered that you should only buy something for someone when you really feel the urge to do so, if you are sure they will like it and if there really is absolutely *nothing* else that you fancy for yourself. Superdad was on form that day.

I became distracted by, and more than a little tight-lipped about, the fact that, in Winchester, there is apparently no such thing as fishing. In the past I have stumbled across, and occasionally bought, some wonderfully arcane and unusual titles in charity shops – *Famous People and Their Illnesses*, *Sewerage Apparatus* or, a personal favourite, *Fangs – The Life of a Gardening Dentist* – and that day I could have added a couple of blinders. I was sorely tempted by the dropped-stitch logic of *Ferro-concrete Boat Building*, and could easily have been distracted by trying to find out whether the rhetorically entitled *What is my Horse Thinking?* really needed any more involved an answer than 'Please get off my back and stop whacking my arse.' However, I held out. We were in the second to last shop of the day, and I had still not found any books on fishing. There were, I guessed, two explanations for this dearth. The first was that, in this corner of Hampshire at least, fishing was a marginal, minority pursuit and therefore the demand for any related literature was negligible. I mentioned this possibility to Dylan, to which he retorted that this was a specious, almost certainly erroneous and fallacious assumption that demonstrated scant regard of the statistical trends concerning the per capita distribution of individuals locally involved in the procuration of foodstuffs or sport by atavistic, if relatively sophisticated, means. Not bad for a seven-year-old.

What he actually said was, 'Whatever. D'you like me gloves?' while waving his hands in the air, but I did reckon that it was a whole lot more likely that killing (or at least catching) scaly things either for sport or for the table was actually going to be pretty high on the agenda of quite few people in this part of the country, and the real reason why there weren't any books on this subject in the charity shops was that they wanted to hang on to them. Miserable bastards. I bet they're the sort who'd take a 96-piece jigsaw puzzle to a children's hospice shop as well.

I had an ace down my waders though. The Oxfam Books and Music shop in Parchment Street is largely staffed by aspiring First Gulf War poets and faded First World War muses. It does tend to charge a little more for its books than the average charity shop, but again, it does seem churlish to complain about this. I know it does – I've tried. This shop also has a huge plus point going for it in that its books are arranged by category, and some sections have even been alphabetized. In fact, when you have trudged in and out of the doors of all eight of the other charity shops in your town and all you've got is cold, empty, gloveless hands, tired feet and kids with no money left, this is more than a plus point. It is a joyous relief from having to scan shabbily-spined titles on sugar-craft, the politically correct use of a fondue or how to knit your own wheelbarrow only to find that there are no bloody books on fishing. In Oxfam Books and Music in Parchment Street, all I had to do to find out that they had no bloody books on fishing was to go and look in the 'fishing' section. This is actually something of an exaggeration. There was one book, *The Compleat Angler*, by Izaak Walton. Now, there are some interesting and, to me, pertinent things to know about this man. The short biography at the beginning of the Penguin Classics edition of this book tells us that Walton (1593–1683) was an 'ironmonger, biographer and writer'. It goes on to say that he was 'born at Stafford, lived much of his life in London (where he was a parishioner of John Donne) but spent the last twenty years of his life at Winchester where he is buried in the cathedral.'

This passage interested me for a number of reasons. Firstly, and most pressingly, what the bloody hell does an ironmonger know about fishing? He couldn't even spell 'complete'. Numpty. Secondly, Stafford was where I grew up, which, combined with the fact that, thirdly, I now live near Winchester, should have made me feel some kind of new-agey, 'some-things-are-meant-to-be' kind of connection but didn't. It merely made me raise an eyebrow and a half-mouthed smile at what is a mere coincidence. Fourthly, why was he *at* Stafford and Winchester, but *in* London? From what I could gather *The Compleat Angler* is about being a trout called Piscator or something like that. The point is that I simply cannot read it. I tried a paragraph or two that day in Oxfam, but even the imagined imploring eyes of some really hungry children who might find relief if only I bought that book could not stop my mind from wandering, as I tried to scan its pages, to more interesting subjects such as the colour of porridge or how long it would take to collect enough belly-button fluff to fill the shop. This was actually a bit of a shame, because for a moment I had hoped that a copy of this book might perhaps inspire my own travels with rod and reel. Having read only a brief snippet, however, I felt that I would far rather sully these trips (which I was otherwise looking forward to wholeheartedly) with the ordeal of eating my own belly-button fluff. Or even porridge if things were going really well.*

Apart from having had a lovely time bimbling around town watching the boys being really nice to each other, the afternoon had been an unmitigated waste of time, so to salvage something from the day, and to assuage my mounting guilt about all those hungry children's eyes, I did buy *The Sporting Gun* referred to in the Introduction. Not that I was particularly interested in shooting by this point, but because the title would serve as a consistent reminder of the elasticity of some words in the English language. I do wonder just how 'sporting' a chance a wood pigeon has against an unchoked twelve-bore at twenty yards.

Despite the fact that my initial attempt to go shopping for porn with my kids had proved so unproductive, I remained resolute. A couple of weeks later, my stomach full of the trepidation and anticipation that always accompany the purchase of a large, brand-new hardback book, I slid out *The Complete Encyclopedia of Fishing* from one of the solid, thick, black ash shelves of my local branch of Waterstones. There is something comfortingly beautiful about a virgin, unbroken, unsullied hardback. It was

---

*   I think Ed Zern had it about right when, in *To Hell With Fishing*, he said 'Izaak Walton pretended to be an expert on fishing. In his introduction, he refers to "the honest angler". That's how much *he* knew.

'*The Compleat Angler* is chock-full of useful information for fishermen. For example, in Part 1, Chapter IV, it says: "And next you are to notice, that the Trout is not like the Crocodile." Walton was observant.

'In Chapter VIII, he tells of a man who caught a pike by using a mule as bait. Fortunately for Ike, it was several hundred years before anybody read beyond Chapter One.'

fifteen quid, the price of maybe half a dozen to ten charity-shop finds, but in this case 'finds' had turned out to be something of a misnomer. Not only did this book promise to be a 'comprehensive guide to coarse fishing, sea angling and game fishing', not only did it weigh nearly four pounds and could kill a fish with a single blow of its spine, but it was also written by people who knew how to spell 'complete'. Much more like it.

'Complete – free from deficiency: perfect: finished: entire: fully equipped: consummate.' That's what Chambers says. To claim a book to be 'complete', or even 'compleat', somehow seems to convey an imperious air of self-importance – arrogance, even. It is as if to say, by implication, that you yourself know absolutely everything about a subject and, consequently, after every page has been digested, so will the reader. To claim 'completeness' is to imply perfection, which in turn is to invite ridicule. Most 'complete' encyclopedias merely deal with the technicalities: the equipment, the locations, the numbers – the prosaics. They are (often indispensable) guides to the practicalities of an activity. My fishing encyclopedia is indeed most informative in terms of knots, rigs, rods and reels, etc., but what it does not even begin to convey is what the juddery thump of a good-sized bite-and-run from the obscured depths feels like in the palms and in the pit of the stomach. It gives no clue to how a landed fish will flip, slippery, spastically and staringly on the scaly, salty, brown blood-stained bench of a boat. Nor does it tell me what it is like to take the life of a fish – to feel its slimy contortions shudder to a stiff, gawping halt in your hands as you club the back of its head. It never even begins to tell me how it feels to sit on a warming stone wharf a million miles in time and space from the rest of my life on a breezy summer afternoon while dangling for coalfish and barbecuing a mackerel whose guts were still warm. No book is complete.

However, just as any half decent page of prose is not possible without a good grasp of grammar, syntax and good old-fashioned spelling, so is any philosophical or aesthetic understanding of fishing not likely without having got to grips with a few of the practical basics. Which is what *The Complete Encyclopedia of Fishing* provides, and this is precisely why I bought it. It is a competent, readable and clear guide to sea, game and coarse fishing. What I knew I should do with it when I got home was to read each paragraph of the relevant sections, make notes and cross-reference the information that I did not fully understand. What I actually did was to scan some of the text, gawp at a few of the illustrations of knots, rigs and tackle and find out a couple of Latin fish names. My favourite of these was the conger eel – *Conger conger* – because this is exactly what I would be shouting while running around in frantic little circles and flapping my arms if I caught one of the toothy, snaky, evil little buggers. I also ogled at a few photographs of the sea with some people and fish in the way of it. After this, I decided that I was bored and surely knew enough by now to go and buy a couple of magazines with adverts, grainy photos, small print, reader's fish and geeks in them.

Pretty much all men are geeks to some extent, and in one discipline or another. All the ones I know are, anyway, and we all agree on one thing – that one of the deepest of joys about any obsession is that of poring over the advertisements in magazines and catalogues and comparing the specifications and prices of gadgets. For some strange reason (I'm not convinced I want to know) this activity is especially fascinating while sitting on the toilet, often carried out long after the original reason for being there has, erm, passed. I have lost count of the number of times that my legs have gone numb to the point of collapse-upon-standing after a good session of tracking down a particular camera lens, seed variety or, new joy of all joys, sinking bass plug.

I was not afraid, and I was not ashamed. I was, I unconvincingly reassured myself, a grown man and had every justification for what I was about to do. I was not going to feel embarrassed or belittled. I was going to walk into the anonymity of a large-chain newsagents and, this time, demand fishing porn. I was going to need to buy tackle at some point, and if I was going to do that, then I needed to know not only where to get it, but also how to ask for it. Because it had been over eight years since I'd even tried to go fishing (and that was with someone else's kit), I was pretty sure that its associated technology would have moved on sufficiently far to make walking into a shop and asking for 'a rod, a reel, some line and some dangly bits' look somewhat foolish. I figured that a magazine or two might provide me with a couple of answers to at least some of the more basic questions I might be asked in order to refine my request. 'How big and shiny would you like your dangly bits, sir?', that sort of thing.

I boldly plucked copies of the oddly unspaced *Sea Angler* and the strangely capitalled and similarly compressed *TOTAL SeaFISHING* from the shelves. Both covers were emblazoned with full-colour photos of really slimy and bizarre-looking gaping-mouthed creatures, both of whom were grinning like idiots and clutching an enormous fish. I didn't get much further with the decision-making process – these were the only ones on offer. I still didn't understand an awful lot of the blurb on the cover, and, more to the point, I could feel the hairs on the back of my neck starting to stand up hotly due to all the disapproving looks from every single person in the shop. All I wanted to do was to get home, sit on the loo and start making some lists.

'Would you like a bag for those?'

What was she trying to say? I'm sure I saw the cashier suppressing a smirk as I handed over my ten-pound note.

'No, thank you. They're fine as they are,' I replied defiantly as I clammily fumbled to put my £4.60 change back into my wallet. I folded the magazines lengthways, the front covers facing boldly outwards, and scuttled back to the car and then home to drool over some pictures of *stuff.*

I don't think it's possible to claim to have fished in Hampshire unless you've at least tried a spot of fly fishing. However, having never done so, its complexities and complications seemed far too daunting and way too distant at the beginning – indeed, they appeared to be conveyed in a different language altogether. Coarse fishing had always been, and continued to be, an utter mystery to me. In terms of tackle (Which? Floats? Wake me up when something interesting happens), location (where? Canals? No thanks), companions (Who? I've spent half my life trying to get away from Brummies in combat jackets), species (What? You mean they're not edible?) and motivation (Why? A day watching a float bobbing about on a scummy, stagnant ditch in the company of people called Nigel or Kevin trying to catch something that tastes like where it came from? Enough said), I had no idea what would persuade anyone into going coarse fishing. I thought that, to ease myself back into the sport as a whole, I should stick to what I knew. Or at least to what I used to con myself into thinking I knew a long time ago.

As far as sea fishing – and sea fishing tackle – is concerned, there are two main definitions: fishing from the shore, and fishing from a boat. Every time I have attempted it, the latter has made me feel so viridian-sick that I have truly wished to die. If it goes on the water, then I have felt violently and distressingly nauseous in it.

From ferries lurching to Sweden to kayaks bobbing around the coast of Pembrokeshire, I have felt so gut-wrenchingly sick that I have truly desired nothing but drowning and peace. As far as initial kitting up was concerned, this, thankfully, narrowed things down further still.

As is often the way with these things, shore fishing can again be broken down into subgroups. These are classified as fishing from a beach or fishing from a mark – a jetty, pier or rocks. There is, naturally, a bewildering array of methods of doing all of these things, especially when you start to think about exactly which species you are hoping to catch, and its inherent level of stupidity. For instance, your average thicky-thumpy mackerel (essentially the sea's answer to sheep) will make the wily and seemingly epicurean grey mullet seem like a reasonable candidate for the average pub quiz team. As far as I could remember, getting a mackerel to leap out of the water and into the coolbox wearing a T-shirt bearing slogans such as 'Shiny and smelly – please use as bait' or 'Great shallow-fried in extra-virgin with shallots and olives' requires no more guile than standing near the sea and whistling for them. In order to stand any chance of coaxing a mullet to within a nautical mile of you, however, it appears that you require the planning skills of a team of architects, the patience of an inner-city teacher and the finesse, poise and stamina of a Russian gymnast.

Whichever species it is, then, that you wish to enjoy with a squeeze of lemon and a slurp of white wine, it pays to do a little homework concerning the correct lures, baits, rigs, etc. The way I see it, the further your tackle gets away from the sea, the less the fish are going to give any kind of toss about it. So, I started at the end that effectively mattered least. Criteria for my rods such as casting distance, flexibility versus stiffness, sensitivity, durability and many other factors gradually became less and less important the more times I saw an advertisement in the catalogue that slid out from one of the magazines I'd bought. All these technical criteria eventually dissipated like raindrops pocking the surface of the ocean once I noticed that two rods, two reels and two icing-on-the-cake, I'm-having-that, I-don't-care-if-it-falls-apart-in-a-month spools of line had been reduced from £104.96 to an irresistible one penny shy of fifty quid. I reasoned that people, myself included, have caught good fish on worse equipment than that, and quite frankly I wasn't sure if I would be able to tell the difference between a rod that theoretically cost £12.50 and one that would swipe three hundred quid out of your wallet before you could cough the word 'gullible'. I was destined to be the owner of a twelve-foot beachcaster, designed for hurling heavy things long distances, and an eight-foot spinning rod primarily intended to lob lighter things less far. In the package came two reels – an 'Okuma 80 fixed spool' and an 'Okuma 50 fixed spool' – and two bulk spools of line. To put it another way, I opted for a big rod and a big reel and a little rod and a little reel. Oh, and some line.

Having decided that my first trip should take me back to where my fishing career had first started in turn narrowed down which 'terminal tackle' (dangly bits: weights, lures, rigs, etc.) would be accompanying me. To assist me further, I made a list of the fish I wanted to catch while I was there (pretty much anything that wasn't going to bite/sting/scare me and/or wasn't going to keep moving after I'd bashed it over the head) and chose tackle that was described in the catalogue as being suitable. The words 'Great for big bass' got a resounding tick, as did 'Pollack can't resist these' or 'Cod love 'em!', whereas anything mentioning that 'Conger will always go for these just before they take the ends of your salty fingers clean off' had me skipping to the next diagram.

The magazines had plenty of articles of interest about rig-tying, locations, readers' fish (no, really) and so forth, but the plethora of advertisements put me into a flat spin of confusion. Comparing camera lenses is one thing – I've been scanning the smalls of *Amateur Photographer* magazine since I was ten, so know my *f*-stop from my focal length. However, differentiating my Shads from my Hokkais was an entirely different arena. Of course, the guys who had produced my catalogue knew this damn well, and its free inclusion was a very smart bit of fishing on their part. It contained everything, it seemed, that I wanted, at what struck me as very reasonable asking prices. I calculated that I could get pretty much everything I needed, and probably an awful lot that I did not, for just over a hundred pounds. At that price, it wasn't exactly disposable, but, on the other hand, it seemed like an eminently justifiable expense considering that I could probably recoup that outlay in the value of the fish I was going to catch in the ensuing thirty years or so.

Ordering the tackle over the phone really did seem so much easier than going into a shop and dealing with someone who knew exactly what they were talking about (proper geek shops tend to be staffed by proper geeks). Face to face, shop staff would try to engage me in a conversation about a subject that I last pursued with any degree of seriousness just before my voice broke, I discovered that girls could be fun and that roll-ups made you look hard. There would be fewer awkward questions on the telephone, and what was more, I could field any that did come along without having to look anyone in the eye while I was bluffing. I could even glance at the catalogue for reassurance before concurring that 27 grams would seem about right for what I'm after, wouldn't it?

The whole process was indeed a doddle. From beginning to end, according to the LCD timer on my telephone, it took me twenty-eight minutes. Seven and a half of these were occupied by being informed that 'all their lines were busy' and would I 'please wait for the next customer services representative', and a further five of these were filled with silence while the chap on the other end of the phone tried to find the code number for the rod and reel deal. After that, I simply rattled off the catalogue numbers of my desired items and their quantities. The act of actually buying (if not choosing) all this gear, then, had taken only a quarter of an hour or so. I reckon that if I'd tried to do the same thing in a fishing tackle shop it would have taken me that long to pluck up the courage to ask for a long, stiff rod with a tip that's sensitive enough to tell me if something's biting.

At one point during the call, the salesman read out a list of the rigs that were being included in my 'rig wallet and ten rigs for fourteen quid' deal. As he enunciated all the names – 'Flapper, Paternoster, Pennell, Running Ledger, Flish Flash Splish Splosh, Double Jiggled Knicker Twister' etc. – I ummed and aahed my assent and approval. *The Complete Encyclopedia of Fishing*, along with a lengthy session with a copy of *SeaAngler* and a can of lager in the bath had acquainted me with these names, but not a great deal more. If I'd had to actually choose them, then I would have done so purely for what they sounded like. Similarly, the criteria for the lures I ordered were picked mainly for how pretty and shiny they were, and how good they would look in the new tackle box I was also treating myself to (£8.99 complete with, mark you, a light inside its lid). In the absence of any other criteria, I wanted my rigs and lures to have pleasantly shaped names that left a sweet taste in the mouth when you told someone what you were using. There was the option of tying my own rigs, and although this was tempting in a really anally retentive, fiddly kind of way, I reckoned that it was unlikely that fish were going to snub a bought rig in preference to one that had been hand-wrought by pixies. I also felt that it would be one step from making your own rigs to crafting your own rods and, let's face it, fish don't know a carbon fibre super-caster from a bean pole. The only piece of tackle a fish really gives two gulps about is your hook when it slices into their mouth. The final temptation when it came to these rigs, however, was the fact that they came separately from the wallet, individually wrapped with a card backing. At the time, I could think of nothing more pleasurable than snipping these open, removing the rig, and sliding it into the translucent sleeves inside the crisply velcroed wallet. This would, in turn, sit purposefully underneath the compartmentalized, regimented lures. Heaven.

The guy on the other end of the phone totalled the order up to £112.94, which included what I thought was a very reasonable five pounds' worth of postage and packing. He also called me 'sir', and did all of it wrapped in a swirling Scottish accent that had all the soothing warmth of an Islay malt in a heavy-bottomed cut-glass tumbler. I assured him that £112.94 was just fine.

'So, when do I get to stack up my lures in the box with the light in the li— Erm, any idea of delivery times?'

'Usually about five working days, Sir.' His 'R's were beautifully and softly burred.

'Oh, bollocks. I wanted to do it tomorrow. Is that the best you ca— No problem, mate. Thanks for all your help.'

I put the phone down, and waited.

I am consistently intrigued by the huge variety of definitions it is possible to place on the term 'working days', as applied to the clearance of cheques or, in this case, the amount of time it takes for just over a hundred quid's worth of fishing kit to arrive. I had hoped that, at a push, and considering that I had ordered it at just after nine o'clock on Monday morning, that it may materialize on, or even before, Friday. Five p.m. on Friday would have been five working days. Towards the end of the week, I fashioned a note explaining that if I was not in then the delivery could be made to Liz and Steve's place two doors up, and pinned it to the front door every time I went out. And every time I came home, I did so to the quite disproportionate disappointment of it still flapping, forlorn and unread, in the breeze.

I reckoned that the following Tuesday afternoon would be a reasonable time to call the Scotsman to give him a gentle nag. Because I do at least a small amount of work on most days, I reasoned that by then it would have been eight working days since I had placed my order and, more crucially, only half that amount of days (industrious or otherwise) until my first fishing trip. I set my mobile phone to remind me, with a violently unpleasant chime, to call them at four o'clock on Tuesday.

No surprise, then, that first thing that Tuesday morning saw me dialling the Glasgow Angling Centre to check on progress. It was a different man I spoke to from before. He was most apologetic, but

'We're still wettin' on a coupla rugs.'

Luckily, before I asked him what relevance their urinating on domestic upholstery had to my order, I realized that they were, in fact, delaying the rest of my order until they had the full complement of rigs. What a relief – I could have made a right duck of myself.

'It should all be wi' ya tomorra, mate.'

'Cracking. Thank you.'

The word 'should' instilled little confidence, but I figured that to press for any more commitment than this would be a little unfair and unreasonable. As it was, though, he could have staked his children's lives on it, because at eight o'clock the next morning I was roused from dreams of salt and seagulls by a blunt rap on the front door. Too early for the postman, and Steve knows better than to attempt any but the most basic forms of grunting with me before ten. This awakening, then, could only logically mean one thing. My rugs had arrived. I threw on the nearest T-shirt and pair of shorts and lumbered downstairs. My hapless hound Charlie skittered down with me as usual and greeted the delivery man in the way he greets everybody except me (i.e. with enthusiasm). The man with the box of new toys at his feet looked about as enamoured with being up at that time of the morning as I did.

'Sign and print here, and here.' He held a smeared sheaf of papers with one tired hand, and stabbed at two boxes containing my name with the forefinger of the other. 'There's another box in the van.'

As he disappeared to rummage for what I assumed to be the rods, I managed to gain sufficient focus and manual dexterity to do as instructed. After a minute or so, he still had not returned, so I entertained myself by glancing at the list of drops he had made already that morning. He must have been up and about for at least three hours already, and after about five minutes of absence I began to suspect that he had actually found himself a cosy nest inside some packages of soft furnishings – a coupla rugs perhaps – and dozed off.

He returned shortly afterwards, though, empty handed and slightly sweaty from his exertions. As he approached, he shrugged with a raised eyebrow and shoulder, two open palms and two downturned mouth corners.

'Must be under everything else. You in later?'

'I'm going out in about half an hour, but should be back by twelve. Can you come back then?' I had to nip out to put a pane of glass in Alex's upstairs window which I had been promising to do 'this week' for about two months.

'Will do.'

This was torture. It was true that I had *some* new gadgets to play with, to take apart, to organize and to break, but no rods? When I was a small boy, I would get so stupid with excitement about the impending arrival of Christmas (around September time), that I would occasionally ask my mother for a stocking, which I then proceeded to fill with some of my favourite possessions. I would leave this by my bed, and try to forget about it until morning, when I would wake up to find a stretchy, staticky, rustling and bulging form next to me, ready to be taken through to my delighted parents at around five-thirty in the morning. This anticipation of ritual, this desire to imitate a yearned for event, has stayed with me. All I wanted to do that Wednesday morning was to remove a new reel from its just-large-enough box and slip it into the seat at the butt end of the rod via its simple screw-clamp mechanism. Then I could have threaded the monofilament line through the guides on the rod, attached a magnet to the end and tried to catch small pieces of steel in the washing-up bowl. But it wasn't to be – I simply had to wait until the afternoon. A large part of me actually deemed this to be a good thing; I am not at my least clumsy in the morning, so playing with items such as fishing hooks is an activity probably best left until later in the day. Quite how and why I thought I would be any better off being fifteen feet up a ladder playing with six square feet of glass escapes me now, but that's what I did.

When I returned home, I was bursting with the energy brought about by the twin factors of having new toys, and of having survived what felt like a near-death experience (the combination of ladders and glass seems to be so diametrically opposed to everything I believe about natural selection). I had left the unopened box of goodies on my sitting-room floor, and returned to find that, remarkably, it had not moved. I somehow thought that it may have shifted slightly due to the vibration of anticipation and excitement, but evidently my feelings were not reciprocated. I sliced through the packaging as carefully as I could in the minimum amount of time possible, and as soon as I could get a grip, tore the box open. Despite my first and best intentions to painstakingly check off each item against the packing list as they came out, I did what any like-minded child would have done – I slid a reel out of its box, attached the handle and wound it round and round while grinning like an loon.

Sea-fishing reels fall into two broad categories: 'fixed spool' and 'multiplier'. I had chosen two of the former for three reasons. Firstly, casting with a multiplier takes more skill than I felt I either had or needed at the time. They are capable of casting slightly further than fixed spools, but not in my hands they weren't. I'd also heard horror stories that any lack of control on the operator's part could result in what is technically known as a 'bird's nest', a term that surely needs no explanation. The second reason for choosing fixed spools was because I actually didn't *have* any choice as they were part of the package deal. Thirdly, and most importantly of all, the way these reels work and move is utterly mesmeric – simultaneously and smoothly rotating and reciprocating. At the front of the reel is a device called the bale arm, which assumes one of two positions: 'cocked' to allow the line to feed from the spool freely when casting and, for the lack of any better description anywhere I can find, 'uncocked' to allow the user to wind the line back in again. The bale arm is fixed via a hinge to a cylindrical housing that in turn orbits the spool onto which the line is wound. When reeling in, the bale arm spins snugly around the spool, which itself slides reciprocally along a splined shaft to ensure even winding of the line. I can watch this for hours, especially when combined with the reassuring 'clack' of the bale arm automatically returning to its winding position upon turning the handle after casting. This whole motion is beautifully concise in its function, and concisely beautiful in its motion.

After I had made sure that both reels went round and round, up and down and made all the right noises, I turned my attention to the tackle and the box with the light in its lid. I managed to resist the temptation of checking the candlepower (approximately three) of the torch until the darkness of later that evening when Liz and Steve came round for the inaugural lighting. They were – Lizzie in particular – quite disturbingly effusive in their excitement. Maybe they just knew how important it was to me.

Before truly making all this gear my own, I did check that I had been sent the correct amount of the correct tackle – evidently they had not bothered to wet on all the rugs after all, as some were missing. I didn't judge this to be a problem, however, as I had no idea how to use them anyway. Apart from this, and having received an extra spool of six-pound breaking strain line in place of something that should have been something else but I've no idea what, all was in order. Consequently I could get on with the crucial task of finding spaces in the tackle box for all the other bits and pieces.

Firstly came the lures. I may have been just a little too heavily seduced by their shininess and prettiness, having ordered a total of fourteen, but any fears were soon allayed by the fact that they all fitted perfectly and shimmeringly in the small compartments in the top tray of the box – ranked, purposeful and deadly for pollack, apparently.

Next to be located were the four different sizes of swivels I had purchased. These small pieces of kit comprise a central barrel from each end of which protrudes an independently rotating eye. These are tied between the terminal tackle and the main line. Fish, as a rule, don't really like having a bloody great barb stuck in their mush and as a consequence tend to flap about a bit when it happens. The swivel prevents the main line from getting as twisted as a bag of eels when the fight is on. They arrived in small, crisp, plastic sachets, adhesive sealed. This is obviously no good at all – with no method of resealing these bags, it would only be a matter of minutes before they would be rattling around the tackle box, and I would have no idea which size was which. Chaos. I found four small, square, polythene snap-lock bags that had remained from a previous stint as a stationery geek, decanted them and, having squeezed the air from the bags and written their respective sizes on some self-adhesive labels, stuffed them into a compartment in the lower tier. The hooks, the largest of which looked as if it had been designed to catch something the size of which I had no intention of ever landing, received a similar treatment, having somewhat inconsiderately arrived in some rather pleasant but hopelessly ill-fitting little plastic boxes. I again labelled the hooks and placed them in the compartment next to the swivels.

Also along for the ride, and largely to act as ballast on the journey to my Scotland, were one pear-shaped lead weight and three 'breakaway' leads. The latter have four hardened steel spikes pointing outwards and upwards from their bases. The dual purposes of these protrusions seemed, on first inspection, to be to make sure the weights did a really good job of getting tangled up in underwater seaweed and boulders and to make fitting them in the tackle box virtually impossible. However, I somehow managed to wedge them into the lower tray before realizing that these spikes were in fact fabricated from two pieces of bent wire which allowed them to be hinged backwards so that they pointed the opposite way. The idea is that they provide sufficient grip against a racing tide to hold the bait in one place, but will release with a good tug from the dry end. This didn't make getting them into the box an awful lot easier, but did give me a thoroughly good idea of exactly why they were called 'breakaway' leads.

It was during the final stages of stowing and labelling all this stuff that I realized that the impulse to contain, arrange, control and personalize is common to all geek activities. What is a model railway, an allotment, a bag of camera gear or a box of fishing tackle if it's not an opportunity to quantify and dominate our own microcosm of an otherwise unpredictable world?

Having said that, I was aware of the fact that I had spent the best part of an hour and a half arranging pretty and/or heavy things in a box. I felt it was really high time I got out a bit more. And did a spot of fishing while I was there.

2   An Isle Full of Familiar Noises

A journey is a person in itself; no two are alike. And all plans, safeguards, policing, and coercion are fruitless. We find after years of struggle that we do not take a trip; a trip takes us.

John Steinbeck, *Travels with Charley*

Steinbeck was right. A trip takes on a life and a personality of its own. It becomes your companion while you take it. It might even turn out to be your friend if you let it take you once in a while. If, like Steinbeck, you are taking off with a pedigree standard poodle called Charley with at least a gram of grey matter, this is all well and good. However, if you happen to be taking a lurcher called Charlie with nothing between his ears but a bone-shaped dog biscuit, well, things can get strained. I was going to need some company, so as well as taking Charlie, I took Charley. And Steinbeck.

In order to settle any confusion over whether I am in any way attempting to compare myself with one of the great voices of American twentieth-century literature, I think a few distinctions are necessary. In the opening chapter of his book, Steinbeck mentions that Charley's full name, having been born in France, was 'Charley le chien'. Not that imaginative, perhaps, but it still has a certain romantic charm. In view of this, and for the purposes of this trip, I have rechristened my dog 'Charlie le merde-tête'. He also tells us that he named his wagon, in which he was to transport himself and 'Charley the dog' around the United States of America, 'Rocinante' after Don Quixote's horse. This truck seemed to be kitted out to cover full-scale atomic warfare as well as the more mundane requirements of eating and sleeping. Conversely, I named my car – in which I and 'Charlie the shit-head' are pottering off to Scotland and which has a fag lighter, a CD player and two and a half seats – 'Horace'. The shame of this would not be quite so great if I could say that I'd named it after the great Roman philosopher, but the car was christened in memory of Gabriel's guinea pig who, after getting to the rare and un-rodent-like old age of seven, pegged it on the same day that I bought the car.

I made, and pedantically ticked off, four packing lists (all of which included the mandatory 'thing that I didn't know I'd need until I got there'). These lists were headed 'Camping and cooking', 'Tackle', 'Work' and the cop-out 'General'. There had been some ugly scenes when it came to a few of the more ambiguous items (did fishing rods come under 'tackle' or 'work'? Or even, by logical retrogression, cooking, for example?). What if I came across some camping tackle or some general cooking items? It was a minefield, and I was staggered and nonplussed that some people around me took the view that buggering off to Scotland with my dog for a few days' fishing in mid July did not strike them as hard work.

After a couple of days with Jacq and Jon, my sister and brother-in-law, who live very roughly halfway between Hampshire and south-west Scotland, I spent a similar number of hours driving along a dry, deserted M6 to a curiously and conversely busy Tebay service station. Maybe Tebay was a destination in itself to some. When I was a child, this place amounted to not a great deal more than an opportunity for my dad to brew tea on his camping stove and for us to urinate and 'stretch our legs' – an expression that meant nothing whatsoever to me then, mainly because as far as I was concerned all this involved was to dangle them over the edge of the back seat of the car.

The M6 is the nearest we have in this country to a 'serious' road – one that is long enough to transport you from one county, or even country, to another, from day to night. Not only was the Isle of Whithorn the furthest away from where I then lived geograph-ically, but was also the most remote in terms of time. I was indeed travelling a good distance away from home, but was also heading for a location that was inhabited by perhaps the least recognizable version of me.

Just after Carlisle, having reached a grand total of forty-four junctions, the M6 gets really bored and transforms quite startlingly quickly into the A74. After about two inches of being green and yellow in my road atlas, the A74 then has a dramatic identity crisis of its own and decides it wants to at least have the right to be the A74(M) and turns blue again. Just after it does so, I should have taken the A75 to Dumfries, but for one reason or another, I missed what turned out to be a gigantic blue sign signalling in no ambiguous way that the next available left turn would take me to 'South West Scotland'. One reason I missed it was that I had been preoccupied and perturbed by an LED billboard advising me to 'check my fuel'. What was wrong with it? Was it dangerous? I mean, it's not combustible or anything, is it? The other reason that I missed the large signpost the first time round was due to my overtaking an even larger lorry that had been obscuring it. When

I did eventually find it, the A75 wound along pleasantly enough, with not an awful lot happening on it apart from two rather intriguing brown road signs. The first almost had me veering very sharply left merely because it was directing me to a 'Devil's Porridge Exhibition'. I speculated as to whether this might be a Scottish euphemism for vomit, or perhaps some other less than pleasant bodily secretion. Or maybe it was some Robbie Burns-ism venting spleen against the English – 'Ach, they've Devil's porridge fer brains, the Sassenachs.' I later found out, with a degree of disappointment, that during the First World War the towns of Eastriggs, Rigg and Gretna were dominated by a huge cordite plant, employing over 20,000 people. Cordite was used as a propellent for high-explosive shells, and when Arthur Conan Doyle (who was, at the time, a war correspondent) visited the place, he described the mixing processes in the factory as 'stirring the Devil's porridge'. I always thought he was a bit weird. The second sign that caught my attention somewhat disturbingly informed me that another turn to the left would take me to the dubious attraction of 'Butterflies and Carnivorous Plants'. Tempting as it was, I needed to press on to the Isle, where I would no doubt be treated to a similar show of 'Fish and Men With Great Big Nets'.

Just past Dumfries, the A75 becomes much less complacent and much more ambiguous when it asks you whether you want to play it safe by staying on the green and flat and yawnsome main road, or whether you would like to check your adrenaline level, pulse and pelvic floor (yes, girls, we have one too) by getting into the racy red twisty bits that make up the A712 to the same place. This goes through a village that would have the Reverend Spooner roaring with delight (Corsock) before leading you to what is quite possibly the most sonorous body of water in the country, Clatteringshaws Loch. I went for the latter option by driving at speeds that would have had my mother clenching knuckle-white tight on the straight bits, and weeping in the corners. I am at pains to point out that I consider myself to be neither a fast nor reckless driver, but I do consider my mother to be the biggest lace doily of a passenger I have ever carried. At anything over forty-five miles an hour, she closes her eyes in a faintly fatalistic kind of way, goes a bit pale and says things like 'I suppose I just have to trust you.' Get anywhere near sixty, and she starts to faint, speak in tongues and get nose bleeds.

She was right about one thing, though. When we were kids, she used to survey scenes such as Clatteringshaws and ask, hands on hips, 'Isn't this beautiful?' Considering she was surrounded by three kids who were, at that point, utter philistines and a husband whose sole purpose on holiday, possibly even in life, was to 'brew up' on every and any available car park, this could be held as some kind of paradigm of a rhetorical question.

As I was standing at the edge of Clatteringshaws Loch, I became aware of an impulse that had brought me there, and that I had only just recognized. The Quiet. Noun. Proper. Anyone who used to visit me at my then home in Twyford from any major town or city would always remark upon how quiet my life is, but all I heard was the regular drone of aeroplanes coming down towards Southampton, the dog in the house behind my flat woofing with a regularity and level of irritation that would do an army of telesales people proud, and everywhere I went the incessant and inevitable thick 'whoosh' of the M3. By Clatteringshaws that day, all I could hear were the lapping wavelets and the occasional, distant hot-clear clunk and banter of cars ejecting their passengers. Admittedly, there was the occasional roar from a car as it sped by at ridiculous speed, no doubt driven by some nobhead who thought he was Stirling bloody Moss, but what additional noise there was came as a surprise, not an accompaniment. I realized that I had, in part at least, come away – had come fishing, had come to place myself by some placid water – in order to hear myself think.

I arrived in the Isle of Whithorn roughly three-quarters of an hour after I might otherwise have done, had my progress not been impeded by two bouncing, bumbling and jolly-looking tractors that I seemed to trail all the way from Clatteringshaws. In reality, it was probably only a few miles, and as it was it didn't matter a jot anyway. Any variety of agricultural vehicle on a main road at home – or for that matter any vehicle travelling at a speed that precludes me from getting to the boys' school in time to pick them up – is an inconvenient, unmitigated and inconsiderate pain in the backside against which I usually feel there ought to be some kind of legislation. However, behind a slow-moving piece of machinery somewhere on the scarlet vein that is the A746 south of Bladnoch and its distillery that day, I didn't seem to mind at all. Slowing down merely represented an opportunity to marvel at this landscape (somewhat unfairly described in the *Rough Guide* as 'disconsolate') of undulating browns and sharp greens under a flat blue sky and to, well, slow down, I suppose.

Upon driving into the Isle, I did the full-blown hunter-gatherer bloke thing and blubbed like an infant. It was a reaction as spontaneous and unfathomable as waking from an instantly forgotten dream laughing. For some reason, crying in public is still something that many men, myself included, feel uncomfortable about doing. However, I was shrouded by the safety of Horace, so I felt quite at liberty to blart my eyes out as I drove along the main drag (which consists of about twenty terraced cottages on one side and a hard-line Church of Scotland and the harder sea on the other) towards the right turn where the road stops and becomes jetty. Why did I cry? I didn't really feel any particular sadness as such, but the tears did not taste of spontaneous elation either. It was more an abstract notion of grief, if anything – a melancholy. A number of possibilities bubbled up: the unrecapturable rapture of youth, a loss of innocence, as well as that of my father, perhaps. It was, I think, the bitter salt of the unrelenting, inevitable and indiscriminate trudge of time. As if that wasn't enough to deal with, I had also just remembered what the 'thing that I didn't know I'd need until I got there' was on the camping and cooking list. How was I supposed to know I was going to need a mallet?

After I'd told myself to stop being such a big wet pair of panties, I parked up on the jetty outside the Steampacket Inn – a low-ceilinged and red-upholstered establishment that still charges 10p a pint less in the public bar than in the not a fat lot more private lounge. I habitually checked the mileometer for interesting readings (palindromics and sequentials are the best ones – double points if you happen to stop on one), performed the necessary but utterly pointless fettling routines with the luggage and headed into the pub with Charlie, who I thought could be relied upon to get me engaged in conversation with some wise local fisher types. Normally I would want to get the tent up first, but as I had only just recovered from an emotional trauma, I felt a pint was necessary. Besides, this was no ordinary pub. This was a place outside which my underaged and scrawny frame was forced to sit, summer after summer, with a glass of lemonade and a bag of crisps while my parents lolled about and got legless inside. Actually, this isn't strictly true, as my father never touched a drop of booze in his life, and I could never help feeling that if all he was going to consume was orange juice, then why didn't *he* come and sit on the cold effing concrete while I went inside and threw up after half a shandy?

I proudly ordered myself a pint, which, considering it had probably had to travel a good 400 miles further, cost me a remarkable fifty pence less than it would at home. Not only was Charlie allowed in the pub, he was also, it seemed, quite welcome to stretch himself out on the cushioned bench seat next to me and rest his long chin in the crook of my arm as I tried to ignore the heavily rowing couple next to me by writing in my journal about the last time I was there.

Just as I was getting to the bit about pretending that I really wanted a little time alone wandering around the headland to 'think' (smoke enough Bensons to make me feel sick and never want to smoke again), the bickering woman approached Charlie and me clutching a good quarter-pound of blue steak between two of her greasy fingers, and asked me if he was allowed to have it. Naturally, I said that he was, and had just finished saying so only a moment after Charlie had licked the remains of it from his chops.

Watching Charlie wallop down the steak, along with all the arguing, had made me realize I was ravenous. There was no way that I could get the tent up without eating, so for a pound less than I had spent a week previously in a local pub for some rubbery microwaved duck, stodgy chips and one of those 'side salads' that are more side than salad, I bagged myself a fillet of haddock that was firm and delicate enough to have been landed the day before with grilled baby plum tomatoes and a Gruyère sauce. This all came with perfectly cooked (which to me means just a sliver more raw than al dente) vegetables, including some beautifully intact broccoli, which I always find a devil to get right.

While I was waiting for my food, Charlie, bless his lovely blue eyes, once again managed to get me embroiled in conversation. A couple who were visiting from Paisley, and who were staying in a cottage just outside Whithorn, had sat themselves next to me. As much as I would love to report that they gave numerous rare insights into the wiles and lore of the local fish population, the conversation instead steered itself from my opening gambit of 'Thank-you, yes, he *is* beautiful, isn't he – half greyhound, half blue merle collie as far as I know' to the lady telling me in quite gratuitous detail about the benefits and drawbacks of the combi-boiler in their holiday cottage. I made a mental note to refine my criteria in terms of who I approach for information, as well as deciding that it may be more beneficial to my cause if I tell people that Charlie is half shit-head, half fish.

Technically, I realize that I should not have driven to the camp-site, having drunk half a pint more than the law says I should have done. However, technically, the road that joins the Isle of Whithorn to Burrow Head campsite is not actually a road, so I adjudged the score to be pretty much even. Besides, I reckon I must have walked off at least half a pint during my hour-long attempt to assuage my guilt at having made Charlie sit in the car all day. Furthermore, the only things anyone is going to be a danger to in a car on that route are themselves, their own vehicle and the hedge. As it turned out, the act of getting the tent up was far more perilous, involving as it did the wielding of bendy, fifteen-foot-long poles, and pushing tent pegs into what amounted to concrete using only a flip-flop.

After I had managed to describe a rough approximation of a dome tent and equip it with the items necessary for as good a night's sleep as could be expected, I took the 86p of the £2.86 in two-pence pieces I had brought along and headed towards the amusement arcade that was situated conveniently next to the campsite store. The arcade had become both physically and metaphorically smaller since the days when, as a child, I would spend what seemed like hours feeding 2p pieces into the three slots of those massively addictive machines whose upper shelf slides backwards and forwards hypnotically, always promising (but rarely delivering) a clanking surge of brown coins in the grey steel tray underneath. As I approached, I realized that, in my absence, the arcade had also become a lot less open than I remember it being over two decades previously. Those ranks of seductive, flashing, spinning and reeling automata stood serried but silent, still and benign, squeezed into a darkened room. This was to be the first of many puzzling and arcane pieces of campsite timing regulations that seemed to conspire against me during my time there. At home, where I am fortunate enough to largely dictate what I do and when I do it, I am prey to few more time constraints than those provided by my legal obligation to ensure the boys are in and out of school roughly when they should be. The powers that held sway on Burrow Head campsite, however, saw to it that as long as I used their facilities, I could shop, eat, and, er, amuse myself only at the times they made these activities available. I hooded my eyes with my hands and tried to peer into the arcade so I could catch a glimpse of the now dormant flash and twirl that had been my childhood, but it was too dark in there, and was obscured by the distracting reflections of the present.

Later, as I zipped myself inside the tent, I sank onto my airbed with a mug of wine, a shot of Steinbeck, a dog as blindly faithful and warmly comforting as some find religion, and a wedge of papers and magazines telling me the best places to catch some fish thereabouts. I concluded from the latter that a good place to start the next day would be the sea. The parts of the tent that had not been correctly pegged or roped down (i.e. the fabric bits) flapped warmly and smoothly in the lethargic breeze outside, and the only other discernible sound was that of adults relaxing after their children had reluctantly and noisily succumbed to sleep. I was in my own torchlit cavern, under my own terms and conditions, having driven my own car the best part of 600 miles to get there. I had legally drunk alcohol and had paid for it, and my dinner, with my own money. I couldn't quite work out why it was, then, that I felt more childlike that evening than I had when I was in the same place as a mere bairn. Maybe it was because the place I had seen that day matched so precisely the image of it that had been lodged in my subconscious for most of my life. Many places change over time, and after a period away are markedly different from before. Not this one. It was every bit the same place as it always had been – same noise, same buildings, same hard concrete jetty, same smell, same colours – but the way in which I perceived my surroundings had been stretched grotesquely tight by imagination, time and memory. Maybe that's why I cried.

I awoke, having had four fitful hours' sleep, at ten to five in the morning. The dawn chorus at Burrow Head campsite seemed to consist of seagulls (understandably), pheasants (inexplicably) and, in my case, a need to pee (urgently). After visiting the toilet block, I wrestled with Charlie for pole position on the airbed. As well as a mallet, I had also forgotten a pillow, so I attempted to grapple for cranial comfort on Jacq and Jon's dog Moose's bed. Jacq had thoughtfully supplied this with Charlie in mind, but when I had plopped it next to the airbed before settling down the previous night and gestured that he should lie in it, he gave me the withering look that he reserves for those occasions when he really, truly believes that he is higher in the food chain than I am, and curled himself in the middle of the airbed, where he stayed until 7.25 in the morning. At 7.30, a Calor Gas lorry arrived to make a scraping, clanking delivery and/or pick-up of canisters. For reasons known only to those with sufficient motivation and powers of speech to find out at that time in the morning, the driver also deemed it necessary to leave his engine running while this swap-over took place.

I resigned myself to the fact that I was awake, so fed and watered Charlie and stumbled over to the cafe in order to gesticulate at the menu in an attempt to procure a bacon roll and a large mug of tea. I also wanted to find out whether it was going to be possible to stash the teeming shoals of fish I was going to catch that day in their freezer.

However, although I'd been awoken at 7.30 in the morning by a bloody great lorry, I was not going to be fed until nine o'clock. True enough, I did have a camping stove, gas, pans, water and even tea bags. However, the organizational urge that had propelled me into buying three bottles of wine for the price of two in Newton Stewart the previous evening had not, for some reason, also prompted me into buying two pints of milk for the price of two at the same time. Probably because drinking a pint of milk didn't then strike me as essential to the process of getting the tent up. I made do with water, and the fact that at least it wasn't raining, to get me through what may otherwise have been a tortuous hour and a quarter.

After I eventually did get breakfast, my tongue actually began to feel as if it belonged to someone who had not died, so I asked the compact, elderly and white-haired chap behind the counter whether there was any chance I could store my ice blocks for the coolbox in his freezer until a little later that day, and possibly some fish later on, and for the next few days until I left.

'Weelll . . . ,' he rubbed his chin between the thumb and forefinger of one hand as he considered the proposition as if it was one with which he was utterly unfamiliar, 'Ye'll be fine 'til lunchtime, bu' aftae tha . . .' He pulled down the corners of his mouth and shook his head with an expression that would not have looked out of place on the face of a doctor in a TV hospital drama who had just stopped resuscitating.

After that, what? Everything melts? I decided not to pursue it. Instead, I reiterated my request about the chances of laying my fish out to freeze. I should have known better, really. I may as well have asked the same doctor whether I could possibly chop off one of the recently deceased's fingers so I could scare girls with it.

'Och, no! There's nay room!'

I should have thought about this before I came – it was clear that if I caught any fish I was going to have to actually use the camping stove.

It was with some surprise that, when I went back – at lunchtime – to pick up the blocks, I noticed a sharp upturn in the demeanour of the chap behind the counter. He even suggested helpfully that I could return the ice blocks later in the day in order to give them a chance to freeze properly in time for the next. Maybe he'd also been woken up by the Calor Gas lorry.

From what I had read, the two hours either side of high tide were the ones worth fishing when doing so from rocks and jetties. I was sure that there were very good technical explanations for this to do with fish feeding habits, the diurnal nature of tidal reciprocations or perhaps even the beautifully arranged law of twelfths, but frankly, the extremely basic hunting rule of not letting what you want to kill see you was enough justification for me. However, I do know that if you put a dead fish under your sweetcorn when you're planting them, they'll grow like buggery. The sweetcorn, not the fish.

Whatever, this meant that I had a few hours to kill before I attempted to do the same thing to anything piscine. Charlie and I drove to the Isle again, and did battle with the morning bustle (someone had left a lobster pot in the way) to carve out a parking space on the jetty. The weather had decided to not so much smile as beam insanely at us. The unmitigatedly light and cloudless sky sharpened and intensified texture, line and colour as much as the heat rendered the unique smell of this place so much more pungent. Occasionally, I have caught a whiff of other places near the coast and thought that perhaps they were imbued with the same mix of ingredients that go to make up the cocktail that pervades the Isle of Whithorn – but they are, I realize now, only *similar*. Nothing smells *the same* as that place, and to try to describe it would be utterly futile. But that's never stopped me in the past. It is, quite simply, the smell that happens when a combination of dairy and arable farming collides with the sea. It is the joint green-brown sweetness of cowshit and seaweed; it is the putrefaction of dead fish; it is the thirst of dried salt on split, painted wood; it is the chugging, metallic nausea of diesel belch; it is the slick detritus of low-tide mud and high-tide guts. It is sweet, it is sick, it is utterly glorious and only one place smells like it.

At the top of the headland that juts out from the south-east of the Isle sits a squat, whitewashed and castellated tower. As a child, because of its then monumental proportions, I had always assumed it to be, well, a monument of some kind. However, it too had (inevitably) shrunk in the intervening years and someone had seen fit to place a whirring weather station and a solar panel the size of a large radiator on top of it. I later learned that this white block was in fact no more than a navigational aid, and the only monumental thing about it were the cock-ups made by the captains of the boats that had foundered on the rocks before it had been built. This became yet another place where my mother would look wistfully out to sea, trying to remember quite why it was that she married our father, while telling us how beautiful it all was. There had been a further addition there, though. A lump of granite had been sliced through and its face polished and engraved with the names of the seven men whose lives had been lost along with the *Solway Harvester* in January 2000. The skipper had been two years younger than I was on the day I stood reading his name, and the combined ages of the two brothers who perished totalled one year less than mine. Life is indeed short, and there is nothing like being reminded that some are shorter than others to give you a good boot up the backside and to stop you feeling so bloody sorry for yourself.

I didn't remember ever having felt nervous prior to going fishing before. It had been eight years since I had done so. I was possibly, having recently forked out over a hundred pounds on gear much of which I didn't even know how to pronounce let alone use, also a little concerned that I may well be a member of that ever-growing fraternity (it *is* usually men) that has all the gear and no idea. Still, another reason for coming here was that nobody else seemed to bother doing so, and those that lived there were far too busy earning a livelihood to care about some soft southern shite prancing about at the end of their jetty. So, it was with a little trepidation but more excitement that I strolled as nonchalantly as I could to the far end of the jetty while carrying two rods, the tackle box, a folding chair, Charlie's blanket, Charlie's water, Charlie's bowl, a bag full of gear, books, wine and a coolbox. Eventually, I made it to the lower section of the two-tier jetty and arranged Charlie's water and furniture before snapping open the metal picnic chair that I had stolen from Steve and Liz's garden before I left.

I know it says 'Beachcaster' on it, and I am fully aware that the sole reason for me being there was in order to fish from a jetty, but it's just that it was so much BIGGER than the other one. I mean, a spindly eight-foot spinning rod is no tool for a real man seeking out real fish, is it? No, I reasoned, it is not, which is precisely why a pretend man in the market for a mackerel or two for his tea should have been using it. Still, I loaded up the other bloody great pole with equally gratuitous twenty-pound line, threading it through the six eyelets from butt to tip. I don't think I have ever even bought a fish weighing anywhere near twenty pounds, let alone caught one, but I figured that it was better to err on the safe side. Besides, the bigger the tackle the better, right?

I delicately lashed a diminutive and pretty 26-gram silver and blue shimmery spinning lure to the end of the line before taking a deep breath or two and relying on distant muscle memory and all-too-familiar blind faith to heave the tip of the rod backwards in what I thought passed as a graceful arc, before cranking my whole body into the explosion of energy of which a good, long cast comprises. So I've been told. On reflection, I think a few things went a bit wrong, which had the cumulative effect of ensuring that the whole thing went quite a lot wrong. Firstly, casting a 26-gram lure with no additional weight is only any good if the total weight of line paid out by doing so is not more than 26 grams. When it is, all sorts of laws of physics involving inertia and mass and moments and all manner of other things the complexity of which makes me feel a bit giddy come into play and the line starts to travel faster than the weight itself. Secondly, 'firstly' does not get any better if you've got about fifty yards too much line on your spool. Thirdly, my timing, strength and overall competence were nowhere near as high as I would have liked them to be. Fourthly, casting twenty-odd grams of something is perhaps not as productive as it might be when using a rod that has 'casting weight 4–6 oz' written on it. The net, and extremely rapid, consequence of all this meant that the line paid off the spool as quickly, simultaneously and excitedly as a horde of liberated schoolchildren, spiralled into a monstrous tangle, hit the bottleneck that was the second eyelet down and stopped. The lure had flown a sweeping five yards or so before being violently yanked back and slapping – just – into the water, which was still a good four yards below my feet. I'm sure I could hear the lure gagging and see its glued-on eye bulging as it dangled impotent and visible just below the surface. Charlie tried to suppress a snort of laughter under one of his front paws, but I heard him well enough. No grilled bass for him that night.

I flicked the spinner back over the side of the jetty and severed it from the the end of the line, the excess of which I paid out from the spool, removed and stashed safely in my gear bag in order that I could dispose of it somewhere slightly more environmentally sensitive. I attached a trace of three feather-type lures to the line on the big rod and dangled it over the wall in an experiment to ascertain whether any animal stupid enough to mistake them for food was actually edible.

While I am on the subject of stupid animals and food, I feel it may be appropriate to digress slightly here in order to relate a salutary anecdote. It is often the case that a pastime will elucidate some truth about life – tripe tropes such as 'It's the taking part that counts, not the winning' spring to mind – but it is rare that life in general will teach you something about a particular pastime. Just over a year before the Scotland trip, Charlie and I had joined Alex and the boys for a few days of their summer holiday in Cornwall. One shimmering morning, we took a picnic to the beach and, after eating, Dylan and I made a 'boat' in the sand and pretended to 'fish' from the side of it. We attached a piece of bread to the hook on his crab line and dangled it over the 'side'. I swore we had a bite or two, but Dyl didn't buy it and consequently got a bit bored. We turned our attentions instead to a remarkably imaginative spot of clam diving in the sand. Meanwhile, Charlie diverted his attentions to the small piece of bread that was still skewered to the hook. Luckily, I noticed what he was doing in time, sort of, and managed to grab it before he swallowed it. My instinct, of course, was to try to pull it out, but it spiked through his tongue near the back of his mouth. The stupid animal that day was me, for sure. I have certain but nebulous ethical misgivings about using live bait for fishing, but also now have a rule that precludes using any bait in which Charlie might take any scoffing interest. Whenever he is around, I also do my best to scout around the area in which I am fishing to ensure that no one else has left any baited hooks lying around, and I can only implore anyone who takes their dog fishing to do the same, and anyone who leaves baited hooks lying around to take the bloody things with them. Charlie was in a good deal of discomfort because of my ignorance that day. I think he has forgiven me, but I'm still finding it difficult to absolve myself, largely because I cannot help but think of – and shudder at – what might have happened had I not got to him before he swallowed.

I attached a different spinner (well, I'd had no luck with the previous one, had I?) to the other rig, comprising the eight-foot spinning rod (casting weight 10–30 g), smaller reel and still wildly optimistic six-pound line. The whole set-up weighed approximately a quarter of the large one, and cast roughly ten times as far. I got a good deal of casting practice that day, and in fact really began to enjoy the steady, rhythmic motion of the slow, precise backswing, the remarkably easily remembered and instinctive timing of whipping the rod overhead and releasing the line from under the left forefinger, the swoop of the spinner and line towards the surface of the water, the tactile click of the bale arm as it does so and you begin to wind back in – either in a steady, slow motion or by using a gentle 'pull, pause, wind' action that mimics the throes of a wounded fish. This pendulum, when it beats smoothly on a cloudless, timeless, salty promontory, is the only measure you need. After an hour or so, though, the fact that I wasn't catching anything, despite my immense enjoyment of the process of trying to do so, slowly began to irk me. I guess the truth is that the process of fishing and the action of catching fish are inextricably linked and, yes, the taking part *does* count, but winning was why I was there. And 'winning' meant outsmarting at least one fish. I began to conclude that either the fish were not as stupid as I thought they were (an unlikely eventuality in my experience) or I was not as clever as some people seem to think I am (an assertion on which I would stake everything I own).

Charlie, however, did sterling work when it came to gleaning a little local knowledge by introducing me to a couple of fellow anglers during the afternoon, both of whom were most forthcoming with advice. None of it, through no fault of their own, turned out to be of any use whatsoever, but it was pleasant to talk to them nonetheless. The fishing gossip is purely functional, but the rest of what complete strangers will tell you when you have a dog and the willingness to listen is what makes it all worthwhile.

As is everyone's opening gambit to someone with a fishing rod in their hand.

Any luck today?

It's always 'luck'. To feast on fresh, organic, home-grown vegetables may take a few months of research, hard work and dedication to get them to 'just grow'. No one stands next to me in my garden come September time and asks me if I've had 'any luck' with my carrots this year, but it seems that all it takes for a fish to 'just get caught' is for you to be a jammy bastard. The man questioning my fortunes that afternoon was a glinting, wiry but broad-shouldered, greying and roll-up tooting Scouser whose mouth had taken on the appearance of one that had found each and every word of its life bitter and bile-laden, but its owner was simultaneously drily humorous. After making overtures towards Charlie (the responses to which which were a wag, a sniff and 'Have you got any food?') he proceeded to tell me about a veritable menagerie of his ex-pets that were buried in his back garden. He then went on to relay the story of his current dog, the synopsis of which was 'Springer spaniel, ex-working dog, now utterly ga-ga', and proceeded to precis the last few years of his own life. Until five years previously, he had lived 'down south' (i.e. in Liverpool), and had run his own chauffeur driving business, but had moved here after early retirement for some peace. He now drove a fish lorry 'part-time' for around fifty hours a week 'to stop him from getting bored'.

'Cool. Have you got any tips on catching fish hereabou—'

'Twenty cars I had. Walked away from it all. Moved up here. Started fishing.'

He was teasing with me. Wily old mullet. I was going to have to be cunning, and strike when he'd taken a little more conversational bait.

'Any regrets?'

'Not one day,' his voice assured me, as his mouth told me that every waking moment had been a pointless and grinding waste of time.

'Tell me about fish, please.'

Still too early. He told me he was called Gerry. He told me where he lived and how to get there. He gave me the low-down on his lorry, which stood idle on the upper jetty while waiting for a trawler to come in. He then told me how beautiful Charlie's eyes were. Finally, he nibbled.

'Any luck today?' It may be everyone else's opening gambit, but after the amount of time I'd spent talking to this guy it felt more like some kind of valediction. He surveyed the square of concrete over a surprising amount of which I had managed to spread my fishing gear, my dog, his accessories and a half-empty bottle of wine. My frustrated and sarcastic side wanted to reply that yes, as he could see, I was knee-deep in a slithery flapping of ocean foodstuffs, and ask him whether he had any idea of where I could dispose of this glut.

'Nah. I don't really know the area. Any pointers?'

'Have you tried Port Logan?'

I knew the name, but couldn't place it. 'Not yet.'

He gave me directions, which I have to admit I only half listened to, and said that on a low tide there I could bag as many bass 'as I could carry'. Gerry had assured me that Port Logan was east of where we were, and concurred when I suggested that I might stop off on the way home to stock up, but upon close inspection of my map later on, it appeared that he assumed I was taking the long road back, quite possibly via Stranraer and Ireland. Port Logan sits bravely on the edge of the hammerhead that forms the very westernmost point of Galloway, a good fifty miles by road west of the Isle, and diametrically opposed to the direction in which I had planned to travel home.

Besides, another man in his early twenties, blond haired, bare chested, tanned, heavily tattooed and thick gold-chained, to whom I got chatting soon after Gerry had scampered off to talk scampi with the now-ashore skipper, assured me that if I were to fish off the end of Burrow Head just before a high tide, I could get 'seven-poond bass'. Why on earth would I want to drive all the way to Port Logan when all I had to do was roll out of my tent and dangle my tackle in the water? When I got back to the campsite, however, I realized that Andy had omitted to tell me how to get near enough to the sea from Burrow Head to fish without using all your line just getting your lures in the water. Everywhere I checked there were nothing but vertiginous drops with seemingly no safe way down. I was even less likely to risk life and limb to catch fish than I was going to drive fifty miles out of my way to do so, and decided that I would spend the next afternoon on the jetty again. It didn't really seem like a hardship to do so, and I had vivid memories of catching a good variety of fish from there in the past. The fish weren't to know that I was nearly two and a half decades older.

Despite the disappointment of the day, I still managed to rustle up a tasty fish supper. I couldn't justify the expense of eating in the Steampacket again (but did manage to convince myself that a quick pint on the way home was entirely within my means) and had, reasonably I feel, assumed that the campsite cafe would be open until the same time as the shop: nine o'clock. However, all cooking activities ceased at eight, so I availed myself of the extensive selection of produce available for self-preparation in the shop. Six slices of white bread and a tin of sardines in tomato sauce may not be everyone's idea of culinary nirvana, but I was on a fishing trip. This wasn't the intended way of procuring them, obviously, but I needed to keep up my intake of omega-3 fatty acids up somehow or another. I'd be bonkers not to.

After 'dinner', I went back to the arcade with my two-pence pieces. Instead of the graceful, hypnotic machines I remembered from my youth with sliding trays and coin slots at the top, there was a single clumsy, ersatz affair with static tiers ranked with coins and a frantically spinning paddle wheel at the bottom, at which all it was possible to do was drop coins randomly through front-mounted apertures. No skill or timing involved whatsoever. That machine fleeced me of 86p faster than either of my kids could manage even in their most imaginative, cute or persuasive form. I wondered what had fascinated me so much about those other machines as a child, and what it is about them that still waylays me as an adult. Maybe it was their similarity to the process of fishing that drew me. It is reasonable to assume that the sea, given the right time, tide and tackle, is as likely to relinquish a proportion of its fish as those machines are of providing money. It is the perceived potential for riches of one kind or another, the process of attaining them and, most importantly, the ease and convenience with which we forget the inevitable law of diminishing returns, that draws all people to their chosen obsession.

My particular obsession the next morning was to get clean. I had already been informed by a handwritten sign on their door that the showers near my tent were 'out of order because of a missing part' (something trivial such as hot water, no doubt). At 8.30 the previous evening, while I was scouring the shop for my 'pain avec poisson', I was told by the same man I had seen there that morning and who had sucked his teeth so thoroughly at my ice blocks that, although the pool showers were now closed, they should reopen at nine o'clock in the morning.

Sometimes you just know that you stink, so at 8.59 I was standing almost patiently with towel and soap waiting for the showers adjacent to the outdoor pool to open. Just outside the block, a man was shuffling wheelie bins around in a manner that led me to believe that at any moment he might sidle up to me and bet me a tenner that I couldn't tell him which one the shit was in.

'Nay opin teel teen, pal.'

'But I was told it was nine last night.'

'I dinna ken who tol' ye tha',' his tone softened as I edged towards him, probably more because of stench than menace, 'but here ye go.'

He unlocked the gate to the pool, which in turn allowed me access to the shower block. Here was my much-needed opportunity for me to stand under hot running water and stop smelling of sardines, sweat and beer. As far as I'm concerned, a shower is purely functional in nature. A bath, whose decadence can last well over an hour with a good book and a tin or two of beer, is a place to relax, reflect, isolate and meditate. A shower is simply a way of removing dirt. At least it should be.

The shower head itself looked promising enough – six inches in diameter and peppered with a plethora of purposeful-looking perforations, ready to have sufficient pounds per square inch of water blasted through them to hose me clean in seconds. The reality, though, was less 'power shower' than 'flower-power shower'. Washing was turned into a strategic-planning exercise of military complexity involving having to figure out the optimum time to press the self-returning button to get the water to come out. When fully depressed I was treated to a pleasantly warm sprinkle and would lather energetically before the button snapped off with an abrupt 'ptfth' leaving me with no more than a dribble. It felt like the Forth Bridge of showering – by the time I'd washed my hair, it felt as if my toes were already dirty again.

The previous evening, after conversation with Charlie had all but dried up, I read him a section from *TOTAL Angler Fishing* that made it quite clear that it is possible to use a 'beachcaster' rod in locations other than a beach, provided you have a suitable amount of line on your spool and a decent amount of weight at the other end of it. So, after my 'shower', I headed into Whithorn, a town some four miles north-west of the Isle, in order to find myself some bait to attach, along with four ounces of lead, to one of what seemed like hundreds of rigs at my disposal.

B. Perks and Son, of 118 George Street, Whithorn, has a door that swishes on a burnt-ochre rush mat underneath it and, when you swing it open, a real bell that dings just above it. The shop contained enough shelves to make negotiating the twelve feet or so from the entrance to the counter a journey worth concentrating on, which in turn carried most domestic aids from boot wax to car body repair products via washing lines, Rawlplugs and plungers. It smelt of metal polish, leather and linseed oil. And fish, which neatly answered my question in Chapter One regarding Izaak Walton and what the bloody hell an ironmonger knows about fishing. Whithorn is the sort of town where it is eminently possible and indeed commercially expedient that the fishmonger also knows a fair bit about ironing.

'Can I help ye?'

An upright and wise-looking man with wild but thinning hair had appeared behind the nut-brown, two-inch-thick, highly polished lift-up and brass-hinged counter with his hands wedged into his beige, zip-fronted cardigan. I was put in mind of both Albert Einstein and Grandpa Joe from the original film version of *Charlie and the Chocolate Factory.*

'What baits do you have at the moment?' It was a daft question, as I didn't really know a great deal about what constituted suitable bait for any kind of fish, except that sand eel are good for bass, and that if mackerel are dappy enough to try to eat feathers then it doesn't matter a hoot what you use as bait for them anyway.

'Squid, mackerel, sand eel, rag, lug and,' he opened the freezer behind him, 'aye, a wee bit o' razor.'

'I'll get some mackerel and a bag of sand eel, if I may please.' I reckoned that if the sand eel didn't work, I could always fry up the mackerel on the camping stove.

'Four pounds, please, my friend.' He really did sound like someone who thought I was just that.

I set myself up at the end of the jetty again, and this time rigged up the beachcaster with a 'wishbone' rig. This has two hooks arranged in a formation looking much as its name might suggest. Onto one of these I wove a strip of mackerel, and impaled a sand eel on the other. I looped a breakaway lead on the end of the whole arrangement and this time lobbed it sixty yards or so onto the bottom in the middle of the harbour, where I let it waft about pointlessly while I set up and set about casting the spinning rig.

After half an hour or so of nothing happening except the exacerbation of some slight strains picked up while casting the day before and the reeling in of the wishbone rig (only to find that half of the sand eel and all but a shimmer of the mackerel had been eaten by something almost certainly crustacean in nature), I began to feel a number of things. Firstly, I started to get that sense about fish similar in nature to what I had felt while digging slippery, weed-infested allotment mud three Novembers previously so I could grow some potatoes. Wouldn't it be easier to go and buy some? My second impulse was that there was a perfectly good pub serving fantastically cold beer not even 200 yards from where I was sitting, in whose comfort and shade I could traditionally embroider a whole quilt of fabrications about the sizes of the One That Got Away and nobody would be any the wiser. Thirdly, having gone to Scotland in search of, among the fishing, silence and stillness, I was instead having to fish to the soundtrack of a dozen or so 'bairns' of ages ranging from around eight to fourteen-ish jumping from the end of the jetty into the rising tide. This they did by noisily hoiking and dramatically spitting (an action that I shall henceforth refer to as 'gralloching') into the water, then using this puddle of unmentionables as some kind of target onto which they took a running jump. At one point, and as I had just started to wrangle in earnest with the pub idea, a girl of around thirteen and what must surely have been her younger brother approached me.

'D'ye think the water's deep enough tae jump intae here?' She gestured to the water at the very end of the jetty where I was fishing from, just around the corner from where the others were gralloching, galloping and gambolling.

'You tell me where to catch fish round here, and I'll tell you whether or not you'll break your ankles by jumping in.'

Unfortunately, she knew about as much about local fishing haunts as she did about the nasty, jagged and invisible rocks just below the surface of the water. I peered over the edge.

'Yeah, you should be fine. Get your brother to go first, though.'

I was ready to pack up when a portly, ruddy, middle-aged man in a black string vest sidled down the steps towards us at a forty-five degree angle – almost crab-like, as if he was vaguely concerned that he might stumble if his belly got too far ahead. Charlie greeted him with barely suppressed pleading, as if he was a dear but distant friend who was guaranteed to look after him better than I ever have, and would he take him home please?

'Hasn't he got beautiful eyes?'

'Yes. Now tell me what in Jesus Christ's name I've got to do to catch some bloody fish round here.'

'Well, I'm off out in a boat with a mate, but if you're struggling here then you should maybe try your hand off the rocks.'

I managed to quell the urge to make like Charlie and beg him to please, please, please take me with him on the boat. Instead, I cajoled him into being a little more specific as to which rocks he would suggest.

'Just over the other side of that headland over there,' he gestured behind him, 'to the left of that monument thing.'

I thanked him before swigging down the last mouthful of the glass or so of wine that had escaped me the night before and packed up my gear. The sun had been obscured by some high, thick and stubborn cloud and sufficient breeze was whipping from the north-east to ensure that Charlie would be cool enough in the car if I left the windows ajar. I spread his blanket out on the rear seat, wedged a bowl of water into one of the rear footwells and stashed all but the spinning rig and a couple of spare spinners in the boot. I also took a plastic bag to carry any catches in, my faux-leatherman multi-tool and a tea towel to help hold fast any flapping, writhing and slippery fish I may catch while I humanely bashed them over the head with my erm . . . aah. Right, hang on – I need a fish-basher. Otherwise known as a 'priest'. I had meant to get one when I ordered all the other gear, but had experienced a moment of parsimony, reasoning that it couldn't be that difficult to find something lying around that may be suitable. Funny how sometimes the simplest of criteria can be to most elusive to fulfil, and I never did manage to find or fashion a suitable implement. I was therefore going to have to kill anything that I caught quite literally with my bare hands. I could not entertain the idea of allowing any animal that I had caught to flap and gasp its way to its demise. I happen to think that any creature that has not been shown the respect of a dignified and rapid death as free from pain as possible tastes kind of funny, and I find it difficult to stomach anything else.

As I was locking the car, I heard a voice from ten yards or so behind me.

'Any luck today?'

I strolled towards the voice's owner and what I assumed was his wife, who was holding what I was convinced was a very sharp-looking eight-inch cook's knife. I panicked momentarily, as I fretted over whether there might be such a thing as a right or wrong answer to his question. But as I looked down I saw what he was busying himself with – a standpipe and a fish that may well have put the strain into my six-pound breaking strain line. She was chief cook, he pollack-washer.

'No more than yesterday.'

He looked at me quizzically. Either he didn't quite understand what I'd said, or he couldn't quite fathom how it was possible for anyone to fish for two consecutive days round there and not catch anything. As I approached, he told me that he'd had twenty or thirty like the one he was washing that day alone, but had put the others back because 'Ye shouldnae tak more than ye need.'

I couldn't have agreed more, and couldn't have cared less

whether or not this was macho exaggeration. One like his would be plenty.

'How d'you manage that then?'

'Spinnin'. Just to the left o' that monument on the other side o' the rocks there.' He pointed in the direction I had already been heading. I thanked him for his help before making my way hurriedly over the headland and the rocks to find myself a suitable vantage point.

As I cast out a blue and silver spinner, a six-inch swell licked and gurgled around the lichen-stained and barnacle-pocked boulders, split and criss-crossed by millennia of upheaval and carved by countless tides. I realized that, for the first time since arriving, I had found one of the things I came looking for. Absolute quiet – or, more accurately, peace. In my version of things, the sucking of a tiny swell, the occasional distant, plaintive 'moo' of a stocky Friesian and the faint shuffle of line paying out from a spool may not technically constitute complete 'quiet', but I don't think I have ever experienced, and have certainly never fully appreciated, such peace. The tide had just reached its second zenith of the day, and after a few speculative casts to different locations using a couple of the spinners I had brought, I remembered something that I'd read in one of my mags. On a dropping tide, a good policy is to cast across the mouth of a gully, into which predatory fish will swim on the rising tide. As it falls, they will make their way out, searching for supper as it is carried past by the ebb. I looked around for a suitable inlet, and soon spotted a likely looking place some sixty yards south of where I stood. I scrambled around the headland a little in order to position myself a little closer, and did as the magazine had instructed.

It was probably the fourth or fifth cast. In all honesty, it could have been a dozen – precious few things in life do not need to be counted. I was performing the 'pull, release, reel in, pull' routine to convince the big fish that this little 'fish' was not only very tasty, but also had little ability or motivation to swim off in a hurry. I'd just let the spinner go into free fall for about the tenth time that cast, and had started to reel in, and there it was. Resistance and a bent rod. Dead weight. I cursed, as I realized that I had let the lure sink too far and had snagged it on either a rock or some thick, rawhide seaweed. There was no familiar judder or thud on the line, just a sullen heaviness. I pulled, struck at the obstruction, and the tip bent like an exaggerated caricature. Then all went slack – surely a lost piece of tackle. Then stiffness again, followed by the taut line darting quickly across the surface of the water. I had good reason to believe that I had indeed found not only peace, but also supper. I reeled in to try to stop whatever it was at the other end from diving for cover somewhere where it really would be impossible to get it back from. For an instant I was tempted to let it try to fight, to 'give it a chance', but remembered quickly that this was actually only going to prolong what was almost certainly the agony of having between one and three of the treble hooks at the tail end of the lure lodged in its mouth. I levered, pulled and reeled in quickly and firmly until I could see the flapping white flag of underbelly and flagging surrender to the inevitable. I could not yet tell what it was – possibly a pollack; maybe a coalfish. It looked too flat and broad to be a mackerel. I reeled in further, until I could hoist it clear of the water. As I did so, despite the fact that it was not a huge fish by any feat of the imagination, the line tightened dramatically and squeaked on its spool as the rod tip quivered and danced to the beat of the fish's gasping contortions. Dropping my rod, I wrapped the tea towel around it as quickly as my trembling hands could manage and, gripping its pulsing, writhing length firmly belly-down against the rock, brought the edge of my right hand down sharply onto its exposed neck, just above its pink and now redundant gills. It spasmed and jerked again. Terrified, shocked, indignant. This could have been reflex, but I had to be sure. I struck it again, and this time it stilled and sagged under my hand. I turned my attention to the mouth in order to remove the two hooks still snagged there. Everything else around me had ceased to exist – no sea, no rocks, no sky, no cow, no monument. Only the creature whose life I had just taken, and me. I grabbed the lure and removed the first of the hooks with my fingers, but the second proved to be more firmly wedged and stubborn. I reached for the multi-tool and opened the pliers in order to get a better grip. As I closed them around the hook, the fish curled and arced, stiff again. I calmed myself with the certainty that this was merely an electrical, post-mortem impulse – blood was seeping from its mouth, gills and eyes and trickling down the shiny black rock to dye the small, drying pools of high-tide salt water. I levered out the hook and stooped down to sea level in order to wash the secreted blood and excrement off its body. As I laid it back on the rock, although quite and unmitigatedly dead, it continued to twitch minutely along its lateral line. For the first time in eight years or so, I had taken the life of an animal for food.

Never before then had I done so at the same time as questioning whether this was a morally defensible thing to do. Or, if I had, the answers had certainly come easier than they did that day. It crossed my mind that if I had qualms about using live bait when contemporary technology had made it was perfectly possible to catch fish using artificial methods, then surely it followed that eating animals was a similarly outdated activity. Then I reminded myself of the last time I ate tofu and redirected my gaze back towards my dinner. It was a small pollack, distinguishable from its cousin the coalfish by its protuberant lower jaw, probably just over a pound in weight. I quite deliberately had not invested in a set of spring scales – as long as I could ascertain whether a fish was large enough to feed me as well as being over prescribed landing sizes, then all other information was somewhat superfluous.*

I fished for a further three-quarters of an hour or so, luckily to no avail – I certainly did not need any more than I already had, but I think the adrenaline had got the better of me. Eventually, the sea decided to even things up a little and snagged my spinner on what really was a large rock or lump of seaweed. Either that, or a fish so large I had no desire to try to land it anyway. I pulled and tugged and yanked, only for the line to finally fall slack and weightless.

Back at the campsite, I realized that my 'camping and cooking' list really was in some serious need of embellishment. I had already established that it needed more in the way of mallets, pillows and corkscrews, but I also discovered that it was somewhat thin in the way of foodstuffs. I had brought olive oil, salt, pepper and, in the hope of fish being on the menu, some home-grown tarragon. Oh, and some Pentland Javelin potatoes from the allotment. As it turned out though, and as any decent chef

---

* A note on minimum landing sizes. Anglers are required by law to return fish that are under the minimum landing size (MLS). This is an essential part of the environmental role of the angler, as important as taking all their crap with them and not leaving it lying around for birds to meet a protracted and painful death by getting wound up in it. The MLS is there for a good reason – most are calculated to be the size a certain species of fish will grow to before it spawns. Killing a fish that has not spawned does not only take that fish from the water, but also its thousands, possibly millions, of offspring. See table opposite for a list of minimum landing sizes for various species.

Minimum Landing Sizes

Below is a selection of some of the more common and/or familiar fish caught around the British Isles. Wherever you're fishing from, boat or shore, if it's not this big you must put it back.

SPECIES	LATIN NAME (nomenclaturus pretensioni)	MLS (cm)
bass	Dicentrarchus labrax	36
coalfish (saithe)	Pollachius virens	35
cod	Gadus morhua	35
dab	Limanda limanda	23
dogfish (huss)	all species, genus Scyliorhinidae	35
common eel	Anguilla anguilla	35
conger eel	Conger conger	58
haddock	Melanogrammus aeglefinus	30
halibut	Hippoglossus hippoglossus	50
ling	Molva molva	72 (Defra 63)
mackerel	Scomber scombrus	20 (North Sea 30)
mullet	all species, genus Mugilidae	30
plaice	Pleuronectes platessa	27
pollack	Pollachius pollachius	35
skate	Raja batis/alba/oxyrinchus	11.35 kg
lemon sole	Mocrostomus kitt	25
dover sole	Solea solea	24
whiting	Merlangius merlangus	27

Sources – Defra, Scottish Fisheries Protection Agency

(not that I claim to be one) will concur, if your ingredients are fresh and chemical-free, then it's really not necessary to do a great deal with them apart from cook them for just as long as it takes and eat them.

I opened a screwtop bottle of wine and connected the gas to the camping stove and proceeded to do something that I had been hankering after for some time – to cook myself a meal consisting solely of ingredients that I had either grown or caught myself. True, I did not evaporate my own salt, nor did I press my own olives for oil (although I did grind my own peppercorns, for those pedantic enough to care), but I don't think that I can remember a meal that tasted quite as succulent, sweet or satisfying as the freshest possible pan-fried pollack and boiled new potatoes I ate that warm evening.

Enough about me, what of Steinbeck? Of his best friend, he says:

> Charley the dog has no nerves. Gunfire or thunder, explosions or high winds leave him utterly unconcerned. In the midst of the howling storm [which had just visited their house], he found a warm place under a table and slept.*

In contrast, I would assert of mine that:

> Charlie the shit-head is a fat stinking jessie. The rustle of a crisp packet or a sneeze, clapping or whispering 'boo' in his ear leave him a jelly-like juddering bag of taut muscle and stretched fur. In the midst of the moderate shower that had just visited our tent, he lay on his back, legs akimbo, and

---

*   John Steinbeck, *Travels with Charley.*

twitched repeatedly like that poor, tasty fish I had karate-chopped the day before.

To be fair to the wee timorous beastie, the tent (like any tent) does tend to amplify the perceived severity of any rainfall, which that morning had ranged from a light drizzle that would have only just dampened after a hundred-yard walk, to a healthy, steady shower that may well have soaked after twenty. However, the tent's outer fabric suggested that it might have been stretched tighter than I had thought. It magnified this range from a moderate downpour to sounding as if someone had slit the belly of the sky as I did last night's fish, and its guts were splatting on the nylon. At one point, I actually began to believe that someone had forgone the evisceration phase and was simply lobbing thousands of fish at the tent.

During a lull, just after nine o'clock, I trudged damply towards the toilet block with Charlie in order that we could perform our morning constitutionals. I fed him when we got back to the tent before opening the car door so that he could sit in its security rather than the tent's precariousness while I went and fixed myself up with another bacon and egg roll. Before he got in the car, he shook himself in the way that dogs do when they are damp – from just a whisker in front of his nose to a vertebra or two behind his tail. He then wagged the latter an extra few times and looked at me as if to say, 'You might have opposable thumbs, but you can't do that, can you?'

'Perhaps not,' I replied, 'but you can't open car doors, and I'm going to get breakfast and a mug of tea somewhere where I can't hear the rain.' I shut the car door and squelched, feeling as grey and flat as the smudged sky, over to the cafe.

I have seen few places that I could accurately describe as

'godforsaken' (mainly because, as a committed atheist, everywhere basks in that status), but Burrow Head campsite that morning really did look as if every deity of every denomination had indeed ceased to give any kind of toss about it whatsoever. Now that someone had seen fit to airbrush out everything beyond the immediate horizon, it looked as if God had not only forsaken the place, but had also been sufficiently contemptuous of it to cut it adrift in a sea of murk. By the time I reached the cafe I was not damp enough to have approached true 'wetness', which somehow I would have minded less as there is a strange comedy in a soaking. However, there's nothing funny about being clammy. I looked back to see Horace, who was barely visible, and who in turn contained Charlie, who was, as usual, barely sentient. For someone who had achieved a long-held ambition the previous night, I was pretty bloody pissed off. Maybe the pollack wasn't oily enough or something.

The same old boy that had been behind the counter since I had arrived – and had quite possibly been there since Edward I had arrived – was still there. He was reading his newspaper and operating two tills, one for the shop and one for the cafe, and treating each customer as two separate people if they availed themselves of both. As he was serving a couple of young lads, I glanced at the front page of his tabloid. It was smothered with CCTV footage of one of the suicide bombers who had torn London apart on 7 July and an unsuitably sensationalist headline. This, along with my mood, put me obliquely in mind of the memorial to the shipwrecked fishermen on the headland. The man behind the counter was called John. He wore tooled, leathery skin under his starched and pressed short-sleeved white shirt and equally stiff, straight and snowy hair. His deep pools of eyes were so dark that they appeared to be all pupil, and his clipped, economical local accent descended at the end of every sentence with an expression of intelligent resignation. I mentioned the memorial to him after I had ordered my breakfast.

'Oh, aye. Terrible thing, that was.'

'Did it hit people very hard round here?' Almost certainly a stupid question, but I was trying to extend sympathy, not extract juicy gossip.

'Och, yes. Wasnae any famlee no touched by it.' He gazed down, as if they had all been his own.

'Did you know any of them?' Considering that seven men from a community of only five hundred or so had perished, this was also a bit of a no-brainer.

'Aye. All of 'em. Since they were bairns.' A pause, and another glance towards the counter. 'Every one of 'em.'

I felt a need to be very sensitive. A gash that large in a community that small can fester for some time – I could sense a strong feeling of injustice from John – either cosmic or legislative.

'There was a court case, wasn't there?'

'Aye, there was.'

The briefest and most telling of pauses suggested that to take this line of conversation any further would be neither wise nor sensitve. As if to underline this, John folded his strong, wiry arms tightly, pursed his lips and looked down at his paper.

'Terrible business, these suicide bombs. D'ye ken anyone there?'

It had been a week, to the nearest ten minutes, since four bombers had scarred London with the sign of a cross – north, east, south, west – killing over fifty people. One death, one minor injury, even, is inexcusable in the name of fundamentalism, but the majority of Londoners were left personally untouched by the tragedy. This is in no way intended to suggest that the deaths of those people in London were any less difficult to bear for those who knew the victims but, as John said, in the Isle, no one was left unscathed – everybody lost a brother, a son, a father, a lover or a friend that they had skipped primary school to go and jump off the jetty and do some hearty gralloching with. I may well have seen them doing it while I was on holiday one year. In a village like this, everyone would have been touched with all the subtlety and innocuousness of a mallet. Maybe they did feel, justifiably, godforsaken.

'No. No, I didn't. I don't live there.'

For some reason I didn't feel like fishing. I tried to tell myself that I must, that this was the primary reason for my being there. But I felt a bit weird, if truth be told, and I couldn't quite place why this was. In order to give myself some thinking time I trundled around the campsite with Charlie and recorded some suitably bleak video footage of the campsite to show the folks back home what a lovely time I'd had. While I did so, I tried to come to terms with the fact that, similar to having set out to dig an allotment and ending up actually growing vegetables, I had now gone fishing and caught fish. But going from preparing soil to pulling out carrots takes months, whereas this had been a matter of a couple of weeks. I decided not to fish again that day, and convinced myself that this was as a result of the lack of refrigeration facilities. I'd planned to have a bar meal at the Queen's Arms pub later, so any fish that I may have caught would have gone off anyway. Catching fish only to put them back felt a little like carting a cow to an abattoir, taking it inside and show-ing it a cleaver or two to scare it witless, then telling it that it was only a joke, and would it like to go back in its field now? There's nothing like a little selective moralizing to avoid having to ask yourself too many difficult questions or to make too many difficult decisions.

So instead I decided to visit a couple of small towns that sat resoundingly (and conveniently) on my list of Places I Must Not Leave Without Seeing. First, I made a quick trip into the Isle to run Charlie around the headland and to check whether the Steampacket Inn (where I was booked in to stay the following night) was more accommodating in its fish-storage facilities than the campsite. It was, which meant that for a mere £22 over and above what one night at the campsite cost, not only was I going to get a bath, a television, a comfortable bed, a decent loo, a large breakfast when it was convenient for me, a harbour view and an absence of screaming and unruly kids while I was trying to get to sleep, but I would also have the opportunity to take some food home for my family.

Unmissable town number one was Wigtown, because it purports to be 'Scotland's national book town'. Just to make sure that people know this, the 'W' of the town's name on the sign-posts consists of two open books depicted end-on. Not only does its high street boast what is surely more than enough parking capacity for its bibliophile clientele, but its central reservation actually diverges to form a large grassy area surrounded by imposing spiked railings and on which stands a very grand Victorian neo-Gothic-esque (i.e. it looks a bit like a gingerbread house) public building, which now accommodates the lending library and council offices. I mention this building specifically because its grandeur and architectural interest sets it quite markedly apart from pretty much all the rest of the place. Indeed, as I sat in Readinglasses – an incongruously charming little bookshop-cum-cafe – I noted in my journal that Wigtown was a 'dreary little place'. True, it was a dreary little day, and at the time I felt like a dreary little man who had, thus far, caught but one dreary little fish and who was attempting to write another dreary little book, but I remember receiving a postcard from my sister Jacqueline, while she and Jon were on a dirty (or was that dreary too?) weekend up there a few years ago. The photographer Martin Parr published a book called *Boring Postcards* recently, and I have to say that he really let this one that Jacq sent me slip through the net. In the background it depicts the library set against a largely white and predominantly dreary sky. In the foreground, just in front of the spikey railings, a number of visually predominant signposts inform you that, in one direction, the A714 will take you to Port William and some of the way towards Whithorn (after which you need the A746). We are also informed by a sign slap bang in the middle of the card that walking a small distance in the same direction will locate us squarely outside the toilets. Travelling 180 degrees in the other direction will take you past the police station on the way to Newton Stewart, some six miles or so to the north. It is a fabulous postcard, on the back of which is printed the slogan 'Wigtown – The Centre of Things'. As I happened to be in town with my camera, I thought perhaps I should start work on a rival card on the reverse of which I could print 'Wigtown – The Middle of Nowhere'.

When I was there, I estimated the number of bookshops in the town to be somewhere between six and ten. Later research, however, suggested that there are in fact more like twenty-five of them, which contain a total of around a quarter of a million books. Before I ended up in Readinglasses for a snack, I had probably been into about 20 per cent of the shops, and had only had to open an infinitesimal percentage of the books in order to find out that either a good majority of them were overpriced, or I was being underpaid. A further possibility was that I was a miserable old tightwad who couldn't look at the price of anything without tutting to myself that I could get it for 50p in a charity shop back home. I did develop an unhealthy interest in one particular two-inch-thick paperback manual simply and almost irresistibly entitled *Medical Anomalies*. This book contained explicit drawings and photos of a range of deformations that made the Elephant Man look decidedly George Clooney. It would have been fully irresistible had it not cost £15 – however, if I wanted to look at people who might put me off my food, why would I want to pay that sort of money to do so when I could go next door and watch my mate Stevie eating his dinner for free?

I finished my cappuccino and made my way back to Horace and to a perpetually patient and perennially puzzled Charlie, and refocused on my road map to figure out the best route to my next destination. Garlieston, like the Isle, is another tiny village geographically and financially arranged around a harbour, which now plays host to more leisure craft than trawlers or merchant shipping. I dimly remembered the place as one more that I'd been dragged to as a kid to watch my dad make tea and because 'it was so beautiful'. Indeed, Jacq had reinforced this the day before my trip. She is now to all intents and purposes a grown-up, and had told me that I should go there. Therefore, in the absence of any more mature suggestions myself, I went there.

As I entered Garlieston – an odd little place, delineated by squat, low and predominantly white houses and overshadowed by a group of eerie, disused harbour buildings – a sign informed me of an exhibition in the 'Forteviot Hall' that promised to spill the beans on all there was to know about 'Garlieston's Secret War'. This sounded appropriate enough. I cannot think of a better way of ensuring a secret remains exactly that than by putting on an exhibition about it in a place like Garlieston. What was still a secret to me, though, was why I still felt so uneasy about going fishing. I suppose that in the absence of the stomach for eating another fish supper or the inclination for cooking one, I just didn't see the point in catching one.

Near the harbour head, I tried to squeeze Horace into as many of the five adjacent parking spaces as I could, and got out of the car. I'd decided to take Charlie on the walk that leads past the old harbour buildings and along a coastal path towards the wonderfully named Cruggleton Bay (which I later learned is a top spot for mackerel) and Sliddery Point. Garlieston's part in the war is probably worthy of an exhibition for good reason, because it would seem that absolutely nothing of any distinction whatsoever has happened there before or since. Charlie meandered heavily, sniffing and stopping and looking at me, saying, 'So what in hell's name made you bring me here, to this no-place of a town?' It was a warm if grey and muggy day, and the two halves of me, which had in the morning felt as if they'd been glued together wrong, seemed to be gradually slipping further and further out of alignment. One of them answered Charlie by saying that we were here because this was a fascinating place because of its local history, beguiling landscape and richness of visual and atmospheric texture. The other said, 'Fuck knows – fancy a pint somewhere else?'

I listened to the first voice for around two hundred yards, before heading up into the village itself to find some food and a point to existence. The former I managed to locate in the local shop, but the latter came thoroughly unexpectedly as I was making my way back from the Forteviot Hall. I had nipped there to see if I could find out what it was that was so secret about Garlieston's war, but it seemed that they really did mean what they said, as it was closed. As I was scrabbling around for one of my loose and metaphorical sheets of recycled paper on which to make a mental note to revisit the place on my way home two days later, my path crossed that of an eighty-umpty-year-old boy who was slowly making his way over the road towards the post office. His crooked walking stick appeared to be of little use. While I strolled along unthinkingly, walking was obviously an activity not to be taken either lightly or hurriedly by this man. As we met, he smiled at me. We struck up a conversation about tennis, as there was a match going on in the court over the road being played by a quartet of people with a combined age of somewhere around 512. We talked about 'rather them than me', 'in this heat, too' and 'I just watch it on telly' before he bid his farewell while agonizingly climbing the two bowed stone steps into the shop and post office. My spirits were unexpectedly lifted by the realization that, despite the utilitarian and often hostile surroundings, perhaps because of them, the people that live – exist – in places such as this seem to have a defiant joviality about them. On the whole, they do not seem somehow resentful at being alive, and do not appear to believe that they are owed anything by anybody except for the common courtesy of a smile and a little polite conversation.

The cloud had lifted, so Charlie and I ensconced ourselves on the lower portion of the jetty with the necessaries: blanket to sit on, water for him, wine for me, camera and tripod in place, Steinbeck to keep me well and truly in mine. I had, on the way back from Garlieston, decided that, after all my internal conjecture, I didn't want to fish that day because I didn't feel like it and that there was, in fact, nothing wrong with this. We'd done another circuit around the headland before we sat ourselves there, so Charlie was content to lie, sigh and rest his head on my thigh while glancing up at me occasionally to check that everything was where it should be. I took a couple of photographs of us on self-timer mode and settled down with Steinbeck. He quoted:

Non fumum ex fulgore, sed ex fumo dare lucem
Cogitat, et speciosa dehinc miracula promat.

I tried to translate this at a later date using an online Latin dictionary, but couldn't really make much sense of it. I'm not too sure whether it matters, but what seemed really important at the time was who wrote that piece of text. None other than Horace! Not the guinea pig, the philosopher (who lived between 65 and 8 BC, so the website wasn't completely useless). There are some moments during a day, however lacklustre the rest of it may have been, when a coincidence reassures you that you are indeed doing at least one right thing at roughly the right time. There are others, however, that can give you exactly the opposite impression. Just as I was topping up my wine, I heard a sploshing noise. I levelled the bottle out a little, thinking that perhaps I was pouring a little too enthusiastically. However, when I stopped pouring altogether, and the watery slapping did not, I looked up to see half a dozen or so fish cavorting and jumping out of the water as if there were so many of them in there that there wasn't quite enough room for all of them. Some might call this irony; I called it taking the piss. I had spent part of the previous two days trying to catch fish from that very spot, and the little bastards decided to turn up and have a frolic on the very day I deigned not to try to kill them. Anybody who knows me well enough will be aware of my tendency to perhaps take things a little too personally at times, but I'll be buggered if those slimy little shitbags weren't sticking their fins in their gills and blowing raspberries at me while they were doing their sodding fishy gymnastics. I was sorely tempted to get my spinning gear out of the car and catch a couple of them just to wipe the silly grins off their faces and to let them know exactly who was in control. Of course, I didn't do anything of the sort, mainly because on that particular score, on that particular day, I really wasn't in the mood to be proved wrong.

The next morning, having already ascertained that I could stash the shoals of fish I was going to haul in later that day in the fridges and/or freezers of the Steampacket Inn, I was feeling much more positive than I had previously. I had also checked whether it was going to be possible to leave Charlie in the cool of the hotel room while I fished from the headland. This meant that I could spend a lazy and productive few hours on the rocks that afternoon reeling in mackerel after mackerel, with the occasional bass to provide a little more sport and weight.

The previous evening, in the bar at Burrow Head while enjoying the spectator sport that was Thursday night bingo, I had got talking to a round, ruddy and expansive Scotsman called Colin who told me that he'd been fishing earlier that day from the very same headland and caught 'just over thirty mackerel, five pollack and one seagull'. Just for a moment, I was less interested in fish than in birds, and asked him to elucidate.

'I'd just cast out,' his right hand came perilously close to my third pint of the evening as he made an explanatory swooping gesture with his arms, 'and just before the lure hit the water . . .' this time he moulded the fingers and thumb of his right hand into a beak shape and made a violent pecking motion into the palm of his left, which obviously represented the spinner.

'What the bloody hell did it think it was doing?' The image had made me chuckle – seagulls come quite some way below cats in my scheme of animals that I feel any kind of pity for, so perhaps my level of concern for animal welfare was not what it might otherwise have been.

'No idea, but the hook got stuck in its beak all right.'

'What did you do?'

'Well, it put up a fight. I pulled it around a bit to try tae free it, and it tried tae get away.' His hands moved from holding an imaginary rod, one in front of the other, to one either side of his body, pulling alternately. 'It was a bit like flying a kite.'

I did the always inadvisable thing and tried to drink something fizzy and laugh simultaneously.

'At one point, it was headed straight towards a rockface.' He pulled his imaginary kite as if he were trying to keep it airborne while too close to the wind, nearly falling off his stool in the process. He recovered his balance at roughly the same time as saving the seagull from a splattering. We both chuckled beerily like old friends recounting a familiar story.

'So what happened?'

He supped his pint, sucked most of the froth from his generous moustache and removed the remainder with a sweep of his thumb and forefinger. As he replaced his half-full glass on the table, he exhaled and said, with a wink and a smile,

'The only one that got away today.'

I bought him another pint before asking him about the ones that didn't, and, more specifically, how I might achieve similar success. He told me that he'd fished with a trace of three feathers alternated with a single spinner when the weight and airy flapping of a trio of mackerel at a time got too much for him. He also said that he'd fished off the headland at 'about ten o'clock'.

'But wasn't it low tide then?'

'Nay, nay. I mean where, not when.' He drew a beery clock-face with the end of his forefinger on the table. 'Here's the headland, yeah?' I nodded. He put his finger in the middle of the circle.

'Monument?'

'Yep.' He moved his finger to the top edge of the circle.

'Twelve o'clock?'

'Uh-huh.' He traced round the edge anticlockwise sixty degrees and prodded firmly twice.

'Ten.'

'Aaaah!' Roughly where I had been on Wednesday and had caught a solitary one-pound pollack. I felt that maybe I was missing something.

'Any other tips?'

'Cast out just between the two buoys, just past 'em.'

'What sort of time?'

'Ooh, coupla hours or so before high tide. You'll get more than you can carry.'

By the time I had packed the tent and the remainder of my things into Horace, munched through a final bacon and egg roll and showered (just), there was still half a day to kill until 'a coupla hours or so before high tide' came around, and I had a purchase to make and a place to visit.

The incident on Wednesday, when I had tried to end the misery of a fish with the edge of my hand, had disturbed me a little. It wasn't quick, accurate or decisive enough – I needed to find a priest, or at least something that looked very much like one. There was only one place to go.

I brushed the bottom of the front door of Brian Perks's hardware shop against the rush mat, and at the 'ding' of the small bell, he appeared from the rear of the shop, hands still tucked half inside the pockets of his cardigan. I felt just a little like Mr Ben.

'Hello there! Any luck the other day?' He had obviously remembered my visit to buy the bait. In fact, it was entirely possible that he'd seen no one else since.

It almost felt churlish to reply that I had caught nothing, as if this might have been interpreted as an indictment more of his bait than of my angling ability. I also did not want to appear rude because he had actually remembered me. It isn't often, in the more populated areas of this country, that this sort of thing happens, nor is it that frequent that you actually get served by the man or woman whose name appears above a shop door. Unless the shop is a pub, of course.

'Oh, this and that. Not much really.' He nodded in sympathy and as a tacit acknowledgement that he knew very well that this meant, 'Bugger all, your bait's crap mate.'

'What can I do fo' ye today, then?'

The fact that I had just virtually admitted that I had caught next to nothing over the last couple of days made my request seem a little silly.

'I'm looking for a priest.' A smile as wispy and transient as dust in a narrow shaft of sunlight flickered across his lips as he blinked blankly at me. I wondered if I should have said 'cosh', 'club' or perhaps even 'fishbasher' instead. I expanded.

'For hitting fish over the head with to kill th—'

'Aye, aye. I ken.' He removed his hands from his pockets and used them to support himself on the counter while he leaned forward, inspecting me a little more closely as if I was a curious plant long thought dormant. 'It's just that you're the first person to've ever come in here and asked fo' one a' them.'

I was amazed. Not only had no one ever deemed the humane killing of fish a priority round there, but it also appeared that while iron bars may well have been an acceptable currency in those parts they were not an acceptable commodity. This man, with all due respect and kindness, must surely have been wearing the floorboards of that shop with the soles of his shoes since before decimalization, yet not once had he been asked for a priest. Staggering.

'Well, I don't suppose you have a length of steel or anything – just something that'll do the job better than my hands.' He looked a little perplexed and a tad troubled, as if he may well have just the thing, but wasn't quite sure what or where it was.

'Oh, hang on. I've got this. It was *made* fo' the job.' He delved under the counter top and resurfaced, beaming, as he held aloft an object that looked as if it may have been unearthed when the foundations for the shop were being dug. He assured me, though, that this thing had, quite literally, been fabricated for the very purpose in question. He was holding up a piece of wood of around ten inches long and of three-quarter-inch diameter that had been slowly patinated by the passage of time and scales. Attached to one end by means of four rough, hand-hammered rivets was a thick-walled length of brass tube, chamfered and dulled by air, blows and blood.

'That's what ye' need.'

I wasn't sure whether he was telling me this in order to sell it to me, or simply to make me insanely jealous.

'Well, that'd be grand, but . . .'

'I'll have tae charge ye fo' it, mind.'

'You don't want to sell me that, do you? I mean, it's yours, isn't it?'

'Ach, well, I can make meself a new one easy enough.'

'Are you sure? How much d'you want for it?'

Brian could not possibly have had any idea just how extraordinary a figure he could have got away with. This was no ordinary fish-basher. This was Brian Perks's fishbasher with about twenty years' worth of fish blood on it, along with the oil and sweat of his, and possibly countless others', cudgelling hands. I had £60 in my wallet, and knew exactly where the nearest cashpoint was. About twenty-five miles away, and I would have walked on my hands to get there if I could then get them on this piece of history.

'Gi' us a coupla quid fo' it.'

I didn't ask for a receipt. I am fairly imaginative when it comes to what might be construed as tax-deductible, but there are certain items that are beyond financial reason or measurement. I was as profuse with my thanks as I thought I could get away with before he began to suspect he could well have asked for much, much more, and I left the shop feeling like a complete bastard because I had accepted his change from my fiver.

Next port of call was Monreith, a cluster of beaches on the west side of the Machars peninsula and around eight miles distant from the Isle. These were our destination beaches when I was a boy, and I remembered them with huge affection and as the places where my father would instruct his family from his beach chair in the art of gathering large quantities of damp driftwood. Some of these he would whittle into vaguely recognizable animal forms with his unwieldy penknife, but most of which ended up being burnt (or, more accurately, 'smouldered') on the annual beach barbecue. I have absolutely no recollection of my dad lifting so much as a tea strainer in the kitchen at home, but give him a pile of damp sticks, a lighter and a packet of value sausages and he immediately transformed into Raymond sodding Blanc. I have never seen a better argument against the adage 'no smoke without fire' than watching my old man trying to light a beach barbecue, and how we avoided food poisoning will forever remain a mystery.

As I was going to be locking Charlie in an unfamiliar room later on, I deemed it only fair that he had the chance to stretch himself and get well and truly knackered beforehand. I left Horace on the Monreith Golf Club (ten quid, nine holes, all impossible) car park and strode up the hill down which we had just driven towards the Gavin Maxwell memorial. For those who are now scratching their heads and wondering just where they've heard that name before, Maxwell was the author who famously penned an enchanting naturalist's tale called *A Ring of Bright Otters*, or something like that. He also, according to the monument, 'loved this place as a boy, and made it famous as an adult' and died in 1969. A happy and kind of symmetrical coincidence, considering I was born in that very year, I too loved that place as a boy and am probably not about to make it any more famous than it is already.

After making our way from the memorial, past the derelict but beautiful Norwegian fishermen's chapel set into the sloping cliff face, along 'front bay' and round to 'back bay', Charlie found himself an enormous patch of firm, low-tide sand and ran around it repeatedly and aimlessly until his eyes and tongue seemed to be involved in the mother of all battles to see which could fall out first. Some distance away, along the high-tide mark, sat the predictable, wide and smelly belt of seaweed, dotted with the usual flotsam and jetsam of careless sailors and mid-July holidaymakers (I saw a grand total of two on the whole walk). Charlie had obviously not had quite enough, and had made it to the seaweed a hundred yards or so before me. As he got there, contrary to how shagged out he had just appeared, he began to sprint towards something as if I had just let him out of the car after a lazy day on the sofa. I spotted what he was after about a second or two before he closed in on it. Pecking and hobbling about in the filth like a tramp rummaging through a Saturday-morning bin was a decidedly pissed-off and bedraggled-looking crow. Now, in my experience, birds have a tendency to fly off when being pursued by Charlie, but this one was either suicidal, ill or just too damn interested in trying to find out whether this particular disposable lighter was any more edible than the last. Charlie hurtled into it and bowled it over before I could yell him off the poor thing. Luckily, as I did so, he acquiesced and left the hapless, dazed hobo bird to stagger about looking for all the world as if he'd found a half-empty bottle of whisky on the ground. Charlie eyed it in a vaguely disgruntled manner as it made a valiant attempt to flap away. Just as its feet were about six inches off the ground, Charlie grabbed its wing-tip, and again I screamed at him to let it go. There was a terrible but undeniably comical moment when I came over all Dr Dolittle and read the expressions on the faces of both beasts. The crow was quite obviously thinking, 'Oh for Christ's sake, what now?', while all Charlie's eyes were saying in reply was, 'Fucking hell – it's a flying rabbit!' Thankfully, Charlie again obeyed, and the now very awake bird managed to make good its escape by doing something that I have never seen a bird do before – limping in flight. I was immediately put in mind of Colin the Seagull Man the previous night – to catch fish requires enormous amounts of gear, guile, luck, timing, nous, knowledge, common sense and seemingly some kind of sixth sense, whereas all you need to bag yourself a bird or two is a stupid dog or a misdirected spinning lure.

I made it to ten o'clock at around ten past three. With me I had the light spinning rod loaded with six-pound line, an assortment of spinners, the God-given priest, my multi-tool, a tea towel to hold the fish and a plastic bag to carry them back in. That was it – no mobile, no laptop, no dog and no responsibilities except trying to provide something for the barbecue at Jacq and Jon's the following day. I had reckoned that ten o'clock was pretty much where I had been a couple of days previously when I'd caught my pollack, so I headed to the same spot. When I got there, however, I couldn't see the buoys that Colin had mentioned. There were a few dotted about, but not an obvious pair to cast between. He'd reliably informed me that they were permanent mooring buoys as opposed to pot markers, so I glanced back to the white cairn on the headland. I was actually a little bit early – about 9.13 at a guess. I scrambled over and around a gully to what I deemed to be five short beeps and one long one and, hey presto – one white sphere, one pink. Bobbing about in the water like a brace of aquatic goalposts that I reckoned even I, with my somewhat erratic casting, could land a lure between. I settled myself into a tranquil, if primal, afternoon of doing hopefully nothing at all except throwing things into the water and hitting whatever came out of it over the head.

One expression that Colin had used in last night's conversation was that this place had been 'boiling with mackerel'. After about half an hour of catching nothing but thin slivers of seaweed, I began to suspect that even 'tepid with sprats' might have been pushing it. If I was to use a shooting analogy, then it would be fair to say that my casting technique that afternoon was 'scattergun'. Another word would be 'crap'. I began to wonder whether I was to return home the next day with no more than an unlikely story. Then, thud. The tip of the rod pulled and bent, almost doubling back on itself. I cursed – this was no sliver of seaweed, it was a bloody great lump of it and it was stuck fast to an even greater lump of rock. But then, like before, the seaweed trembled and pulsed. Then went slack. Then moved. Whatever was snagged on the other end of the line was no more vegetable or mineral than I am; at that moment, we were both very definitely animal, and both acting purely on impulse. The only difference between us was our position in the food chain. I reeled in fast, lest sure-hooked fish number two tried to dive for cover in the murky rocks below, and kept the line as tight as my instantly wound nerves. As the fish slapped and flapped inevitably towards me, I saw the same sand-camouflage and white-silver gibbousness of another pollack – twice the size of the last one. I swung it above the rocks, and wrapped the tea towel around it, exposing the two inches or so behind its uncomprehending eyes in order that I could end its suffering. I brought the priest down with a slimy but resounding and reassuring thud; the creature spasmed, curled and stopped dead. All that remained of it was fresh flesh and reflex.

I didn't even stop to wash my hands. Instead, feeling some kind of atavistic bloodlust, I proceeded to frantically cast out over and over again in an attempt to bring home a haul. The primary sign of manhood had now ceased to be the volume of my car engine, the size of my wallet or even my sexual prowess (convenient for me on all three counts) and was now solely dependent on how many fish I could catch in one afternoon. After a while, though, I began to think that maybe I should either invest in a very loud exhaust for my car, get a proper job with a proper salary or even consider some kind of surgery after all, because a two-pound pollack wasn't going to lure anyone back to my cave, was it?

Then, again, thump-thump. A more definite, positive and streamlined hit this time. More direct. 'Hit' was the word – adrenaline was coursing through me as hard as any drug. This fish was perhaps not as heavy as the last, but it seemed to pack more pounds per square inch. It was faster too. It dove, it darted, it traversed and it lulled me by slacking off before it fought back again. I didn't want to let this one get away – any animal this toned, this lithe and this fit for its purpose was sure to taste good.

Keeping the line tight, I eventually managed to reel it in. A mackerel weighing, at a rough guess, a shade over a pound. A handsome torpedo of a fish – a chrysoprase green and oil-slick black striped pearlescent beauty, kicking and spitting angrily to the last. Whereas the pollack had seemed to chug lugubriously to the rock and the priest, as if it had been brought up to accept that this was a part of its fate, the mackerel just kept on flailing, trying to stick one of those remaining hooks into me out of spite.

I fished until 6.15. I had promised myself that this would be when I would stop. I had spent three magically quiet hours (apart from the violent deaths, obviously) atop a rocky plateau as it had gently lowered itself into the running sea, whose tiny ripples had nibbled and lapped lasciviously at its foot. It was just after high tide, and high time I went to get clean and sink a pint or two.

I had caught a further two mackerel, slightly smaller than the first but equally entertaining in their indignation at being got. The pollack was headed for the freezer, until it could be enjoyed with some home-grown mashed potatoes and some prawns in a hearty fish pie. The mackerel went straight into the Steampacket's fridge and were eaten, one each, by myself, Jacq and Jon just a shade over twenty-four hours later stuffed with all manner of complementary pleasantness and baked in foil over a barbecue. It is correct and received wisdom that, when buying 'fresh' mackerel in most supermarkets, it is as well to look at the eyes; they should be clear and bright. This is indeed true, but is overcomplicating the case. All that is necessary is to look at the colour of the animal. Most fish you will see on a shop slab are blue. Fresh mackerel's skin is a startling emerald green, as clear and light as the water it came from. Everything else is sharkbait.

I woke the next morning somewhat blearily, largely because I had spent the previous evening somewhat beerily, but also because I had had a good amount of sleep to catch up on. After checking out of the Steampacket, packing Horace full of fishing tackle and coolboxes, and encouraging Charlie to check out some of the more precipitous drops over the headland, I left the Isle of Whithorn for the first time in twenty-one years. When I was a child, being driven into that place for a fortnight of ice cream, sandy toes and suntans free from the worry of carcinomas, I did so with a bellyful of excitement and anticipation. When I was ferried out, I would cry because of the speed at that that bliss had that raced by, and at the seemingly uncrossable chasm of time that lay between that holiday and the next. As I had driven Horace and Charlie into the Isle five days previously, I had found myself weeping at the seemingly infinitesimal period of time between then and those always bright-blue days. Conversely, as I steered my car away from there that Saturday morning, I smiled contentedly at the prospect of the life I was returning to. When I had planned the trip, I expected that while I was there I was going to be exorcizing some ghosts; having spent five days fishing in the past, I came to realize that, in actual fact, I had gone a good way towards accommodating them.

I had one final visit to make. As it turned out, the Forteviot Hall in Garlieston had put on a fascinating and revelatory display, elucidating in engrossing and illuminating detail exactly what role that plucky little town had played during the war. I'm not going to divulge what it was, though. It's a secret.

Pollack and Potatoes

You will need

1 pollack, recently deceased

a few potatoes, freshly dug and scrubbed

a little olive oil, salt, pepper and some herbs that go with pollack
   – try some thyme, fennel or parsley

Hook up your two-burner camping stove to your over-large gas bottle and sniff for leaks. Fire it up and get a pan of water going. In point of fact, get this on the go while you're looking for a corkscrew because both activities will take roughly the same amount of time. Chop the spuds small enough to give you a fighting chance of catching last orders after they've simmered, and get them in the water. On the other burner, warm a little olive oil in the bottom of your flakey non-stick frying pan that smells suspiciously of bacon and that has a wobbly handle no matter how tightly you do up the screw. Actually, 'warming' a little olive oil is a little inaccurate in this context, as all camping stoves, in my experience, are either off or really bloody hot. Not hot enough to manage to boil water in less than an hour, but quite enough to burn oil. Odd.

Spill the guts of your catch onto your chopping board (tray, flattened beer can, newspaper, grass, etc.) and hack out two fillets. These will both still have bones in them because there is no way you are taking *that* filleting knife camping with you. Not at that price, and not while it's rattling bluntly around in the back of the car with the remainder of the items on the packing lists, which seem to have got all mixed up.

Season the oil with salt, pepper and whatever herbs you have remembered. If you had the presence of mind to include tarragon, parsley, chives or even bay leaves then well done. If you brought rosemary or one of those hideous dried mixed herb concoctions, then make sure the fish is well done. It will hide the flavour. Place the fillets skin side up in the pan. Then scrape them frantically to remove them from the non-stick layer of the pan, which has probably non-stuck itself and become intrinsically attached to the fish. Once you have managed to flip all nineteen small pieces of now chemically enhanced flesh so that the skin is now replacing the non-stick coating of the pan, turn off the gas under the fish. Prod the by now lukewarm potatoes with the sharpest implement you have available (in my case a wooden spoon). Using a sharp implement engenders the false belief that, due to ease of insertion, the potatoes are ready to eat without giving you stomach cramps at 3.30 the following morning.

Strangely, this will be the best fish supper you have ever tasted.

Barbecued Whole Mackerel

You will need

1 *fresh* mackerel per person

a good handful of fennel for each mackerel, bruised and generally offended

a slosh of Pernod

a couple of sprigs of fresh thyme

a squeeze of lemon

maybe a few chopped black olives

sea salt and ground black pepper

Sometimes (and it is only sometimes) you will find really fresh mackerel on a fishmonger's or, even more rarely, on a supermarket's slab. It used to be that Billingsgate fish market used to open on a Sunday only in order that it could sell fresh mackerel – if it had been caught on the Saturday, then by Monday it was deemed fit only for the cat. Land a mackerel yourself and you will see – they are the most remarkable colour. Green as the sea they come from on a clear day. They become a cloudy blue very rapidly – those that I took back for my family after the Scotland trip had already become distinctly overcast. The cat didn't get a look-in, however. Mainly because the fish were still four days fresher than most for sale, but also because the cat (Snidge, rest his soul) had died some six months previously.

You should have gutted the fish as soon as it was dead – any later and they start to flavour the flesh in a non-beneficial manner. Any sooner and you clearly have some unpleasant bloodlust issues. Get the barbecue lit and open a bottle of white wine. Place each fish onto sufficient foil to wrap it in loosely and turn up the sides so the liquid won't escape. Slice some shallow nicks into the skin of the fish to allow the flavours to work their way in. Then stuff the cavity with the fennel, thyme and olives if you fancy them. Splash over the Pernod and lemon juice, followed by the salt and pepper. Wrap each fish up in the foil. The aim is to seal it well enough to keep the steam in, but giving sufficient space for it to be able to circulate. This recipe will work equally well in the oven, as in actual fact you are steaming the fish rather than barbecuing it. However, the ritual and occasion of the barbecue allows you to buy much cheaper wine (as well as, more pertinently perhaps, crappier beer) so you don't need to feel quite so guilty about splashing out on the Pernod that you know will only ever get used for cooking anyway.

Over a decent amount of heat, about 15–20 minutes should do it. As with all fresh fish, under is so much better than over. If it's properly done, the skin, flesh and bones should just peel away from one another. Best eaten immediately with a hunk of ciabatta (wasn't that the big furry one in *Star Wars*?) and a good salad containing plenty of rocket and some baby plum tomatoes.

3   Thinking Like a Fish

There is a common myth amongst the non-fishing populace that fish have very short memories that can be measured in seconds. If you fish or work with fish you will know that this is complete fiction and that fish not only have memories but are quite quick learners.

Mark Burdass, *Trout Fisherman* magazine

My next excursion was to St David's in Pembrokeshire (or Dyfed, depending on which side of the border you are on), in order to try my 'luck' at some beach fishing. It was November, and the warm and fuzzy days of mark fishing in Scotland felt like the memory of a dear friend whose phone number I had carelessly mislaid. The fall in temperature and decrease of the daylight hours seemed to widen this chasm, and the fact that the mackerel had all but disappeared until the following spring, with most of the bass slipstreaming voraciously behind them, only seemed to lever it open further. There would be a few pollack and wrasse to be had from the rocks but my magazines and books informed me that winter was all about standing around on a grey and windswept beach questioning the Point of it All for hours on end while squinting googly-eyed at the fluorescent tip of my twelve-foot beachcaster nestling in an aluminium tripod, waiting for a telltale twitch from the lips of an enormous and lugubrious cod.

In order to maximize my chances of what I could call 'success', my target species definition had not, so far, got much narrower than 'fish'. I felt perhaps that from here on in I should begin to be a little more specific as to what exactly I wanted to be eating later in the day. I also felt that it was about time that I used the beachcasting rod for exactly that, rather than as a means of lure-strangling or as a semi-permanent fixture in Horace – albeit one that had proved most useful when it came to tripping Charlie up when he jumped in and out of the back seat. This branching out in terms of technique, along with the fact that I had not done so for a while, obviously necessitated the buying of more gear.

It was gear that I previously hadn't even been aware that I would require, but I had been dipping into my slowly growing selection of angling literature that I had begun to pick up when and wherever I could find it. Charity shops were still proving to be either overfished or understocked, but I was getting more bites from the independent second-hand shops. I had also hauled down from my mother's loft the four complete volumes of *The New Fisherman's Handbook*. Dating from the early eighties, judging by the mullets (and I don't mean the fish), these A4-size partworks, with binders, weigh just over a kilo and a half apiece. This fact, quite apart from the ambiguity of the title (was it the fisherman who was supposed to be new or the book?), surely suggests that the average fisherman's hands are enormous. Maybe that's why I was the only person ever to have asked Brian Perks for a priest. My father had lovingly bought each issue for me over a period of sixty weeks, which had meant that for more than a year he'd watched me lovingly look at one or two of the pictures in every issue before slipping it into its plastic retainer inside the binder and then, when full, equally affectionately closing each one. What he didn't live long enough to be aware of was that these tomes would then remain dustless and unread until nearly twenty years after he died. I figured that this obsession more with owning and organizing information than with its practical application is a habit I really should be dealing with. So, armed with as much knowledge from these books (as well as magazines such as *tOTAlSeAfishANGlerinG*) as I could cram inside my head without bits of it falling out of my ears, I reasonably confidently made my way to Rover's Tackle Shop in Fareham. It was time to feed my growing obsession with owning and organizing unused equipment instead.

As it happened, the first item on the list was never in danger of underemployment. I was in desperate need of a new pair of wellies. My pair of ribbed black Dunlops with red soles had done sterling work on the allotment, but had developed a split that had widened from a just-penetrating nick to a flapping mouth that seemed to grin at me as if to say 'Hello, your right sock is now as wet as your dog' every other pace. Not only was I getting a bit fed up with wearing footwear about as effective at its job as a pair of carpet slippers, but I was also buggered if I was going to stand around on a wild and windy beach for any amount of time while running the risk of chilblains, foot rot, sock chafe, toe freeze or any other ailment, even if I *had* made it up. And I certainly wasn't going to pass up the opportunity of buying any kind of footwear for £6.50, which was all Rover's was asking for a pair of green size 9s.

I'm not sure what it is about finding something in a shop for considerably less money than expected, but somehow I always feel literally better off as a result – not just that I have *saved* money, but as if I actually have more of it weighing my pocket down than before. If, just before entering Rover's, I had been expecting to pay, say, fifteen quid for a pair of wellies, then by my warped logic I had instantly become nearly ten pounds richer as soon as I picked up the boots. This meant that I could spend slightly longer than necessary spending even more money than I needed to on things most of which I probably didn't require in the first place. In my excitement and new-found flushness, I selected a variety of additional breakaway lead weights just in case some of the other (as yet largely unused) examples didn't break away when I asked them to and also because I think that they are pleasing pieces of design. What's more, I like fiddling with them in a manner that probably suggests that I have nothing better to do with my time and that I am in imminent danger of breaking them. They also happen to make rearranging the gear in the tackle box that much more challenging, and I'd hate for life to become too easy for the sake of £1.50 a shot.

I also bagged some lighter, pear-shaped weights in case I fancied a spot of float fishing. I'd bought the float itself in Stafford on the way to Scotland, along with a weight that, I was assured by the boy of around twelve who served me, would balance – or 'cock' – it perfectly. I tried it. It didn't. Cocked it up, perhaps. Or, more accurately, down – the float plummeted towards the seabed like a dead mafioso. I got some three-way swivels in order that I could try my hand at tying some of my own rigs and so that I could use the Eddystone Eel lures, which I had bought on some quarter-remembered whim in Scotland. These strips of rubber are enormous but relatively light – by using a three-way swivel I could rig the lures in conjunction with a weight for increased casting distance. These swivels, as the name implies, have three eyelets as opposed to the usual two. This means that, as well as allowing for rotation between the terminal tackle and the main line, it is possible to attach a line and a weight 'straight through' from the main line and a separate trace perpendicular to the main line for attaching bait or a lure.

A number of throat-slittingly boring Sunday afternoons at my paternal grandparents' house in the Cotswolds during childhood taught me early on that it is perfectly possible to have too much of The Spinners, whereas, thus far on my foray into arranging shiny things in boxes, I had yet to find a point where I found myself with a surfeit of spinners. Somehow their shimmering and sinuous shapes and various methods of inducing movement when retrieved had me gazing at the display board with an expression that probably wasn't far away from Homer Simpson's when presented with a can of 'Duff Beer'. Eyes like ping-pong balls, a small bead of saliva running from the corner of my mouth and uttering a dull mantra along the lines of 'Mmmm . . . bright and shiny' (the spoonerism of which might appositely describe a poor day's sea fishing). I chose a Mepps Aglia, which was of French origin, weighed a mere 10g, had a treble hook and a red rubber 'skirt' type thing and which was topped by a silver metal 'spoon'. The packet told me that it was 'par excellence for all fish in all waters'. It continued to inform me that 'it's a marvellous lure engineered to start spinning the instant it hits the water and to emit a maximum vibrating effect. No other lure has caught so many record fish all over the world.'

A high recommendation indeed, although I was slightly suspicious that nowhere in the French version of the blurb were the words 'par excellence' to be found. There was something that I didn't quite get about 'les gros Rosbifs très crédules', though.

I also bought a brace of Wildeye Rippin' Shad Swim Baits,

which had been produced in Finland. These weighed 20 g apiece and were made of that tacky, squidgy kind of rubber that can, if you play with it and sniff it for long enough, make you come over a bit queasy. With the exception of the bloody great hook protruding from their back, and the smaller treble dangling from their belly, these things really do look quite convincing in their fishiness, and I reckoned that whether or not they ended up landing anything larger, the piece of advice on the front of the packaging was worth £3.99 in itself. 'Always think like a fish, no matter how weird it gets' is a motto well worth bearing in mind, up to the point where you get an enormous hook wedged in your gob, of course. Lastly, I could not possibly resist the £2.79 and 28g worth of metal that was a silver Dexter wedge. I'm not exactly sure why I chose this – I think its density and sinuous shape were satisfying and reassuring and it did seem to shimmer in its packaging in a remarkably fishy, if ersatz, kind of way. I also like the word 'Dexter'. Anyway, a good selection of different types of lures is handy to have in your armoury – the more lures you have at your disposal to swap about endlessly, the greater chance you have at becoming completely flummoxed as to what the hell actually *is* going to catch any fish, and therefore why you are trying in the first place.

All of these items of tackle are, however, largely superfluous when it comes to beach fishing, and were really bought as supplementary items. This is a lie. They were bought because somebody as good as gave me eight and a half quid when I picked up the wellies. I was in Rover's primarily, though, to buy some beach-specific items. First on the list, and something that I had, up until that point, twice resisted buying previously, was a tripod. A simple device consisting of three long, spiked legs at the top of which sit two rod rests. Anyone who has wandered along a beach in the early evening will recognize these devices as much as their physically and metaphysically slightly detached owners. A tripod's function is basically to enable the fisherman to get very cold feet indeed while standing next to his rod for hours and hours because he does not have to hold it still himself. It also, on a more practical note, keeps your reel away from the sand, which is by no means nature's most effective lubricant. I had nearly bought one for the Scottish jaunt along with the other tackle, and had come close to picking one up in Whithorn from a shop that for some reason also sold watercolour paints and pet food. Possibly because the only other shop there is B. Perks, Hardware. It wasn't until I went into Rover's that I realized why I had resisted. It was because I had adjudged a fishing tripod to represent something similar to those used for cameras; that their ownership implies that you know what you are doing, and up until that point, in an odd way, I hadn't felt as if I had deserved – or earned – one. But now I'd actually caught something, had got my hands on Brian's fish-basher and I knew what a wishbone rig was, I deemed myself to be ready. Rover's had two types, so the selection process, after the preliminary 'Do I want to spend twenty quid or thirty-five quid?' question and its rapid 'The wellies weren't that cheap' answer, consisted of whether I wanted the one near the window, or the one just next to the expensive one.

Also necessary for beachcasting is something called a shock leader. The stresses involved when casting half a pound of lead and dead fishbait out to sea are quite considerable: G force, inertia, momentum, Barker's law, that kind of thing. Anyway, whatever the technicalities of the matter, when you bang out any kind of mass, it momentarily multiplies in weight, and if you place that much stress on your poor, feeble twenty-pound line it will, to use a technical term, go ping. A shock leader is a length of line with a much higher breaking strain than the main line, which takes the 'Ooomph' of the cast. I went for the sixty-pound as opposed to the fifty-pound line not, obviously, because of my Herculean strength, my perfect casting technique, nor indeed the colossal weight of the fish I envisaged catching, but because it was a nice shade of fluorescent yellow. Buying this stuff also meant that I got to learn a new knot, and the last time I did that was up in Scotland when the tent wouldn't stay put. The unimaginatively named shock-leader knot is a doddle to tie as long as you've got a picture or two in front of you, but considering that it took a good-sized paragraph to describe what a shock leader actually is, and bearing in mind that most people don't actually care, I'm not even going to try to explain it here. Suffice to say that it ends up as a kind of self-tightening, tapered affair so that when you cast out it doesn't get stuck in the line guides and pull your rod out of your hands or your arms out of their sockets.

Another item that for a while I had had a suspicion that I would need was a multiplier reel. They have the ability to cast much further than my fixed-spools, but there were still a few issues holding me back. Firstly, they may well be capable of casting further than the reels I already had, but I was less than convinced that I was able to do so – there seemed to be little point in spending money on equipment if I could not use it to its full potential. I also still had concerns over the potential for 'bird's nests' if the line overran on casting, and furthermore I was mindful that I had to be a bit careful about how much money I was spending – this gear, along with what I'd had delivered before I went to Scotland, had so far set me back £160 and had so far landed me a total of about six pounds of fairly ordinary fish. I had some more learning and some more earning to do before I could justify this particular bit of kit.

I laid out the gear on the counter. Considering the fact that the price of most of the items had ended in awkward numbers such as 'nine' or 'four', and taking into account the cursory manner in which the chap behind the till had surveyed my purchases and pointed vaguely at a few of them while pursing his lips and squinting, I was a little nonplussed that the total came to 'Forty-eight pound please, mate'. I wondered how it was that when it comes to weighing fish, most anglers demand accuracy to the nearest grain, but in financial matters they are generally happy to round up or down to the nearest pound. Perhaps that's the way it should be. I warmed to the guy as he swiped my card (not something I do that frequently), and as he awaited authorization he struck up conversation.

'What you after then – mullet?' He evidently *did* mean the fish.

I wasn't even sufficiently well informed to know that this species was still around at that time of year, let alone catch one of them, and I told him as much.

'Oh yeah, they're still out there,' he assured me in a manner that suggested that he might be wondering whether I knew what all this gear was for, and with all the zeal of a man who was not, under any circumstances, going to allow me out of the shop until he had told me absolutely everything he knew about these fish.

'Yer mullet', he continued authoritatively, pushing his glasses up the bridge of his nose, 'fall into two main types – yer grey mullet and yer red mullet.'

'Aaah. Right.'

'Yer red mullet are, in fact, not related to the grey mullet at all.'

'Oh.' I nodded slowly while raising an eyebrow and lowering the corners of my mouth in what I hoped suggested sage interest.

Red mullet must therefore, I surmised, be assumed to be an impostor, or possibly even a red herring. In addition to this, later research told me, they predominantly swim about in the Mediterranean – even the best multiplier in the world isn't going to get my bait that far.

I entered my PIN, foolishly assuming that this would bring the matter to a close. But no.

'Yer grey mullet, on the other hand, comes in three different varieties. Yer thin-lipped, yer thick-lipped and yer golden.' So, yer red mullet is not actually a mullet, but yer grey mullet can be golden. I didn't ask.

I didn't need to, because it got even stranger. Just as I was about to politely curtail the conversation by telling him that I was actually off to the wilds of Pembrokeshire, he went on to tell me the line of demarcation between 'thin' and 'thick' when it comes to mulletness. I'm thoroughly glad he did, because what makes the difference, apparently, is the size of the top lip in relation to the diameter of the eye. Less than half, and you are in thin-lipped territory – more than half . . . ? Well, you can guess the rest. Needless to say, I didn't have to.

'What about golden mullet?' I forwent the 'yer' in case he thought I was taking the piss.

'What about them?' He pushed his inexplicably slid glasses back up his nose with his forefinger, folded his arms and shook his head almost imperceptibly before looking at me as if I had just asked him what colour underpants he was wearing.

'Well, do they have thick or thin lips?'

'I'm not sure really. I've never really thought of it like that. They're just, well, gold, I suppose.' Of course. Silly me. Bloody typical. Just as I had got to the point where I was actually interested, he had reached a juncture where he had run out of information. As he handed me my receipt, he struck out on a different path.

He continued to tell me that 'yer mullet' are remarkably hardy and adaptable creatures – they can tolerate water brackish enough to kill most salt-loving species and can survive murky, oxygen-depleted water better than most. He also tried to convince me that they can even survive by gulping air through their gills, but either I do not believe that, or I do not want to believe it. The reason, he said, that taking mullet along certain stretches of the south coast was possible all year round (they generally scoot off for deeper water as soon as October hits), is twofold: firstly, cooling water from power stations (such as Fawley near Southampton) keeps the water at a mullet-friendly level, and secondly, some fish can become virtually land- (or water-) locked by any dock system more complicated than a harbour wall. And there was me thinking that mullet were supposed to be smart.

'Are they really as difficult to catch as I've heard?'

'Weelll . . .' He leant against the glass counter-top and puckered his thin lips. 'They're not impossible, but,' a tap of the nose with the same forefinger that had adjusted his glasses and a hint of a wink, 'you've got to be canny.'

I could only assume that he meant that if I wanted to bag a mullet or two I had better start thinking like a fish an awful lot harder than I had been.

'So, what *are* you after?'

'I'm off to Pembrokeshire for a spot of beach fishing, maybe some spinning.'

'Bit of early cod then, huh?'

I plucked my carrier bag full of goodies from the counter and wrapped my other hand around the three cold tubes of the tripod.

'I'm hoping so. Maybe the odd late bass too.'

'Well, best of luck to you.' His tone had a ring of 'you'll be needing all you can get' to it.

'Thanks.'

When I got home, I had a peek inside one of my growing number of catalogues in order to check what the hell a Dexter wedge actually was and what I might want to use one for. I noticed that they cost 29p less via mail order than I had just paid, but also found out that they have an 'irresistible wobbling action'. What is more, the larger sizes are also excellent for jigging, which I would have found extremely comforting if I'd known what it meant. Also in their favour as far as I was concerned was that they were apparently great for whatever bass were around at that time of year, and even if they weren't, the one I had bought had some fancy, trancy holographic sticky-backed stuff on it, which I found utterly mesmerizing as I rocked the lure back and forth. Think like a fish, huh? I was getting into it already.

Possibly one of Robert Louis Stevenson's more famous quotes is the one about it being a better thing to travel than to arrive. I beg to differ. Frankly, unless I'm taking the dog for a walk, I don't see the point of travelling unless I plan to be somewhere other than where I started. Secondly, when I arrive, I sure as hell don't want to be feeling ever so slightly disgruntled about the fact that I'm not trying to get there any more, and thirdly, Stevenson had patently never tried to travel any distance westbound along the M4 in weather so atrociously squally that to be attempting it in anything but a narrowboat seemed plain foolish. At one point, I had a horrible feeling that something was going terribly awry with the rear end of the car, but as I glanced round I saw Charlie, who had developed something terribly awry with his ability to stop himself from quivering like a jelly. I was clearly to blame for the facts that a) he was not on his sofa, b) he did not have any idea where he was going and c) even if he did, he probably did not want to go there in the first place. I did my best to calm him with one hand while the other attempted to guide the car, which had essentially become an aquaplaning craft, down the motorway, which in turn had transformed into a tributary of the River Severn.

I also part company with Stevenson because when I travel anywhere, I always have an urge to just, well, get there. True enough, I did take a break at Leigh Delamere services as well as at Sarn Park, although this latter was as much to bale the water out of the car as it was for getting coffee into me. But I always feel a need to 'settle in' when I arrive somewhere – to at least unload (if not unpack) my bags, pee in the corners of the room and generally establish where it is I am going to be sleeping after I have gone off for a sniff around, a meal and a pint or two.

The place in question that day was Twr-y-Felin (pronounced 'turr-e-vellin') Outdoor Centre in St David's, Dyfed. Or, as it had been somewhat jauntily renamed in my absence, the TYF Hotel. This establishment had been set up by a guy called Andy Middleton in 1985, and it was here that I spent the summer of 1989 doing my damnedest to look really cool while nonchalantly teaching people how to surf. A time of life without responsibility, without fatherhood either given or received, without any real care, without stress and without the ever-present spectre of any form of mental ill health. The time that I remember as being one when I felt truly, unmitigatedly *alive*.

For some reason, it felt a good deal stranger returning to this place than it had when I had gone back to Scotland: there were no tears this time, possibly because there was far less innocence to be recaptured or mourned for there (or, indeed, no tent pegs to be pushed in with flip-flops), but there were certainly some ghosts. The first spectre that hit me as I entered the blue, thick and solid front door snuck up on me through a sense that I was not altogether expecting – I had assumed that as soon as I saw the place again my excruciating transition from adolescence to some semblance of adulthood would assault me head-on visually through the tiled floor perhaps, or maybe the imposing mahogany staircase or even the peculiar creak of the door to the bar, but the past is much more devious than that. After the seaweed and shit stench of the Isle of Whithorn, it shouldn't really have come as any surprise that, again, it was the smell that hauled the remainder of my consciousness inexorably backwards. But the smell of the Isle was something that I had actually remembered throughout my life, and which I could almost recreate – somehow reconstruct from its component parts – in my mind, whereas the peculiar odour of those walls had, I thought, become lost in the nasal passage of time. It is perhaps telling that I couldn't even begin to describe it now, except to say that it smelled like Twr-y-Felin Outdoor Centre, Pembrokeshire, at the same time as smelling like the TYF Hotel, Pembrokeshire. True, it had fifteen years of polish, a lick of paint or two and the combined odours of a few thousand sweaty, briny and at times mildly scared people sucked into its walls, but like the subtly altered features of a friend from another life, another time, it was unmistakable.

I crossed the intricately tessellated floor (a couple of extra tiles had started to rock underfoot from the last time I had walked on it) to the bar, from where I could hear two female voices involved in tea-break banter. After I introduced myself, they informed me that there was no one else staying at the Twr for the next couple of nights, and that none of the staff slept on site either. I was therefore going to be in that large, eerie building – accompanied only by its groans and bumps of age, central heating and settling – alone. Not for the first time: when I'd first arrived there back in the wild, windy and uncommonly dark January of 1989, I lived there on my own for a while before anyone else appeared, either to work the summer season or to be scared silly by abseiling instructors who had a keen penchant for telling them, halfway down a steep and slippery rockface, that the word 'gullible' had been taken out of the English dictionary. The Twr was full of ghosts back then and, it turned out, over the two nights I stayed there, to have crammed in a few more hackle-raisers of my own invention during the intervening years.

The name of the establishment I was staying in may have been changed as much as my reasons for being there, but the exterior of the building – the same eponymous and imposing grey-rendered twr, or tower – had not. This had originally been a windmill, built in the early nineteenth century, but its one round wall has, for the last hundred years or so, thickly shrouded four storeys of circular rooms of cave-like proportions and illumination. The equally imposing extended front of the hotel, added at the same time as the mill was stripped of its sails, and which houses bar and dining areas as well as the majority of the sleeping accommodation, also looked familiar. In the grounds were dotted the usual kayaks, surfboards and other outdoor-pursuits paraphernalia, along with the enormous original millstones and some transport that looked somewhat more reliable and salubrious than the Series II Land Rover that I had rattled about in during my days there.

I was shown to my room by one of the ladies taking a tea break at the bar. She introduced herself as Angie, and was most helpful when it came to reminding me of the locations of the facilities, including the kitchen that would, she said, be serving breakfast between seven and nine the next morning. Considering the fact that the person cooking it would roundly double the number of souls on the premises during my stay, it struck me as a little unfair that he should have to turn up while it was still dark in order to cook breakfast for a man who would rather eat his own toes than get out of bed before he absolutely had to. Either Andy, with whom I had made contact prior to my visit, had forgotten how bloody lazy I am, or he'd forgotten to tell his staff.

Once I'd transferred all the relevant bags from the boot of the car to my room, I made my way to the TYF shop in St David's itself (the Twr reaches squatly skyward about half a mile or so from the city centre). This is where Angie had told me that I would be most likely to find Andy. In fifteen years, he had taken a small outdoor venture and turned it into a business encompassing not just an outdoor centre, but now including a hotel, two shops and a proposal for a large 'eco-building'. I remembered him as a focused and driven individual, sometimes seemingly ruthlessly so. When I moved to St David's, my father had been dead just three years, and it was not until I returned for this fishing trip that I realized that Andy, ten years my senior, had represented one of a string of attempts at finding some kind of replacement male role model. However superfluous the 'in-law' bit of 'brother-in-law' was and is when it comes to my sister's husband Jon, this has not stopped me from feeling that the early demise of my dad has deprived me of something that so many other people take for granted. I perceived Andy to be self-assured, ambitious, a touch ruthless and strong enough, if push came to shove, to beat me convincingly in a fight. He had been, in short, many things that my father had not. I therefore sought approval and respect from Andy, and the fact that I was too callow and naive at the time to know how to go about getting it, in conjunction with this apparent aloofness and single-mindedness that he displayed, meant that I simply didn't get it. While I'd worked for him, I'd always got the impression that anything I'd had to say was not worthy of attention (probably because I didn't have a clue what I was talking about) and always felt physically inadequate in comparison with him. He was, although I didn't spot this at the time, also a thoroughly charming and affable bloke. It was no wonder I hated him.

On arrival at the shop (which used to be a restaurant called Digby's to where Andy, in an unusually paternal gesture, had once taken all his instructors, including me, for dinner), I paused for a moment to consider whether I was truly ready for this – what if I felt rejected by him again and felt once again clueless and childlike? Worse, what if he didn't recognize me? I jerked the handbrake, told myself to stop being such an arse and that I was a grown-up now, told Charlie that he will always be more of an arse than I am and headed towards the shop.

Andy was busy selling a surfboard on the opposite side of the double-fronted shop from the till. Finding him was as easy as finding my reasons for being there – I followed the voices. He had his back to me, and was doing what he does best – convincing someone that what they want is actually what they need – and I felt no desire to interrupt him while he was doing so. In Japanese martial arts there is the expression *zanshin*, which translates roughly as 'awareness: of self, of environment and of others'. I was reminded then that Andy also had this in spades. He turned from his flawless patter with a smile.

'With you in a minute.'

He turned, briefly clocked me, and swivelled back to his conversation. All the time I had known him previously, I had been desperate to get his attention like a child with piece of clumsy woodwork, but it had always seemed that he'd manage to find someone with something more important and/or interesting to say. That time, I'd hoped that because I was older than he had been when I had first met him, and because by then he was exactly the age my father had been when he died, we might be greeting each other on more level terms. A cursory 'With you in a minute' and the resumption of his previous conversation didn't exactly reassure me that this might be the case. I felt my stomach tense in a similar way that it had one morning in Scotland – what the hell did I think I was doing? The past is just that, right? Sleeping dogs? Bygones? I was about to run back to the car and chase the rain back home when Andy slowly turned back, beaming. He had obviously taken me to be just some punter or other, but had performed a double take.

'Hello mate!' He beamed.

'Hi Andy, how's it going?'

'Good, good. You?'

'Just fine.'

He took two paces towards me and extended his right hand for me to shake firmly, while putting his left arm around my shoulders in a greeting that may have suggested a long-lost brotherhood. He then gestured towards the stairs behind me to my left.

'Go on up and make yourself at home. I'll be with you shortly.'

He came up about five minutes after me, and I would like to say at this juncture that time had not treated him at all kindly. This would, however, be an outrageous lie. He was just as tanned, chiselled and boyish as he had ever been. His teeth were still white, straight and (as far as I could ascertain without tugging at them) all his own. Bastard. Still, contrary to my youth, I found it impossible to dislike him. Predominantly because of the warmth of his greeting and the way in which he talked with me that afternoon –

he listened attentively, laughed at the bits that were meant to be vaguely amusing and generally gave me the impression that he took what I said seriously and valued my opinions. I felt something that I had never felt in that city before. I felt accepted.

Despite the fact that I'd had a lengthy, undisturbed sleep, I still awoke with a sense of nebulous unease in my stomach. Not even Charlie had disturbed me during the night, and because I had slept so well, I was feeling sharper than usual. Because of this, that nebulous unease soon turned into a quite specific set of sentences starting with 'Oh bollocks, I haven't/didn't/forgot to', etc., ending with phrases such as 'got any bait', 'buy a tide table' or 'bring my map or any of that careful research I did into fishing in the area'. In addition to these omissions, which were in themselves fundamental enough to make forgetting a mallet for your tent pegs look pretty astute, by the sounds of the windows and the trees it was (to use common parlance) blowing a hooley outside.

However, as is often enough the way of things when you don't worry too much, I needn't have worried too much. After letting Charlie out for his early morning necessities and shutting him back in the room with his breakfast, I went in search of my own. It didn't take long. The dining room was exactly where it had always been, and even my sense of smell – permanently dulled by two decades of smoking until I'd finally quit three years previously – was not going to deny me the joy that is thick slices of bacon spitting under a commercial grill.

As I entered the dining room, I was greeted by a truly gargantuan and genuinely jolly-looking man who was in the process of drying his ham hands on his blue and white striped pinny as he stepped out of the kitchen. He extended his right paw, and said simply,

'Hello mate. Paul.'

I reciprocated by clasping his hand and telling him my name. It wasn't that he was fat, and nor was he particularly muscular – it was simply that he was so much larger than average that I couldn't help thinking that he was in fact standing an awful lot closer to me than I'd first imagined. Realistically, he was probably half as large again as most folk, and he turned out to be a corresponding 50 per cent more pleasant than many people I've met.

'What d'you fancy for breakfast?' He didn't really seem to be the sort of bloke who would be giving me the option of muesli and a low-fat yoghurt.

'Oh, just chuck it on the plate and I'll eat it, thanks Paul.'

'No worries. Coming right up!'

With that, he disappeared into the kitchen while I helped myself to the muesli and yoghurt towards which he had gestured and suggested that I avail myself of while I was waiting. When I'm at home, I find it utterly impossible to even consider breakfast until at least three large mugs of tea have lined my stomach. It has therefore always been a bit of a mystery that when I'm away I will quite happily scoff an amount of food that would constitute a hearty evening meal before I have even found a kettle. Maybe it is something to do with me wanting to perpetuate my father's astonishing ability to extract a pound of flesh wherever there was one to be had. He didn't brew up in the back of the car out of some frontiersman mentality. He did it because he was a skinflint. I may not have inherited his almost xenophobic loathing of foreign travel or his penchant for Val Doonican, but if I'm paying for bed and breakfast, I'm going to make bloody sure that the bed is comfy and the breakfast is as large as I can stomach.

When Paul returned, it was apparent that he had done his

utmost to make sure that my father's memory was honoured in no uncertain fashion. Breakfast was, like the man who had created it, huge. If, like the staff and clientele of TYF, you are an outdoorsy type person, a meal this large first thing in the morning is probably something of a necessity. When, on the other hand, you are a slight lightweight whose idea of exercise is a bit of digging, a dog walk and a few hours of three-finger typing, a meal of this size at any time of the day constitutes a reasonably generous week's shopping.

'Wow! Thanks mate. This should keep me going!'

'No worries. I'll just get your coffee and some juice.'

I shudder to think how many orange groves had been denuded in order to provide the latter, and 'coffee' turned out to be a cafetiere of sufficient capacity to keep half a dozen narcoleptic bears on edge for weeks. I had, for the first time in my life, been served a meal of which I was just the tiniest bit scared.

'Can I get you anything else?'

Short of knives and forks for himself and a few hungry friends and a doggy (bin) bag, nothing sprang to mind, so instead I engaged him in conversation in order to take my mind off the task ahead. It turned out that Paul was not, in fact, a chef (food was obviously more of a hobby as far as he was concerned) but had just been roped in for the two mornings I was to be there. His job description was as mine had been – as an instructor of all things that fly in the face of common sense and natural selection. We therefore chatted briefly about why I was there, why I had been there fifteen years before, and why I had absolutely no intention of doing those things again. Common sense and natural selection would have been convenient excuses, but the truth of the matter was that I had turned into a great big girl's blouse who really didn't like cold water, heights, mild peril or being too far from a pub with a log fire. But when I mentioned fishing, he began to look very excited indeed.

'Fantastic! I do loads of fishing round here! What you after?'

'Ooh, well, anything really – but a late-season bass or some early cod would be nice.'

At this, he was off. Had I known what a treasure trove of information regarding species, locations, baits, tides, etc. was lurking downstairs and garrotting my squealing breakfast, I could have spent those ten fretful minutes in bed being much more productive by worrying about something much more trivial instead. Any fishing was going to be tricky, he said, because of recent and present weather conditions. The water was pretty lively – and therefore murky and churned up – and had been for the previous few days. The best beach fishing, he said, was to be had just after, rather than slap-bang in the middle of, a big blow. However, he said that he'd be willing to show me some spots that might be a little more sheltered on the map in the office. He was unsure that I would have any luck just yet in my quest for cod of any size, but rather fancied my chances of a pollack or two off the rocks, and possibly even a bass if I was really lucky.

I had really been hoping to fish from Whitesands beach, a crescent of sand approximately one and a half miles from south to north, on a low spring tide, and the same bay that I had surfed and hung out on with my friends during the summers of 1989 and 1990. At its northern extremity juts a protuberance of rock called the Ram's Nose, and beyond this St David's Head spits out grandiosely into the Atlantic. Beyond Point St John to the south west lies the bird sanctuary of Ramsey Island, and directly west of the beach lie the Bishops and Clerks rocks. I had fished from the Ram's Nose and St David's Head with an old surfing buddy called Dafydd, and remember catching a good many mackerel and the

odd pollack from these points. I was hoping that the beach itself
would prove as productive.

I told Paul of my desire to return there and he suggested that
if I did want to try Whitesands, I would be better off doing so
during the last couple of hours of the incoming tide. For the next
day or so, this meant either an early morning start or a similar
time in the evening. Now, if the waves had not been as enormous
as they had been the day before when I took Charlie for a run on
the beach, and if Paul had suggested that there was a good chance
of my catching a healthy amount of decent sized fish, I may well
have been willing to drag myself out of bed to catch the morning
tide. However, everything I have read suggests that real beach
fishermen (in search of real fish) only venture out at night. That,
apparently, is when the majority of fish are caught from shore,
blow or no blow. However, in my mind, there was an equally good
reason for not beach fishing at night; my level of expertise at the
time meant that I was more than a little wary of not only very
sharp and unpleasantly barbed hooks flying around in the dark,
but also mindful of the fact that some fish, bass included, are
armed with some pretty sore-looking pointy bits of their own to
contend with. Daylight may not be the best time to catch fish, but
it sure as hell struck me as a less likely time to be skewered by them
if you did.

Trying to ignore this conundrum, I ate as much breakfast as
I could (which had the net result of looking as if I hadn't started
it), and followed Paul into the office, where he pointed out a few
spots. Some of these I recognized from my kayak-wrestling days,
but the further afield and less familiar locations I jotted down
lest I forgot. He told me that my best chance of codling was at a
place called Hobbs Point in Pembroke Dock; if I travelled south
to Dale I could have bagged 'fifteen or sixteen different species',

including a fish whose name I have obliterated from my mind, largely because it apparently looks like a foot-long tadpole, and I think I would rather deal with a conger eel than try to land three pounds of ugly, thrashing jelly. There is a spot just to the west of Caerfai Bay – just down the road from the Twr – with the improbable and to some impossible name of Pen-y-Cyrfrwy that may have yielded some pollack and bass, as may St. Non's, two miles distant. There, apparently, I was to take the coast path to the left of the car park, stand on the 'great big slabs of rock' that I 'couldn't miss', and cast out into the equally obvious gully. Finally, said Paul, if all else failed, I should go to Fishguard and lob virtually anything out from the breakwater there and I would be 'pretty much guaranteed' of catching something.

By the time I had prepared myself I was going to be too late to even try any beach action even if I had deemed it viable. Besides, I had never done any beachcasting before – certainly not while battling against a stiff onshore wind and solid six-foot waves – so my chances of success were perhaps even less than those of anyone else in a similar situation. Six feet may not sound like much, but I was still in the surfer's habit of measuring waves from the back, not the front. From the back, they appear appreciably smaller. Most people would have looked at these waves from the beach and declare them as being 'over eight feet'. They certainly look bigger a) when you are considering yourself to be a fisher-man and b) when you know yourself to have turned into a great fat pansy who is no more capable of casting any appreciable distance than of eating a hearty breakfast.

Just as I was wandering about my room, scratching my head and trying to ready myself, my clothes and my dog for a morning of mark fishing somewhere really quite cold indeed, there was a knock on the door. It was Paul, wanting to let me know that, if

I did catch any fish, then I was more than welcome to wrap them in the cling-film that was on top of the fridge and stash them inside it. Chef had just arrived, and had said that I was also at liberty to avail myself of the kitchen tomorrow lunchtime if I wanted to cook them, or she would do so in the evening. I mentioned to Paul that I was off to Caerfai to try spinning for some bass. He screwed up his nose.

'Better off at St Non's mate.'

'Yeah?'

'Hmmm. I've seen guys lure fishing at Caerfai for hours – half a dozen of 'em at a time and not one of 'em has caught a thing.'

'Oh.'

'I mean, I've had plenty there myself, spear fishing and all, but sometimes . . . I dunno, they just don't seem to want to take the bait.'

Great. Fan-effing-tastic. Just dandy. I had accumulated a good deal of the gear but still had no real idea. All I had was my poncey book and tax-deductible spinners and there I was, face to face with a bloke who can not only eat five times more than me but can also catch fish simply by throwing sharp things at them. Sodding great. Super. Absolutely bloody marvello—

Hang on. Actually, yes – absolutely bloody marvellous! I was there for beach fishing, and if night-time was the best part of the day to do so, then so be it.

'What you up to tomorrow night, Paul?'

He squinted quizzically at the space just above my head as if he had just spied a cobweb on the wall behind me that had not been there a moment before and recited, 'Tomorrow. Thursday, Thursday, Thursday,' like the name of a forgotten face. Then he redirected his gaze towards me and gave a small shake of his large head.

'Nope. Nothing springs to mind, mate. Why?'

'Fancy a spot of beach fishing?'

'Love to.'

We agreed that we would make further arrangements while he was waiting for planning permission to come through for my breakfast the following morning. After he'd gone, Charlie and I headed towards St Non's via the local tackle shop in order to rectify the bait and headtorch deficit in anticipation of our adventure.

St Non became mother to St David himself in around AD 500. Despite having given birth to the patron saint of Wales (St David, or Dewi, was originally worshipped as a sea god, whose symbol was the Great Red Serpent – now to be seen on sandcastle flags up and down the country's summer beaches), St Non does not appear to have been important enough to have been given a patronage of her own. If I was on speaking terms with the Catholic Church, I would implore it to consider letting her have full English – or Welsh – breakfasts. There is now a Catholic retreat at the reputed place of St David's birth, complete with a convenient nearby car park that is used by anglers, retreaters and walkers alike. I pulled up near the retreat and as near to the as yet invisible coast path as I could get and set about rigging up the spinning gear and donning as many layers of clothes as I could while retaining usable movement of my arms.

Locking Charlie in the car, I attempted (and twice failed) to find the footpath that led to the coastal path. When I eventually did locate it, I strode to a suitable vantage point from which to survey the coastline to the left. Paul had indeed been correct – the great big slabs of rock were there all right. Well, they were a second ago. Ah, hang on, yes, there they are again . . . No, wait, they've disappeared once more under a swell running at a good ten feet high. And a ten-foot swell is a ten-foot swell to a fisherman every bit as much as it is to a surfer. More pertinently, both surfers and fishermen know equally well that a ten-foot swell is not too fussy about whether you are wearing waders or a wetsuit when it plucks you off the cliffs like a child absent-mindedly choosing pick and mix. This churning rise and fall made the coastline look like an enormous bath, and the sea the running water through which someone was stirring a hand to even out the temperature, and I actually began to feel a little nauseous just looking at it. At a point in the distance the sea was squeezing itself through a rocky gully with an ominous 'boom' and issuing forth majestic sprays of aerated water at the same time as laying itself in foamy, dribbling sheets over the rocks, then withdrawing and sucking down a fathom or so before surging again. I rapidly decided that, in the absence of a drysuit, some belaying equipment and a frontal lobotomy, perhaps there would be more sensible methods of procuring lunch that day. Such as buying it.

All the other locations that Paul had suggested were either going to be suffering from a similar problem to St Non's or were too far away to get to before the tide (along with the fish) had started to race away in earnest. But as I was heading, despondent, to the local mini-market to buy myself something fishy but probably filipino, I had a flash of inspiration. Porthclais! The place where I had first been convinced that the act of launching yourself over the edge of a cliff with nothing but eighty feet of air and sheer terror between you and the water below was a perfectly acceptable thing to do. I was amazed that Paul had not suggested this sheltered harbour inlet himself, considering the weather conditions. I surmised that this was probably due to the fact that Porthclais is a little-known spot, jealously guarded by the local fishermen in case of conditions like these. Porthclais itself is no more than a car park, a seasonal loo, a plucky National Trust signpost and a tiny and forlorn little boatyard occupied by boats destined to only ever get wet when it rains. Park up and walk along the coast path atop the steep-sided inlet for a mile or so, though, and you come to a small jetty protruding forty feet into the mouth of a gully not much more than sixty feet wide. Charlie and I did just this, and discovered that it was indeed a little-known spot. So little known that there was no one else there. Not exactly brimful of confidence that I was going to 'have any luck', nor that I was going to be encountering anyone asking me whether or not I had had any (no bad thing in itself), I carried on anyway. Although it was chilly, the sun still had strength enough to take any real keenness from the edge of the wind. Naturally, this didn't stop Charlie from slouching around for half an hour or so looking as enamoured with the situation as a teenager dragged to a stately home by its parents. Eventually, though, he managed to find a grassy spot where he could lie in the sun and out of the wind and look imperiously at me down his Superdog paws for a while as if to say, 'What a lovely spot – we should come here more often!'

After I'd cast out a few dozen times and had gone through the phase that all fisherpeople must surely endure at least on an occasional basis – that what I was doing was more than a bit silly – I noticed a gathering of gulls bobbing about on the surface of the sea just to the left of the outlet. They seemed to be waiting for something, jostling for position like impatient commuters on a train platform. Now, I'm no twitcher, but I do happen to know (having lost at least one Cornish pasty to the little buggers) which bodily organ seagulls think with. I reckoned that it was no coincidence that they had turned up just after I had, and I also deduced that if seagulls – who eat small fish – deemed this a good spot for lunch, then it stood to reason that other species of animal – such as big fish – might think the same way. Therefore, so should I. As master of all I surveyed, I flashed a look over to Charlie to suggest that he may like to reassess his position in the pecking order. In turn, he looked back at me in a manner that almost certainly intimated that I may, in turn, like to reflect on who it is that pays for his food and healthcare and who it is that usually gets to lie on the sofa for twenty-three hours a day.

It was ten minutes before high tide, and therefore ten minutes until all those pounds upon pounds of fish that had swum upstream as far as their brackish tolerance would allow, would inevitably start to think about teeming back again towards the sea. I had already lost the diminutive Aglia lure due to the fact that it turned out to be par excellence at getting snagged on submarine boulders. In its place, I had been trying a Dexter wedge for a few minutes when I remembered – think like a fish! Admittedly, I had been doing my best to get inside the mind of a seagull, but to switch to the rubbery Shad lure just seemed like the right thing to do. Unbelievably, on my very first cast with it, the rod jolted and juddered. Just as I was concentrating on not blinking, looking a bit gormless and desperately trying to forget what it was that had been going through my mind three seconds previously, I got a firm, solid bite. Not a tickle, but a definitive and unequivocal chomp.

As is the way of fishing lore, I am now virtually morally bound to say that this was quite the heaviest bite from positively the largest fish that I have ever been connected with. I am bound to say this because I was not connected with it for very long. I'm not sure whether it was lucky enough to be thinking like a human at the time and carrying a pair of pliers, but after an impressive traverse along the jetty wall, a couple of decidedly ostentatious loop-the-loops and a tantalizingly plump glimpse of its white belly, it was free. Of course I did what all people who know not quite enough about fishing do in such circumstances – I hopelessly dangled the tangled lure in the water and jiggled it about a bit in the hope that the fish may come back for more instead of swimming as far and as fast as it could in the opposite direction. I consoled myself with the fact that now I wouldn't have to trouble myself to fabricate a story about a fish that got away. If ever I got stuck for banal truisms (an unlikely event, admittedly), I could now relate this event at will before wistfully and allegoric-ally wittering on about how it's always the ones you don't get that are the biggest/best/richest/quietest/least likely to give you a hard time if you spend the gas money on lager. Delete as appropriate.

But it's that bite, that tug, which keeps you in the game. It is that very thrill that motivates me to be there in the first place – no one (save for a tiny minority of the upper classes) goes fishing merely in order that they can bash defenceless animals over the head. Nor, I suspect, does anyone really go fishing to 'pit their wits' against the fish – for most, this is hardly a fair or interesting com-petition (ditto previous brackets). There is no denying that the scenery, solitude and serenity play their part, but the majority of the joy and justification, to me at least, of the activity of fishing lies in that one gripping moment – the bite – that you feel from within, and which immediately spreads to become a singular, meditative awareness of where you are and what you are doing. It is an example of the precious few moments we experience when everything else in our life freezes, fades and falls away from our consciousness towards complete unimportance. Some people get their fix by going fishing, some by surfing and yet others find Zen in activities such as line dancing. It may be true that you are occupying a different space, and you are watching from a different angle, when you are battling a fish from when you are swooping down a wave, or even from when you are slapping your thighs and yee-hawing, but the enjoyment of each certainly originates from a similar corner of your mind.

I tried a few different lures and banged them out to a few different places, but nothing else happened. The gulls didn't seem to be having much luck either, and when a small fishing boat chugged past them, they all beat a fairly torpid retreat. Charlie was also starting to get cold as the sun was now absorbing itself with the water, so I packed up and we started to make our way up the boulders that lay between us and the coast path. As we neared the top, I turned back to grab a last look at the place. While I'd been fishing, a guillemot had been gliding about, occasionally diving and bringing up the odd sand eel to slither down its gullet. This had further encouraged my theory about the presence of my fellow predators for a while, but after four or five launches had been necked I began to wonder, with the exception of my One That Got Away (yeah, right), whether there was anything worth catching there at all. As I looked back from the clifftop, this bird had just resurfaced with a decent-sized flatfish that, after the slim sandeels, looked a little cumbersome for its lithe neck. Think like a fish, no matter how weird it gets? It doesn't get a lot weirder than when you convince yourself that you've just seen a guillemot wink and look at you smugly.

On the way back along the cliff top, I asked Charlie what he thought of my seagull theory. Firstly, he commented that he'd always thought that gulls are actually more inclined towards scavenging than predating. Secondly, he made the gentle suggestion that, if he were a seagull and had a choice of either being slammed about by the high winds and angry seas or bobbing about with his mates while having a giggle at some nob flailing about hopelessly with a stick and a shiny thing, he knew which one he would choose, and indeed had chosen. Finally, and rather more pointedly, I felt, he gratuitously reminded me that so far I had spent the best part of two hundred quid on fishing gear and I was still buying lunch, whereas the seagulls would, as always, be getting theirs for nothing.

I bumped into Paul at the Twr later.

'Aah! Hello mate. Any luck today?'

'Nah.'

'Where d'you end up?'

'Well, I tried St Nons . . .'

'A bit bumpy?'

'You could say that.'

'So?'

'I went to Porthclais – I figured it was sheltered.'

Paul laughed, not unkindly, and shook his head while making a face often creased by the more polite football fans when the ref has just got it wrong.

'Just about the worst place to go fishing round here, I'd say.'

'Oh? Why's that?'

'Weeeelll, it's too shallow for a start, but mainly because there's a massive great shitpipe just upstream – didn't ya smell it?'

My nose may be tuned in to bacon, but sniffing out decent places to fish, it seemed, was going to need some working on.

As he was winching my breakfast into place the following morning, Paul informed me that he'd seen the forecast. In fact he'd seen two of them, and they both said, 'Unless you are a duck or an umbrella tester, don't bother'. Neither the still stout breeze nor the as yet fine drizzle were going to get any better and were set to deteriorate quite dramatically over the next day or so. Quite how the weather had the nerve to think it could get any worse than it had been on my journey there I had no idea, but we decided that our beach fishing jaunt was, so to speak, on the rocks. I did have the option of staying another day if the forecast had been favourable, but one thing that I had gleaned in my absence from St David's was when to quit. I could see little point in sticking around unless there were fish to be had, or, more specifically, any worthwhile beach fishing to be done.

As I was settling up before leaving, Paul and I exchanged fish recipes. His was a simple but, as it turned out, very tasty affair involving some mackerel, a dusting of flour mixed with some herbs of choice and a medium-hot grill. I'm not being cagey here – this is pretty much what he gave me. In turn, I jotted down my version of Hugh Fearnley-Whittingstall's mackerel with shallots, olives and thyme. 'My version' means whatever I could remember of it, which was not an awful lot more than what Paul gave me in return. We parted like old muckers, with Paul assuring me that I would be more than welcome to come out boat fishing with him on my next trip down.

'What you up to today?'

'Well, I want to fish, but . . .' I gesticulated towards the front door and, by implication, the filth outside.

'Fishguard, mate. Plenty of shelter if you go off the break-water – and you don't want to go home empty-handed, do you?'

I was heading back to my girlfriend Jackie's place that evening. Thankfully she is the not the sort of person who gives two hoots whether I return home with a club in one hand and freshly slaughtered dinner in the other or whether I had grabbed a takeaway on the way home. However, what was left of my male pride was not going to be punctured by returning to my woman without having killed something first, and if I had to brave the wind and rain to do so then so be it. In fact, so much the better. Paul extended his hand which I shook heartily before beating my chest and dragging my knuckles off to Fishguard.

I made it in good time, and it was still two hours until high tide by the time I had taken Charlie for a reconnaissance stroll down the breakwater, ensconced him inside Horace and walked back down the spit again to set myself up on a conveniently placed slope of concrete that I had spied about two-thirds of the way along the loosely arranged defensive boulders. On the way down with Charlie, I had spotted a waterproof-clad angler huddled into the rock, busying himself with rigging up. I took heart, as I reckoned that two seemingly quite rational people such as he and I could surely not both be wrong. He had been so focused on what he was doing that he was oblivious to my steps as I strolled past, and I didn't like to bother him largely because I knew I was going to have to walk past him again a few minutes later. This in turn would necessitate saying hello to the same person twice in a short space of time. I'm never quite sure how to greet someone a second time only minutes after the first without going all silly and Hugh Grant and babbling about the weather. As I struggled past him the second time with my fishing gear, and therefore with my fellow-geek status visible, he had finished tying tiny knots with numb fingers and was tidying up in readiness to cast out. I thought that it would be foolish not to attempt conversation with another optimistic masochist.

'Hi there.'

He turned to me with a large grin and eyes so saucer-like that they suggested he may have been thinking like a fish for just a little too long. His hair, which had previously been hidden by his hood, was the colour of a satsuma and his accent so thickly Welsh that for a moment I thought he might have been sending up the locals.

'Hallooow.'

'What you using?'

'Dug some luvlee fresh 'arbour raag s'mornin', see.' He held up a Tupperware box, the inside of which was alive with a wormy wriggle of serrated pink and brown ribbons, while his grin and eyes widened even further. I wasn't sure whether he was going to think me rude if I didn't try nibbling on one myself.

'Hmmm, yeah. I can see. Smashing.'

'What you got then?'

'Oh, just some squid and a bit of mackerel.'

'Luvlee job, then.' He turned back to the business in hand of casting. Whether in this context this meant lobbing out fishing gear or concocting spells I didn't hang around for long enough to ascertain. Instead, I lumbered off to my bit of concrete while revising the 'seemingly quite rational' bit about one or possibly both of the two people fishing there that day.

I had struggled the good half-mile or so down the breakwater carrying pretty much my full complement of tackle: two rods, tackle box, coolbox (even though the air temperature was probably lower than the water), tripod, landing net and tackle bag containing reels, line, flask and fish-basher along with anything else that did not fit anywhere else. Although this may sound like a lot, I did think to stash some of the smaller items inside the coolbox, and I managed to lash the rods, net and tripod together with Charlie's lead so, although the gear was fairly heavy, it wasn't as awkward as it might have been.

As it transpired, I could have made it even easier, as all the tripod's unadjustable legs were good for on that slope was assisting me in lowering the tip of the beachcaster in a rapidly accelerating if geometrically accurate arc towards the water. I folded it up again, and worked out that the butt of the rod would instead wedge quite happily and securely between the rocks.

Although it was evident by the white horses out at sea that there was still a decent breeze blowing, the combined effect of this breakwater, the much larger one a little further out where things roll on and off ferries to and from Rosslare, and the cliffs between the two meant that the stretch of water that I was fishing was relatively placid. It also, Paul had assured me, had a sandy bottom, which meant that I could finally give the beachcaster (and, more importantly, my beachcasting) a proper outing not only without having to worry about any big waves but also free from any nagging snagging doubts. However, the rain had increased to the extent that I had begun to question whether I would be a little drier if I swam the bait out rather than threw it. For the time being, though, the latter was preferable. Fractionally.

I attached the business end of my shock leader to one of the rugs that I'd been wettin' to use for some time – a 'three-hook flapper'. This arrangement has, unsurprisingly, three hooks tied at regular intervals along its main line, onto which the weight is looped at the bottom with a swivel at the top. Attach this swivel to the shockleader, bang the whole lot out into the sea and, I could only assume at the time, the bait (which you will have remembered to attach to the hooks before you bang them out) will, well, flap about in an alluring fashion in front of the fish. The joy of this rig, apparently, is that you can attach different baits at different depths in order to ascertain what the fish are going for and at what height from the bed. The packet told me that this rig would get me 'bites when all others failed'. In conjunction with the fact that I was in a location where I had been 'guaranteed to catch fish', I was filled with feelings of supreme confidence and inevitable failure in equal measures.

I secured a slice of squid to the bottom and top hooks, and laced a good-sized fillet of mackerel to the one in the middle. With a four-ounce breakaway lead pendulously rounding the whole thing off, I heaved the whole affair out the kind of distance that may, had I been on a beach and not too far from the breakers, have plopped down somewhere between an infant paddler and about where Charlie would get to before remembering that he hates water. Still, considering the fact that, where I was fishing, the bottom was as flat, and shelved about as steeply, as the average office desk it didn't seem to make a great deal of difference how far it went, so I jammed the end of the rod into the gaps in the rocks, wound in until the wires on the breakaway lead bit into the sand and set about some lure fishing with a trace of feathers.

I think that what I value most about going fishing is the opportunity to just stop thinking. I am often consumed by a devouring plethora of (often self-invented) worries, concerns, anxieties, variables, unknowns, possibilities and hyperbole – often sublimely late at night when I am trying to get to sleep or ridiculously early in the morning when I would happily donate a limb just to not be awake. But by rekindling my interest in fishing I have discovered why people will sit for hours on a canal bank, roll around in a boat, or stand waist deep in a river for hours doing – apparently – virtually nothing. It is not, as I had previously assumed, so that they can reflect and make decisions about the rest of their lives. Quite the opposite – it is because this is the only chance they get to stop doing just that and think exclusively, solely and selfishly about fishing.

And so it was for a couple of cold, drizzly hours or so in Fishguard. 'Pay attention to little rod while casting, look at big rod while reeling in line on little rod' was all my mind had to deal with for the first twenty minutes or so. Then the tip of the big rod went bendy and its butt began to graunch against the rocks. I hastily dropped the spinning rod onto the concrete, skipped over to cautiously remove the beachcaster and crouched, wedging its bottom end into the top of my thigh while bracing it just above the reel seat with my right hand and reeling in the slack that had mysteriously appeared with my left. There was nothing there.

Then, another couple of pecks and yet more slack, which again I reeled in tight enough to make the rod tip curve very slightly. Then stillness again – a false alarm. I waited for thirty seconds or so before replacing the rod between the rocks and went to reassess the lure situation. I removed the feathers and lashed on a spinner the like of which had landed me a couple of pollack in Scotland, and settled back into the now-familiar routine for ten minutes or so before a thought struck me. I had certainly had a bite, which in turn led to the possibility that a good deal of my bait had been half-inched by some no doubt large and tasty fish. I put the spinning gear down again, more gently this time, and reeled in the flapper. It appeared that although the bed was indeed free of rocks thereabouts, it was not devoid of seaweed, as I seemed to be reeling about two pounds of the stuff in. But it rapidly became apparent that a lesser spotted, greatly evolved and just a tad scary member of the shark family had attached itself to my line. Not seaweed, but roughly two pounds of dogfish.

'Roughly', when it comes to dogfish, is a remarkably appropriate term – their skin is a little like 60-grit sandpaper, and they don't half writhe about when you pull them out of the water. The last time I had caught one was when I was boat fishing and vomiting just off the coast of Scotland at the age of thirteen. I didn't remember it tasting all that good (yes, the dogfish and, no, not the vomit), but I've got a feeling that this was because my mother had done nothing more with it than boil it in dirty sock water and serve it with mushy sprouts. However, if I land a fish I didn't have any previous interest in eating I see this as my problem to be solved by a bit of culinary imagination, not by saying, 'Sorry, my mistake,' and putting it back. Besides, having had previous first-hand experience of the abrasive writhings of dogfish (also known as huss or rock salmon) before, I wasn't even going to try to get a hook out of this animal until it was very dead indeed and decidedly still.

It might have come out looking a bit sluggish, but as soon as I plopped it onto the concrete it began to do a very creditable impression of a sidewinder on hot sand. All sharks (with the possible exception of the hammerhead, which to me just looks a bit daft) carry with them an air of knowing just how further evolved and fit for their purpose they are than us. They have no less than nine senses, and I had a feeling that this particular specimen had all of them yelling at it that it was about to be hit over the head with a fish-basher. As I placed my foot on its back and reached for Brian Perks's finest, I had a sudden surge of doubt – not so much moral this time as practical. When I had last held this priest over the head of a fish on a warm Scottish rock in July, it had carried some kind of authority and looked quite able to immediately pacify the fish in question. Mainly because the fish in question was a rather smaller, shinier and altogether more acquiescent-looking mackerel. In contrast, poised above this refined, fearsome and very abrasive killing machine, it looked as if it was about to have all the impact of a limp stick of celery. I brought it down hard on the fish's neck three or four times. Not an awful lot seemed to happen really. The brass of the fish-basher got a good sanding and the fish arched itself a bit but did not look a great deal more dead than it had before. A bit pissed off perhaps, but this wasn't quite what I'd hoped for – it had looked less than happy when I'd dragged it out of the water. I didn't want this creature to suffer any more than it had to in order that I could feel like a real man and, far more importantly, I didn't want it slithering down the concrete so that it could tell its mates that the mackerel was best left alone today (the squid was untouched).

Without thinking, I grabbed the six-inch cook's knife that I had brought along to prepare bait with and placed its point just behind the head of the fish and pushed firmly until the steel tip grated on the concrete below. The fish didn't do a great deal more than slow down a little, but by then I assumed that it simply had to be dead, and that any residual movement was down to nervous reflex. Quite why I bothered to put it into a plastic bag before I put it in the coolbox I don't know. This is not an easy operation when your fingers are slimy and numb, the wind is conspiring to billow out the bag like a bedsheet and the fish you are trying to put in it refuses to die in any recognizable way and insists on thrashing its now bloody head around and from side to side. It carried on moving for some time afterwards.

I was less than convinced that I should continue. For a start, I really wasn't sure how good dogfish was to eat, and I was ever mindful of the chap in Scotland who had said that you 'shouldnae tak more than ye need'. The 'death' of this fish had felt strangely traumatic (more so for the fish, I'm sure), and I wasn't sure that I had the heart or will to take another of these Terminators on – the last one had looked at me in a really funny way. However, I was spurred on by four things. Firstly, that maybe I was a little more adventurous in the fish-cooking department than my ma had been twenty years previously, and I had yet to encounter any kind of white fish that doesn't taste good with a splash of lime and a few chillies. Secondly, I've read that dogfish are a bloody nuisance to those whose quarry is bigger/tastier/ harder-fighting, so even if only on altruistic grounds I felt I ought to persevere. Thirdly, in the age of the deep-freeze, 'more than ye need' is something of an elastic concept. Finally, and perhaps most convincingly to my mind, any fish that would rather eat a ropey old bit of mackerel than a nice piece of baby squid probably deserves a knife in its neck anyway.

While it was quite plain that dogfish would catch themselves given half a chance, this didn't strike me as being nearly as much fun as feeling the first nudgings of a bite, cautiously lifting the rod when its tip begins to pulse and tremble, then striking to set the hook at just the right moment. Not that this was exactly what happened with the second dog of the day either. I had thought that it would make sense to continue with the spinning rod, just in case I managed to catch something else that may have the good grace to stay still and at least look as if it had met its maker when I walloped it over the head. Still nothing happened, though, and by the time the next bite came on the big rod, I had become sufficiently disinterested in the small one to get to the beachcaster in time for the rest of the action. Striking, it seemed, was again largely superfluous, as this fish also seemed to become a victim to nothing but its own greed. This one was bigger, though, and more energetic (i.e. less drowned) than the last, so winding it in took more brute force and a little less ignorance. Possibly about three pounds, but I have no idea. The concept of weighing fish was still an alien one to me. As far as I was concerned, a fish was either big enough to eat or it wasn't, and considering the fact that whitebait is deemed edible, I just didn't see the point.

The third fish was about the same size, and this one was as reluctant to succumb to the big sleep as the first two. With both second and third there was no ceremony, hesitation or attempt to tickle them with the fish-basher – I plunged the knife into them with no sense of pleasure or remorse, and all three of them carried on squirming about in the coolbox with no sense of mortality or quite how irrationally pissed off I was getting with them. I don't recall whether I really did shout, 'Why don't you just bloody die' at them at one point, but I was certainly thinking it.

By this time, I had packed up the spinning rod and tackle in order that I could concentrate on the dogfish. Because I knew that they were technically dead as soon as I put the knife through them, and because also I knew that Jackie can eat for Hampshire and also had a spare drawer in her freezer, my conscience was relatively clear about bagging as many as I could. I also felt that the previous couple of hours had been a little brutal – that I had descended to little higher than savagery as a means of providing food. A bit like your average supermarket on a Saturday afternoon. I guess I wanted to feel that the position I had perhaps arrogantly assumed in the food chain over these creatures was justified. They certainly had the edge over me when it came to surviving in the water, and somehow they still had an air of dignity, tenacity and sophistication about them on land that escapes a good deal of humans. I thought, maybe, that I would feel better (and they would taste better) if I had outwitted, rather than out-thugged, at least one of them.

Sure enough, five minutes after what I had sworn would be my last cast, there came the gentlest pluckings at the bait. It almost felt as if a fish had inadvertently knocked it as it glided past and perhaps said, 'Sorry, Madam' on its way through. But the nibbles became more insistent and more regular, every few seconds or so, as if the fish was trying to tug the bait from the hook. Then it would seem to take a swim back, cup its mouth with a fin and try to figure out what to do next. I waited what I thought was patiently – to strike too soon would simply rip the bait from the quarry's mouth and scare it, along with any others, off. All the while I was being treated to the background hullabaloo of three supposedly dead fish rustling and slapping around in the coolbox behind me. Finally, my patience (all forty seconds or so of it) paid off, and the rod tip bent powerfully. I reciprocated by hauling back and winding in, turn after levered turn, until the fourth huss broke clear of the water. Larger than the first, but not as big as the middle pair, I swung it onto the relatively smooth concrete.

I'm not sure what came over me next – it could have been irritation, atavism or possibly even compassion, but something made me reach for the knife and, with a boot holding the fish as still as it needed to be, hack its head clean off. I think that, after the incessant and ambiguous writhings of the others, the decapitation of an animal seemed pretty much unequivocal. Surely any kind of suffering exists only in the mind of the animal in question, and if that mind is no longer attached to that animal then, except for a very brief period, any humanitarian concerns are laid to rest. I chucked the head back into the water for the crabs to bicker over and dropped the (you've guessed it) still sinuously snaking body into the coolbox.

After packing everything up and walking back to the car, I again remembered the anonymous Scotsman's advice about not taking 'more than ye need', and thought that in fact it should be modified. 'Ye shouldnae tak more than ye can carry'. I hadn't accounted for this when I had lugged all of that (mostly redundant) gear down the breakwater and, despite the frequent swapping of hands, by the time I returned to Horace and Charlie, my knuckles were indeed noticeably nearer the ground than they had been before I left the Twr. As soon as I regained control of my arms to the extent that they did not feel like wings, I secured everything in the boot of the car, and headed home.

On the way there, I dropped into your average supermarket in order to buy some bags of ice to keep the fish as fresh as possible. But when I located them, I wondered what earthly sense there was in spending just over three quid on something that would, by the time I got home, have turned into something I could get out of the tap. Surely, I thought, a bag of oven chips and one of frozen peas would do the same job at the same time as completing the meal. Genius. To top it off, I also grabbed a bottle of Chardonnay, which, I reckoned, would have chilled nicely on the way home. As I wandered around the supermarket, I'd had slight misgivings about whether, when I opened the boot and the cool-box, the fish would still be squirming and jostling about in there as if they were trying to get comfortable. I needn't have worried – by the time I opened the lid they had succumbed. Tonight they slept with the humans.

One of the reasons why I value Jackie as much as I do is that I am generally at liberty to bugger off to a place she has never heard of and reappear three days later unshaven, gibbering, knackered and reeking of fish without a great deal more in the way of comment than, 'Have you got anything to go in the laundry?' I am then quite at liberty, it seems, to proceed to spray fish blood and guts around her bathroom without her doing so much as popping her head round the door and saying, 'Fancy a cuppa while you're doing that?'

I'm not the most stern-stomached of people, but for some reason I've never really objected to gutting fish. In fact, I have to confess I actually quite enjoy doing it, up to a point. This might go back to the murky past when, as a kid, I would sit in the garden with my sister and perform grizzly experiments with mackerel heads. I especially like the parts of the process that call for the use of the fingers – taking a very sharp knife to the belly of a fish has its charms, as does the snap of a backbone, but you really can't beat the tactile qualities of what's inside. I've never got to grips with what it all is or does – it's all guts to me – but there really are some rather pleasant and diverting textures in there, from globular to squishy via slippery and stringy. All I know is that you should remove everything that looks as if it might be something that your mother tried to feed you when you were nine.

The evisceration of many species of fish is relatively straightforward. It's possible to simultaneously decapitate and eviscerate a mackerel, for instance, simply with a judicious bit of knifework through the backbone and around the rest of the body. With practice, a quick tug of the head will also have the guts plopping onto the chopping board with the most satisfying of grallochs. In my experience, the whole ensemble is especially effective when it comes to scaring young children.

Dogfish, however, are different. Not only does their skin actually blunt your knife quite dramatically (I had to resharpen after the second head), but they seem to be just as keen to hang on to their guts after death as they are unwilling to let go of life. Pulling, twisting and picking them out of the cavity with your bloody, slimy fingers is a labour of, if not love, exactly, then one of bloodlust. Eventually, though, the job was done, and after I had consigned three heads and four lots of guts to the dustbin, washed down the bath and coolbox, had a slurp of tea and slooshed the carcasses under the cold tap to remove the last of the viscera and blood I was left with four clean, fresh, lesser-spotted dogfi—

Oh, shit. No. You must be bloody well joking. How . . . ? But that's not possi— Run away. Hide. Don't look.

They were still twitching. As brainless and gutless as a school bully, but pulsing and glistening wet under the halogen lighting.

I'd heard stories about conger steaks still acting on similar impulse until they went under the grill, but had dismissed them as gory, macho apocrypha. But there, in the bath, were four creatures (whose lives I had undeniably and emphatically ended at least a good seven hours previously) still alive with the surging electricity of Darwinian struggle. Even after I had doused them with half a glass of wine, the juice of a lime and some dried chilli flakes the kitchen lights were still dancing over their tensing flesh like tiny darts of quicksilver.

Twenty-five minutes at 180°C saw to that. There was no way I was going to eat them if it hadn't. They were – finally – quieted, and quite delicious; so much so, in fact, that the chilli and lime were not only superfluous, but actually detracted from what would otherwise have been some of the firmest, most tender and delicate fish I'd tasted for a while. Inevitably, I couldn't help thinking, while I was eating them, about the experience of procuring them. I smiled at the comfort and warmth of the environment in which I was consuming them compared with the harsh surroundings of where they had been caught. It was funny – the way their bodies had contracted and pulsed in the bath almost made it look as if they somehow remembered what it was like to be alive, and responsible for feeding only themselves.

Paul's Grilled Mackerel with Chips and Horseradish Sauce

First make the chips. Half fill a large bowl with water and cut about that many potatoes into slices about as thick as those you might find in a fast 'food' joint if you were of a mind to eat substances liable to induce at best constipation and at worst cancer. Put the chips into the water as you cut them – this will a) rinse them of starch, which would otherwise make them stick together when you fry them, and b) stop them from going a funny colour. While the chips are de-starchifying, heat a little more than enough sunflower oil in a large pan to 140°C and try to find that chip basket that you are sure your mother gave to you about twenty years ago. You have probably never used it because oven chips are so much easier. However, you have become pedantic in your middle age. It's probably in the loft. If there are any kids about make sure the pan handle is in a safe position before you get the ladder out. Alternatively, get the kids to go and rummage in the loft for you while you open a beer and wonder what the hell you have done with your life since your mum gave you all those kitchen utensils.

Bung the chips into the basket a good handful at a time and fry them for four or five minutes until they are about the consistency of a bar of chocolate left on the front seat of a car on a warm, late-spring day. Remove them from the basket and put them on a few layers of kitchen roll laid flat. Or a T-shirt. Ignore the chips now and turn your attention to the mackerel, which should already have been filleted. Heat equal amounts of butter and olive oil in a heavy-bottomed frying pan until it is doing what all self-respecting thirteen-year-olds do – trying to smoke. Then turn the heat down so that it looks as if its father has caught it and smacked it round the head. Place an unspecified quantity (but nowhere near a whole bag) of plain flour in a large bowl and add fresh herbs of choice. Mackerel has an utterly distinctive flavour and therefore doesn't need a whole lot of help, but try a combination of any or all of these: fennel, thyme, lemon grass, coriander, dill or thyme – again (you can never have too much thyme). Salt and pepper blah blah blah.

Cut the fish fillets into two or three depending on the size of the fish, what sort of mood you are in and how many you can count to. Give them a good roll about in the flour and herb mix, shake off the excess and shallow-fry them. Oh, I should have said – put the oven on low before you do any of this (about 100°C should do it). I say 'about' because most domestic ovens are hilariously inaccurate when it comes to thermostatic control: '100°C' comes roughly halfway along the scale of obscenity of the word that comes between 'Jesus' and 'Christ' when you touch the inside. If 'bloody' comes out, it isn't hot enough, but 'bastarding shitting bollocking arsing wanking' is just a tad too warm. A good, solid, heartfelt 'fucking', accompanied by a shake of the burnt extremity, is about right. As the bits of fish become ready – i.e. golden and a bit tricky to pick up without them falling apart – place them in the oven to keep them nice and warm.

As you drop the last three or four pieces of fish in the pan, shout 'Oh shit – I forgot the bloody chips!' Crank up the heat under the oil so that it gets to a really quite alarming and fizzing 190°C. Drop the chips into the basket in roughly the same sized batches as before, and fry them until they look like Roger Moore's skin. Put them in the oven with the fish while you prepare the horseradish sauce.

A word on horseradish sauce. Do not use if the seal is broken or if you can pop the little button on the lid before opening. Grate my own horseradish? I'm not that middle-aged and pedantic, but I am fully aware that it's only a matter of time.

Baked Rock Salmon

You will need (per person)

the main body section of a dogfish – from the neck to just behind
where the guts used to be

the juice of one-eighth of a lime

a slurp of half-decent white wine

sea salt and ground black pepper

A doddle this one. The difficult bits are getting the guts out of the fish and coming to terms with the fact that it still looks alive when it goes into the oven, which should be pre-set to around 170°C.

Place the fish sections into a thick, sturdy roasting tin (the one whose provenence you are not sure about, but it looks as if it might have come from a car boot sale). It is infinitely easier to bake two or more at the same time, as then you can lean them against each other to stop them from falling over when you place them belly-up in the tin. If you are on your ownsome, then by all means slice a carrot in half lengthways and wedge the strips either side of the carcass. Failing that, and considering the fact that you are probably hungry after all that gut wrenching and moral conjecture, eat two of the little bastards.

Throw the wine, lime juice and seasoning over them before loosely covering the tin with a sheet of kitchen foil. Bake for about 30 minutes, or at least until they have quit with their convulsing malarkey. What you eat it with is up to you, but I can thoroughly recommend oven chips, frozen peas, a good dollop of mayonnaise and a cheap (rather than inexpensive) bottle of white wine.

4 Take

In the world of minor lunacy the behaviour of both the utterly rational and the totally insane seems equally odd.

J. K. Galbraith, *The Affluent Society*

I'd had to leave Horace at home. As far as seating arrangements in 'sports' cars go, I never have been able to figure out why 'two plus two' isn't the same as 'four'. It is in every other sane part of the world. There is a further distinction, sports-car wise – that of the 'two-plus'. What this means is also beyond me, but I always wondered about 'plus *what*' exactly? In Horace's case, this meant 'plus a dog's bed'. By the time I'd packed about ten times more gear than I was going to be needing (I couldn't possibly leave it at home – it would have felt left out), luggage for two humans and a dog plus a spare human, it was all getting a bit tight, no matter how much I tried to rationalize the packing lists. At one point, my chosen spare human tried to make alternative luggage-stowing suggestions. This was, of course, greeted with snorts of both derision and indignation – not because Jackie is a woman, but because one of the golden rules to happy existence is (man or woman), YOU DO NOT INTERFERE WITH ANOTHER MAN'S PACKING. Or woman's.

Everything we were going to be requiring, including all items we didn't know we'd be needing until we got there, fitted easily in Jackie's car. A small, Japanese 'supermini'-type affair that did 0–60 in roughly three days but also managed to eke out each gallon of fuel for at least fifty miles. Practical, economical, plenty of room, comfy enough and easy on the fuel if not the eye. Super. Oh shit. I *am* my dad.

'Hello?'

It had been only half an hour since we had turned off the ever-widening A30, fourteen miles or so before it greyly decides that there is just no point any more and slips towards the sea at Penzance. My phone had rung only a minute or so after we had let ourselves into our home for the week – a small, white flat lined with foot-worn swirly carpets and car-boot-sale books. The aged glass that slumped inside the frames of the large bay window was so rippled that the creased, lichen-quilted rooftops of St Ives appeared even more distorted than they truly were. These gingerbread roofs led the eye crazily to the long stone arm of Smeaton's Pier that in turn embraces the harbour. As Jackie fired up the kettle, I took the call the maker of which was a complete mystery. Who the hell would be calling me at 6.45 on a Saturday evening? When I was on holiday?

'Hallo.'

As far as accents go, some regions can be a little ambiguous. It is perfectly possible, for example, to live in my branch of the tree and encounter someone who will swear until he is blue from head to toe that he comes from ''Aaampsheer'. It is equally likely that next to him in the post office queue will be standing a lady (never a 'woman'), just as indigenous, who will politely point out that she lives in 'Hampshah'. She will possibly also call you 'dahling'.

However, the tones of anyone born and raised in Cornwall will soothingly betray this fact every time. You come from Carnwaall. 'Come from' in this particular context is a little misleading – the bloke on the other end of the phone didn't sound as if he'd ever made it much further than Bodmin. There was an expectant pause, as if I had been the one that had called him.

'Hello, who's this?' My mobile and absurdly retentive memory for dialling codes had told me that it was a Penzance number, but I didn't actually know anyone from Penzance.

'You waanted t'go out 'n a boat trip.'

Not strictly true, as it happens. My enthusiasm for fishing in general had been going from strength to strength, but as far as I was concerned boats equalled feeling really very sick. I had indeed called a couple of skippers a few weeks previously with a view to finding out the availablity of boat fishing, but had never really thought that it would transpire. A large part of me *did* want to go out on a boat, but I remembered that awful, gaseous, churning, heaving without actually heaving feeling that I felt would be inevitable. However, because of the uncanny timing of this call, I suddenly felt, in a way that would make a moth in the thrall of a candle look decidedly rational, inexorably drawn to subjecting myself to a day of feeling violently and debilitatingly nauseous in the company of total strangers.

On reflection, I think that this sudden masochistic compulsion (apart from feeling the sickly hand of fate on my shoulder) was derived from a couple of other sources. Firstly, when I had lived in Cornwall between 1996 and 1998, with Alex and the boys, I had perhaps not made the best of my time and opportunities. Actually, as euphemisms go, this is first class – I cocked things up quite a bit. It was here that I was first made most painfully aware of how great an impact the loss of my dad had made on me. Largely because this was the place in which I began to nurture the seeds of my own divorce and consequent estrangement from the boys. They are strange enough without needing any help from me. I think I therefore felt that this return to battle with motion sickness was in some part a kind of atonement. Secondly, I was perhaps intrigued to find out whether the literally gut-wrenching experiences of childhood fishing trips were quite as bad as I remembered them, or whether I had just been a fat stinking jessie. No, I didn't strictly *want* to go out on a boat, but it didn't really sound as if this guy was in the mood for 'Firstly, secondly and thirdly'. It was 6.45 on a cold January Saturday evening, and he probably just wanted a pint.

'Oh, yes. Love to. Can you help?'

'That's the thing, see . . . I mean, I know it's short notice 'nall, but, well, like, we're goin' out 'morrow.'

This was ideal. No time to chicken out, more time to recover and simper in pleasant surroundings with Jackie and Charlie.

'No problem,' I used the most masculine, least queasy voice I could muster. 'What time you heading out?'

'I gotta talk t'my brother. He's the skipper, see. I'll call you back.'

'Lovely, thanks.'

Jackie had made the tea while I was on the phone, and sat a mug next to me.

'Lovely, thanks.'

When I had been making enquiries about going out on a boat, no one had been in any position to make any promises. I had managed to get a week in the flat for a bargain price through a local holiday letting agency, but had needed to book this well in advance. Therefore I simply had to hope that the weather, tides and relevant whims of the skippers would be unfavourable for when we were there and I would simply have to stay on dry land with my beachcasters and spinning rods. I had initially emailed a chap called Rob who ran a business called Segue Charters advertised in one of my angling-porn mags. However, it turned out that he couldn't make up the numbers to make it worth his while, so he rapidly segued from having my fifty quid in his back pocket to being twenty pints worse off. Next on the list was a guy called Dave, to whom I spoke just before we came away. Dave sounded like a smashing bloke who I reckoned would've made decent company on board a boat, and said that he would do what he could. We had a quick chat about Cornwall and the fact that I had once lived there.

'Oh yeah? Whereabouts?'

'Tiny little hamlet near Helston.'

'Right on. What was it called?'

'Sithney.'

'Well, bugger me. My ma lives in Sithney.'

'No!'

'Yep. Small world, eh?'

Small indeed. So small, unfortunately for Dave, that no one else seemed to want to go out on his boat either. But I do like coincidences like this, though. Strangely, considering my penchant for wordplay, it wasn't until after I had left Cornwall that I realized that 'Helston' is a very obvious anagram of my surname. It took me even more time to figure out exactly what this meant – sod all, like all other coincidences.

Thankfully, it had seemed that on this particular holiday my size 9 wellies were destined to remain on terra firma, but skipper number three called me back as promised just as I had swilled the last of my tea around the bottom of the cup and poured it down my throat.

'Hello?' Although I recognized the number from the previous call, I did not know this particular guy's name at this point. Most Cornishmen's names begin with 's', though.

'Hi, 'sDave 'ere.'

'Hi, Dave.'

'Right on. I've 'aad a word with my brother, an' 'e's goin' out at seven 'morrow mornin'.'

'Right.' I was feeling unsettled already. 'Okay, ahem. Er, fine. Whereabouts shall I meet him?'

Yes, I know. I was going out to sea on a boat from Penzance, so the likelihood of congregating in the parish hall was slim. Maybe I was just stalling while I tried to figure out at what unholy hour I would have to be up on a cold Sunday morning to do something I felt at best ambivalent about in the first place.

'Well, at th' 'arbour,' answered Dave, in a tone that suggested he had never had to do so before. Thankfully, he didn't patronize me further by giving me directions along the lines of 'It's the large wet area full of boats next to the town – you can't miss it.' Lucky, that is, because saying to me 'you can't miss it' is a little like saying 'they couldn't hit an elephant at this dist—'

I had a few further questions.

'I'm a bit of a beginner – have you got all the gear I need?'

'No praablem. We'll sort y'out.'

'How long are we going out for?'

'Should be back 'bout fourish.'

'Oh shit. Can't we just nip out for a couple of hours, catch a pollack or two and be back in time for a pub lunch by an open fire' was tempting, but instead I came out with some real pseudo-macho lunacy:

'Any chance of some conger?'

'Doubt it. Might be some ling, though. And plenty of pollack.'

'Thank Christ for tha— Sorry, er, yeah, great. Seven-thirty, then.'

'Seven.'

'Of course, seven. Right. Erm, What's your boat called?'

'*Take*.'

'*Take*, right. And your brother's name – the skipper?'

''sCharlie.'

Now there's a coincidence. Jackie and I took Charlie le merde-tête out before heading to the nearest pub for a farewell dinner and a couple of pints. I tried to get an early night, but couldn't sleep. Partly because I was excited, partly because I knew I was going to have to drag myself out of bed at a time that should, in a civilized society, be illegal, but what kept my eyes stretched wide most of all was that I had forgotten to ask Sdave about The Green Thing.

Some preliminary research had told me that commercial fishermen are a bunch of people so superstitious as to be bordering on the neurotic, possibly even paranoid. Not that I can blame them – I guess that the more peril you expose yourself to on a frequent basis, the more talismans you cling to in order to balance the danger. On this basis, I am quite happy to walk under a ladder carrying thirteen black cats while whistling 'Don't Fear the Reaper' by Blue Öyster Cult, but I guess that the average trawlerman (yes, 'man') is entitled to his (yes, 'his') ritual ticks and devotions if it makes him a little more optimistic about a safe return. One of these rules is that not only are animals not allowed on board (for fairly obvious health and safety reasons – all I had to do was to just *think* of the havoc Charlie could wreak on board a boat if only it was possible to get his skinny, hydrophobic frame anywhere near water and I immediately understood), but it is also *streng verboten* to even mention any type of beast. Except fish, of course. Although I couldn't help wondering how conversation might go had fish been included in this linguistic embargo: 'Okay, boys, let's get out there and bag ourselves some of those, er, you know, er, well, some of those little flappy things.' On the way to Penzance at six o'clock that morning, the thirtieth after the latest dawn of the previous year, I knew that if any of my fellow anglers leaned towards this bestial superstition, they would be safe on that score at least. Not only had I had the good sense to leave my best friend in bed with my woman, I had also sworn to myself that I would not gibber on about him as I often do when stuck for anything more interesting to say. Which is alarmingly frequently. He does have beautiful blue eyes, though. And very unusual markings.

Another no-no as far as fishing boats are concerned, apparently, is The Green Thing. On no account must you wear, carry or possibly even think about anything green while on board. This particular idiosyncrasy had been troubling me for as long as I'd being planning the trip. I had refrained from asking any of the three skippers about it, though, for what seemed like eminently good reasons. In my mind, there were two possible responses to my asking 'Is it all right to wear my green wellies?', and both of them, to me, belied not only my specific incompetence, but also would have made me look generally very stupid. On the one hand, I imagined 'Anyone who doesn't even know that wearing green in a boat is likely to result in the death of everyone on board is a total liability and is not setting foot on my vessel' might be a likely retort, whereas on the other, 'Anyone who is gullible enough to swallow that pack of horse shit is obviously a total liability and is not setting foot on my vessel' seemed equally feasible. There is, of course, a third possible response of 'I don't give a toss what colour your wellies are – your fifty quid will still taste the same down the Smuggler's Arms as anyone else's,' but we often don't think of these things while they actually matter.

On the outskirts of Penzance, I pulled into a puffy-eyed, fluorescently lit petrol station in order to get some lunch. I also really did need some directions to the harbour – I hadn't been to Penzance for seven years or so, in addition to which it was still inky dark. On the subject of lunch, and more precisely why I was bothering to buy it when it was almost certainly going to be coming back up shortly after it went down, I had decided to take some seasickness tablets, both down my throat before I departed and in my rucksack for the rest of the day. If seasickness really was going to turn out to be as bad I as I remembered it then my capacity to fish – or indeed to do anything except sit in a corner snivelling and wanting my mummy – would be drastically reduced. I therefore stocked up with a roasted vegetable wrap containing encouraging things such as salsa, sour cream and sweetcorn, a packet of diesel and fish-gut crisps and a hearty raw egg, diced carrot, tomato skin and off-ish milk health drink to wash it all down with. When I asked for directions to the harbour, the guy behind the till, who looked as if he may have got 'waking up' and 'getting up' a little muddled, told me, limply rotating an arm vaguely behind his back that,

'It's the large wet area full of boats next to the town – you can't miss it.'

Because I had not clarified The Green Thing situation beforehand, upon arrival in Penzance at a time in the morning when usually the only decision I was capable of making was which side I should continue sleeping on, I was faced with a shocking dilemma. I had carefully put my brown walking boots by the back door the previous evening, but had even more studiously left them there as I walked out of it that morning. I therefore had the choice of meeting my skipper for the day sporting £6.50's worth of green wellington boots or a brace of extravagantly expensive and therefore still quite pristine skateboarding shoes. Whatever I slipped over my knee-high walking socks would immediately signify me as one of two things, both of which I would have trouble denying convincingly – a clueless up-country numpty who knows bugger all about the lore of the sea or a namby-pamby landlubber who probably has some half-cocked moral qualms about killing things. That's how it felt, anyway. I went for the skateboard shoes on the marginal grounds that I would rather spend the day being viewed with ambivalent pity than with murderous intent.

After I'd parked up near what certainly looked like a harbour, I stuffed all my gear – flask, lunch, Stugeron tablets, waterproof trousers – into my bag and hoisted it onto my shoulders over my bought-for-the-purpose grey and orange waterproof jacket and ambled around the large wet area full of boats. The west end of the harbour was home to the mighty, towering, rust-seeped hulls of trawlers and passenger charters, some high in dry dock – impotent but still somehow menacing against the blue-black of the morning. The sodium street lights seemed only to darken the surrounding sky while exacerbating the enforced stillness of the boats, angry at their suspension. I hurried through the public car park to a quay of more human scale, at the top of which I had spotted a flurry of folk being jettisoned from cars with all the noise and activity of those excited at the prospect of a day's fish-bashing. I was still unsure of exactly where I was going, so I asked one of the contingent if they were also headed out with Charlie. They all fell silent, as if I had just painted myself green and run around reeling off the entire contents of Noah's ark.

'No.'

'Oh.'

'I think his boat's down there,' one of them pointed to the bottom of the quay. Or possibly to the bottom of the harbour.

'Thank you.'

For a quintet of people who were just about to embark on a day of optional recreation, they didn't half seem miserable. They were probably just jealous of my skate shoes. There will be no further fish/clothing-based puns.

There were two boats jostling for position and phutting cold, thick, blue-grey clods of diesel smoke that hung in sulking clouds over the black water near the end of the eastern quay. Each of the skippers were attending to their pre-trip safety and equipment checks. It soon became apparent that one of these was preparing for the glee club I had encountered on the way down, as he and they began loading up enough bait and tackle to start a floating shop. I could only assume that the other boat was, for that day at least, partly mine. Either that, or 'You can't miss it' was about to become a contender in that week's 'How Wrong Can You Be?' competition, and I really was in the wrong place. But sure enough, as the 38-foot-long wedge of fibreglass was expertly steered alongside the harbour wall, I could make out, in the now indigo light, the word *Take* on her stern. When he had lashed her fast to the waisted, rusted stanchions, the skipper (olive green trousers, unambiguously green gilet) began dancing with diesel drums and fettling with fish boxes.

'Hi! Are you Charlie?'

''smee.' He replied through one corner of his mouth as he kicked a box from just behind the wheelhouse in a well-judged scrape along the deck. It turned through a sweeping ninety degrees on the way and stopped broadside against the stern with a shudder and a plastic clack, magnified by the violet stillness.

'Hello there. My dog's called Charlie!' I know, but it was still, as far as I was concerned, yesterday.

'Right on.' He didn't look up. Did he say, 'So what'?

'I spoke to your brother, Dave. Last night?' I watched as he teed up another crate.

He curled the crate along the deck, and as it nudged up against the first, he put his hands on his hips and squinted up at me as if he still wasn't convinced. As if he needed to recognize my unfamiliar face.

''sright. Says you're down from up country an' waants a day's fishin'.' He shielded his eyes from the glare of the yellow harbour light behind me and twitched a half-smile before returning to this chores.

'Yeah, cracking. I'm a bit of a novice, though.'

''sno praablem.' He squeezed this out through the clenched teeth and protruding lower jaw of waddling a full drum of diesel from one side of the boat to the other. The morning light, which had started to move sluggishly towards a deep mauve, revealed him as a sharply handsome man – no more than twenty-five years old with pink, fresh skin and a slow, expressive face that suggested that, of all its features, its mouth did the least talking. All his movements were precise, practised and unhurried in their brevity.

It was 6.45, and in the time it had taken for us to carry out this preliminary interchange, the fun-loving five had stacked their boat to the gunwales, donned full waterproof gear of various shades of green, and tally-ho'd off towards the horizon.

'How many of us are going out?'

''nother four after you. Be with you dreckly.'

This word (roughly and entirely misleadingly translated as 'directly'), in Cornwall, is one of the most flexible I have come across in any language. It is comparable to the Spanish *mañana*, but implies considerably less urgency or predictability. The Inuits may need forty-odd words for snow, but in Cornwall there is need for only one *dreckly*. To understand its often frustrating ramifications fully, it is really necessary to live among the natives for a while, but it loosely translates as 'when I feel like it'. Charlie disappeared into the cabin in order to (it transpired dreckly) roll and light a cigarette. While he busied himself I pulled on my – oh my God, I hadn't even realized – *green* waterproof trousers in an attempt to distract attention from the incongruousness of the shoes, and sat myself on a nearby always-cold granite bollard. I swivelled myself round, the seat of my pants scraping on the stone, so that I could see my pen trace itself across the page in my journal in an effort to remind me that Charlie was 'one of those people who doesn't have to say a great deal to get you to like him'.

Just as soon as I'd written another line or two about the option of not liking him possibly leading to my unnnatural deselection, I met up with the first of the other guys who was to be coming out with us. Geoff was a slim, avuncular (possibly, in true West Country style, also paternal) and friendly chap of around sixty. He wore an orange flotation suit and a happy, lined expression around watery blue eyes. His kindly, patient face suggested that although his life thus far had been, on the whole, good, he still had a working knowledge of what might politely be called its ironies. He was keen to introduce himself, and to engage in conversation, as if he knew what it might be like to spend eight hours on a small boat with someone having not made the effort to do so. Because I was similarly keen to enjoy the day, and because I'm a sucker for anyone a similar age to my father, we had got quite carried away with conversation by the time Third Fisherman entered, stage right.

'Aaaah! There you are, you fat bastard!' Geoff obviously knew the corpulent and stereotypically jolly-looking man who had just joined us. His salt-and-pepper swept-back hair was, unlike the rest of him, thinning.

'How you doin', y'old git!'

'Robin, my dear boy,' commenced Geoff, mock-grandly, 'this is the fattest man in Cornwall. May I introduce you to T—'

'*Tim* Simpson?' Tim extended his enormous, raw-sausage right hand as he told me his name. He italicized the 'Tim' and interrogatively intoned the 'Simpson', as if there were a local clan of that name of which I must have heard mention and of whom he, specifically, was Tim. He nodded toward me and smiled, gap-toothed, as if to reaffirm this, at the same time as suggesting that I should reply by introducing myself as '*Robin* Shelton?'

'Good to meet you.'

'Likewise.' A surprisingly flaccid handshake, a predictably stiff pause and another, slightly disappointed, nod, as if he was giving me another chance to reciprocate.

'No Potty?' Geoff redirected Tim's attention.

'Oh, oh, er – he's on 'is way. Only got the nod 'alf an hour ago.'

'Terry,' Geoff explained, turning back to me. Not much of an elucidation, so I tilted my head and raised an eyebrow.

'Another member of our club,' Geoff gurgled secretively. 'No one calls him Terry – we all call him Potty.'

'How come?'

Tim laughed, all the way from his hand-clasped belly to his nostrils, and Geoff tutted and arced his head as if Terry was an errant but dearly loved son.

'Ask him yourself. Here he comes.'

For a man who had only been sentient for half an hour or so,

Terry looked to be remarkably together and in control of himself as he measured his pace towards us. Perhaps so much so as to be a little contrived. Charlie spotted him from the boat.

'POTTY!'

So, Tim knew Geoff. Geoff knew Tim. Both knew Terry. Charlie was also on nickname terms with him, and it had become evident that he was also familiar with the other two. I began to feel distinctly English.

'Mornin', Chaarlie.' Terry smiled down at the skipper as he drew level with the rest of us. 'Geoff,' he intoned amicably.

'Potty.'

'How ya' doin', Pots?'

'Right on, Simps. You?'

'Fat, warm and breathin'.'

'Can't have everythin', I s'pose.'

Terry was around my age, and had an unruffled blonde calmness about him that suggested two things – firstly, that not a great deal troubled him overmuch, and secondly, that he was as unhinged as a barn door in a tornado. He looked at me politely, and I noticed that he did so with placid, piercingly blue eyes the like of which usually stare out from a face in the newspaper alongside a caption that reads 'He always seemed so *quiet*, says horrified neighbour.' He extended his bony hand.

'Hi. I'm Terry.'

Not 'Potty'. I was not, I realized then, in their club.

'Robin,' I replied.

'Hi, Robin,' and then to Tim and Geoff, ''s Mike comin'?'

Both men shrugged and all three turned to look down to Charlie, who was arranging some short, stout, stiff rods vertically in holsters on the deck in echo of the lines of the radio masts atop the wheelhouse.

''s Mike comin' out today?'

Charlie pulled down the corners of his mouth and shrugged nonchalantly, 'Spoke to 'im laast night an' 'e said 'e were up f'rit, but,' another hunched and indifferent shoulder, 'oo knows wi' Mike?' He slotted the last rod into the rack and its tip quivered as its butt hit the deck.

'HALLLOOOOO! AHOY THERE!'

On the fingertip of the western arm of the harbour stood a figure, waving a fat rod not much taller than he was in one hand and a tackle box in the other. The other four members of the club tittered and looked up towards who I surmised to be Mike. All that stood between him and us was a sixty-foot stretch of water and the ability to be in the right place at the right time. Tim cupped a hand round his mouth.

'What ya' doin' over there, ya' wanker?'

Mike managed indignance at twenty paces as his rod and box exaggerated his shrug and splayed arms. 'Whaddya mean? I'm in exactly the right place. 'sjust you buggers are wrong, 'sall.' There was something in his reply and demeanour that had more than the merest suggestion that he truly believed this. Charlie solved the dilemma by signalling to the rest of us that he was ready for us to get on board and calling to Mike that he would come and pick him up before we headed out.

We chugged over to Mike, a middle-aged man whose neatly combed hair was not so much wavy as tightly rippled and flecked with white horses. He boarded the boat in no graceful fashion using a found ladder and laden, erratic, counterbalancing arms. He stumbled onto the boat, adjusted his spectacles (which had been ground and framed to somewhere between milk bottle and windowpane), nodded to everyone else and made the most emphatic physical contact between any of us that day by slapping and clasping my shoulder. He looked me up and down as a pirate captain might survey a new cabin boy, smiled and said,

'New boy, huh? You gonna show us all how it's done, eh?' He nudged me with a wink and a smile. Maybe I could be in Mike's club. If I wanted to be.

The sun ascended somewhat reluctantly towards daylight, rendering the sky a cornflower grey fading to a steely lilac at the crisp, gunmetal blue horizon as we hit the olive chop of open water. While the others caught up on fishing gossip, I thought about this odd lack of physical demonstration between these bonded and bonding men. At first, I wondered whether this was due to some kind of macho posturing, but later appreciated that when you are occupying the same 200 square feet or so of deck as five other souls from sunrise to sunset, you need to start out with all the personal space you can get.

The hull accelerated surprisingly quickly from lumbering displacement to cruising planing craft, and we made our way rapidly past the hub of the Cornish fishing industry that is Newlyn and the fashionable but still functional villages of Mousehole and Lamorna, familiar from previous times from the other side of the coastline and the opposite end of the day. As we all unwittingly settled ourselves into our roles for the next few hours, I truant-mindedly attempted to make anagrams of the the word 'Stugeron'. After I decided that I could do no better than 'Er, no guts', I struck up conversation with Tim, who was busy rigging up while Charlie did the same for me.

'Last time I was out on a fishing boat, I felt so goddam sick I wanted to die.'

Tim looked up from his traces and lures. 'You too, huh?'

I rolled my eyes and held my stomach while biliously billowing out my cheeks in mock vomit mode.

'Gets me too. Every bloody time,' continued Tim. 'Know what?'

'What?'

'Tuna sandwiches.'

'Does that cure it then?'

'Nope – but they taste the same on the way up as on the way down, so it don't feel as bad.'

I doubted that my vegetable wrap was going to do the same trick, but as yet had had no queasy qualms. When I was a child, all I had to do was sit on a throbbing, belching, rotten charter hull and I would be greening with nausea. Maybe I had grown out of it.

Tim disappeared inside the wheelhouse, where Mike was guiding the boat towards the first hunting ground of the day while Charlie was rigging up my gear for me. In truth, I could have done it myself, but I figured that if I did so, it might also be assumed that I was in possession of further information, which I most certainly wasn't. In front of Mike was a console housing some pretty sophisticated-looking sonar, GPS and countless other digital aids that went 'blip' or displayed a mesmerizing array of sweeping, flashing or pulsating lights. Between them all, and in Mike's insouciant left hand, was an incongruously traditional spoked ship's wheel, the majority of which I had assumed now languished above seaside bars or were wedged inside job-lot boxes in auction houses. It looked as if 95 per cent of the dash had been subjected to a refit, but when it had come to the wheel, whoever had been responsible had run out of either money or inspiration and left it where it was. Maybe there is some stuff that just can't be improved on.

Half an hour or so of three-quarter throttle later saw us at our first destination. A wreck lodged on a piece of ground known as Epsom Shoals. All of us were fishing with lures known as 'jelly eels' – brightly coloured flexible rubber rockets that imitate highly edible small fish when reeled in. Charlie presented me with an eight-foot boat rod with a multiplier reel at the opposite end to the eel. He demonstrated how to use the multiplier, which in this context (involving nothing more complicated than dropping the lure over the side of the boat and letting it plummet) turned out to be unexpectedly straightforward. I was instructed to allow the spool to run freely until the weight hit the bottom then, after immediately putting the reel into gear and winding frantically for two or three turns to avoid snagging, to reel in slowly and smoothly for another forty turns or so. Above this height, apparently, there was little chance of catching anything worthwhile, so the process was to be repeated.

Charlie positioned the boat uptide of the wreck four or five times, and each time nothing happened, save for the occasional and optimistic flutter of excitement from one or other of the more experienced fishermen on board when they thought they had a 'take', the preferred word that day to describe what I had always called a 'bite'. That explained why the boat was called *Take*. I had been wondering about the odd name, so open to being misconstrued as an instruction to pilfer. I once spent a night in a police cell for urinating in a public place after making a similar mistake next to a 'Wet paint' sign.

We all (including me, in my infinite wisdom) agreed that, this day at least, Epsom Shoals was, in Mike's words, a bag of fucking shit. As we motored on to our next hunting ground, it dawned on me that – of course – I was in a boat. With five other blokes. Not 'dawned on me' in the 'How the bloody hell did I get here then?' sense, but rather the implications of where I was, what I was doing and with whom I was doing it hit me like a slap from a wet kipper.

When I had been in Scotland, I had at first been puzzled by the fact that explicit profanity seemed to be as much an acceptable conversational tender as 'please' or 'thank you'. Everyone swore. Men, women, children. I swore. At one point I even thought I heard a local dog call Charlie a fookin' soft sassenach bastard as I strolled past it. This last could, of course, be put down to the lack of omega-3s at the time, but the notion stayed with me nonetheless. The rowing couple whom I had overheard that first evening in the Steampacket could, in retrospect, just have been having a perfectly pleasant and ordinary Monday evening out. It took me a while to figure out, though, that the locals conversed like this on land simply because they spent so much time doing so on a boat, where 'normal' social conventions are irrelevant. On a boat men will swear, shout, brawl and generally act in a way that most blokes would behave were they not bound by the prevailing social mores. Because these people live – metaphorically and physically – so close to their work, it is in part inevitable that it seeps into their domestic parlance.

I happen to think that, when used correctly and in the appropriate context, swearing is a perfectly acceptable (indeed, essential) part of any language. Personally, I would be lost without 'bollocks', especially when I crack my head on the corner of a garage door that hasn't been opened quite far enough. However, I try to be circumspect with my expletives, partly because of the sensibilities of others, but mainly because that way they are so much more effective when I'm giving the kids a good bollocking (you see, indispensable!). I could see that, while aboard *Take*, I was going to have to put this 'time and place' attitude to swearing into action if I was going to stand a reasonable chance of fitting in. To put it another way, that day, in that boat, I could see that I was probably going to need to wheel out the odd cunt or two. It soon became clear that the occasional conversation about exaggerated sexual exploits, penis size and how many pints I could drink was going to be fundamental to social survival. Maybe it's not just the sizes of the 'ones that got away' that fishermen lie about.

Considering the fact that every one of us on board was wearing at least one item of green clothing, it was evident that I was not among a superstitious bunch of people. This was compounded further by the fact that our next watery port of call was a place called Thirteens. As we neared it, I asked Terry, who was (along with Geoff and Tim) busying himself with changing his lure with a penknife, why this place was so named.

'You wanna know why they call me "Potty"?'

The way he asked me this – unexpectedly, incongruously and in a way shadily reminiscent of a man attempting to sell me something illicit in a bar where it might be difficult to say no – had me thinking very carefully indeed about whether, in all honesty, I wanted to know or not.

'No, I mean, no I don't know why . . . er . . . yes. No that I don't want to . . . Yes, why is that, Terry? Yes. Why?' I might have giggled just a little at this point. Terry opened an Arian blue eye so wide that its iris was entirely surrounded by white. And, I noticed, filigrees of sleep-deprived red. He tapped his temple repeatedly with his forefinger.

'Because I am.'

Oh Christ. It's often said that only the truly mad have no concept of their condition, but in my experience it's the ones that insist on telling complete strangers, unbid, just how cuckoo they are that often give maximum cause for concern. Especially when they use the word 'Potty' to describe their condition.

'Oh,' another 'Well, shucks, there's a thing' chuckle, 'Right.'

I had no idea what else I was supposed to say next to such self-confessed and therefore self-evident Bedlam fodder. Furthermore, I obviously couldn't run away, and he had a knife and thin, garrottingly strong nylon line in his hands.

'What makes you say that?'

The quite straightforward answer to this is again, of course – in the best tradition of missed-beat logic – 'Because I am', but even now I still can't think of a better question in the circumstances.

'Because I am.' Terry winked, and his face broke into a beaming smile as he gently nudged my upper arm with his bony elbow.

'Just kidding, mate. I have done some pretty daft stuff in me time, though.'

Now I knew I was in deep trouble. I was in the confined company of someone who had gone from telling me he was bonkers to telling me that he was only joking. Surely this territory is normally reserved only for those whose mental soundness is limited to plasticine pot-making.

'Oh yeah? Such as?' Humour him. Then dive and swim as fast as you can. Not just yet, though – I wanted to see if he'd manage to top my own all-time, dumb-ass, no-brain, I'm-immortal-because-I'm-nineteen exploit of putting my head inside a rotating concrete mixer full of wet mortar just to see what it looked like.

'Went fishing in a Force 10 once.'

Pah! Nancy boy. He could see I was unimpressed.

'Twelve-foot swell running.'

So? I remembered when I had considered, albeit briefly, fishing from the rocks near St David's in that kind of sea before dismissing the idea due to lack of abseiling equipment.

'Off the rocks, it was.'

Hmmm. That *is* pretty barmy, I suppose.

'Abseiling.'

'You went rock fishing in a twelve-foot swell and a Force 10 gale while dangling off a cliff?'

'Hundred-foot cliff.'

'I see what you mean. You're as mad as a box of frogs. Catch anything?'

'Huh?'

'Did you catch any fish?'

'What – in a sea that big?' He grinned and shook his head twitchily. 'No chance!'

'You went fishing in a hooley while dangling from a bit of dental floss when you pretty much knew you weren't going to catch anything?'

'Had a fair idea, yeah.'

I still thought that my escapades with the concrete mixer surpassed this in most departments, but I reckoned that to even try to out-loony this guy would be more foolish than both put together.

'All right then, lads – tackle out.' Mike breezed out of the wheelhouse, where it seemed he had all but taken control of the boat while Charlie had been rigging and chatting. Mike clapped and rubbed his hands together before slapping me between the shoulder blades just a little too hard with one of them. He bent down, retrieved his lure (orange, like mine) and, with a deft slice, tug and a push, replaced it with a red one.

'Have you got the time on you, Mike?'

'Eh?'

'Time?' I pulled up my sleeve and tapped my empty wrist with my finger. I had left my watch coiled snugly inside my left walking boot.

'Oh, er . . .' Mike put down his rod and pulled his phone from his waterproof-coat pocket. 'Half eight.'

It was only eight-thirty on a Sunday morning, and not only had I already got up, been fishing and made it to an unfamiliar place on time, but I'd also had a conversation with a nutter. My stomach gave a slight and ambiguous rumble. I thought that perhaps I was getting peckish.

'Right on, lads.' Charlie had made some final adjustments to the boat's position by means of sonar and some delicate thraps and blips of forward and reverse gears. The engine chugged lack-adaisically on idle while we dropped our brightly coloured lures once more. As the lead weights dragged them down, I tried to work out whether I really did need some lunch at 8.30 in the morning, or whether I was actually beginning to feel sick. While I pondered, Terry, Geoff and Charlie remained quiet, observant, while Tim and Mike bantered.

'You wouldn't know what to do with her!' asserted Tim.

'You give me 'alf an hour wi' your missus, I'll show you what I can do!'

You mean you'd want him to watch?

'You're bloody welcome to my missus!' Tim looked suddenly saddened, as if through saying it he had only just realized that he might mean it.

I thought of Jackie still curled up with the other Charlie – all warm, musty and oblivious. Gits.

'Whoaaaeeeeayyyy!' My reaction to what felt like something with all the hydrodynamic efficiency of a bucket being attached to my line came from as deep within me as my lure was below the surface.

Throughout the day, when someone had a real or suspected bi— (sorry – *take*) Charlie would automatically and inquisitively say 'Fish, ... ?', followed by the name of whoever was claiming that they had something. Not me, though. Despite the fact that he actually shared my dog's name, Charlie rechristened me 'Avvee' for the day.

'Fish, 'avvee?' In Hampshire (certainly in Hampshah), this would translate roughly as 'I say, my good man, do you think you may have connected with something of a piscine nature?' 'Fish, 'avvee?' in this context, worked just as well.

'No, it's a bloody bucket,' was tempting, but I resisted with similar tenacity to that of the leaden, thickly quivering mass at the other end of the line. This was, I could tell already, by far the largest fish I had ever snagged.

'I guess.'

Charlie came over to stand next to me as I puffed and pulled and panted and ranted about how bloody heavy it was.

'Jus' keep windin' 'im,' encouraged Charlie, while he flipped gum around his mouth with an air of excitedness bordering on the barely visible and the others seemed to fish just a little bit harder in a nebulous kind of way, muttering barely audible thoughts containing words such as 'fucking', 'jammy', 'up-country' and 'bastard'.

I kept windin' 'im.

'Pull 'im up, then, as ye let the rod down, woind like buggery.' They don't give you advice like that in *The New Fisherman's Handbook*. I did as I was bid – there was no real sport or technique in hauling this lump in. In terms of skill, it reminded me of a more strenuous version of the children's fishing game where the cardboard 'fish' have a small piece of steel glued to their heads and, instead of a lure, the 'rod' has a magnet dangling from it. The knack to this type of fishing is all in finding the fish in the first place, and I had Charlie to thank for that.

'Don't let the line go slack, wha'e'er you do. Just 'ang on to 'e wi' all you got.'

At that point, he could have been talking about various things – fish, rod, sanity, contents of stomach – but all I could think about was keeping that fish on the end of that line. If I landed it, I could tell myself that I'd done what I'd set out to do, I could relax for the day and concentrate on more important things such as staring at the horizon and avoiding being out-weirded by Terry. I kept the line tight, and made sure that whatever was on the other end stayed there. It wasn't exactly fighting, but was certainly making life as difficult as possible for me on its way up by the simple expedient of being quite stubbornly heavy and uncooperative.

I began to regret that I had started winding in quite so enthu-siastically. However, despite (possibly because of) the fact that I had had no concept of how to pace myself, and because I am too stubborn and far too vain to do anything else, I kept reeling at the same frenetic pace. I didn't want the others to feel any more inad-equate than they already did. Having been beaten to the first fish of the day by a novice is one thing – being pipped by a namby-pamby novice is another type of ignominy altogether.

Eventually, the fish neared the surface, and I drew its lateral sluggishness in close to the boat. Charlie reached over the side, wrapped the cheese-wire line round his hand and heaved what later turned out to be just over seven pounds of pollack over the gun-wale. As he expertly unhooked the fish at the same time as fling-ing its bends-dead form into one of the plastic boxes he had earlier kicked to the stern of the boat, everyone else eyed my catch with what I took to be envy. At this point I realized that I was sur-rounded by three things – firstly, and most immediately, five people who knew a lot more about boat fishing than I did. Beyond that, we were all buoyed by around 400 square feet of fibreglass and ultimately we were, along with roughly 30 per cent of the rest of the planet, dwarfed by salt water. I reasoned that my chances of not being ejected into number three from number two by number one would be greatly improved if I did not, at this point, dance around, waggle my fingers in my ears and chant 'I caught the first fish, I caught the first fish, so-oo there.' I remained as diffident as was possible having just caught the heaviest fish that I had ever managed. I allowed myself a little bit of masculine pride, though. No matter that this catch was perhaps an insignificant event for the other folk on board – to me it represented not only a good-sized dinner for everyone I know plus a couple of strangers, but it also seemed to break my boat curse in some way. And, what the hell – man come, kill beast. I was on a boat full of very blokey blokes, and (balls to the lot of 'em) I *had* caught the first fish. What's more, I'd done it without faffing about with my lures and talking about how good I was in bed. I was the alpha male. I was hunter and gatherer. I was Ernest effing Hemingway. Bloody hell – I was even good in bed. I was . . . I was, ah. Glob. I was . . . bock. Er – glug. I was starting to feel really quite sick. I was also going to deny that fact and talk about *my* fish that *I* had caught instead. Tim was kneeling next to me, once again switching lures and munching on a tuna sandwich.

'That's the biggest fish I've ever caught!' Retaining the contents of my stomach and those of my excited mind was just too much to deal with at once.

'Ish it.' Tim's masticating reply, which obviously didn't warrant a question mark, was ejected through a gooey paste of tuna sandwich that could well have been either on the way down or up.

'Schpessmin weight fr'our clubsh 'bout twiche that big.'

A 'specimen' weight for a fish is basically that at which an official body will stop sniggering at it.

Specimen Weights of Selected Species – Cornwall

The table below lists the weights at which most people will take what you have caught seriously. This is not to be confused with the table of minimum landing sizes on p. 69 – the measurements listed there are the bare minimum at which fish should be taken. Any fish under this size will not only result in derision, but also in a hearty slap for assisting in buggering up the marine ecosystem.

SPECIES	LATIN NAME	BOAT (lb)	SHORE (lb)
bass	Dicentrarchus labrax	7	7
coalfish	Pollachius virens	16	2.75
cod	Gadus morhua	20	8
dab	Limanda limanda	1	1
eel, conger	Conger conger	40	20
garfish	Belone belone	1.5	1.5
haddock	Melanogrammus aeglefinus	9	1
lesser-spotted dogfish	Scyliorhinus canicula	3	2.75
ling	Molva molva	20	4
mackerel	Scomber scombrus	2	1.75
mullet (yer thin-lipped)	Liza ramada	3.5	3.5
mullet (yer thick-lipped)	Chelon labrosus	4	4
mullet (yer golden)	Liza aurata	1.875	2
plaice	Pleuronectes platessa	3.5	2.75
pollack	Pollachius pollachius	14	4.4
pouting	Trisopterus luscus	3	1.5
whiting	Merlangius merlangus	3.25	1.25
wrasse, cuckoo	Labrus mixtus	1.25	1.25

Sources – National Federation of Sea Anglers

'Oh.'

'Schtill,' a gulp and a wipe of the mouth with the back of the hand, 'not a bad fish for a beginner,' Tim smiled. He was being kind, but I suspected that most fish might have trouble differentiating between a lure dangled by a novice and one expertly placed in front of it. I also wondered why, considering I had caught a good-sized fish using the same orange rubber lure that I had been given in the beginning, everyone else (none of whom had caught a thing) continued to switch around as if the fish might have put out the warning, '*Don't go for the orange ones – they've got sharp bits in and Larry's just gone to the Great White Freezer in the air.*'

Then, an unexpected flurry of fish. First Geoff, who up until that point had remained drily quiet, suddenly became animated as he hauled a fish just a little smaller than mine into the box. Then Mike, who landed a similar-sized pollack through a combination of brute force and persuasive conversation: 'Come on, my little beauty,' and 'That's the way,' and, a tad disturbingly, 'Come to daddy.'

It then became apparent that Charlie was capable not only of finding the fish in the first place, but also of catching them as he silently, and seemingly with scant pleasure or satisfaction, lobbed another eight-pounder into the box. I hadn't even realized that he was fishing until I heard it slap against the plastic. We fished for another period of time (which could have been anything between ten minutes and an hour) to no avail. The consensus was to move on to the next spot. In this case, the 'consensus' meant two-thirds of the party were, having sorted out their dinner already, happy to try somewhere else. The other third – Terry and *Tim* Simpson? – didn't seem quite so keen. Tim assented through a smile that suggested that if he did not grin idiotically then he may well cry, and Terry simply replied with a slight tick and a twitch of the temple.

'Got the time, Geoff?'

Geoff moved his wrist to a comfortable distance from his eyes and viewed it along his nose. 'Eleven forty-five, son.' He looked at me and smiled. 'You okay?'

'Me, yeah, fine. Bit peckish, though.'

I swerved into the wheelhouse and retrieved the sandwiches and crisps from my rucksack. I sat myself down to eat across from Charlie, who played autopilot with the boat's controls while engaging in gear, gadget and gizmo talk with Tim and Terry. If only I could eat, then this awful, hollow churning might abate, at least a little. I thought I'd start slowly, and squirrelled a morsel from the edge – a little bread, a piece of sweetcorn, a soupçon of salsa, a dribble of soured cream. It was no good – it felt as if it was already on the way up before it even thought about going down. I chewed for what seemed like hours, all the while desperately trying not to imagine what it might look like all mushed up and sicky, before swallowing. I slugged some water, resigned myself to a day's fasting and went back out on deck to breathe in the cold, salty ozone through wide, gulping nostrils.

Next stop was an eery outcrop called Wolf Rock. Green; Thirteens; Wolf Rock. One of us hadn't done their homework. Either that or we were all going to be dead by the end of the day. Some seven miles south-west of the glib travesty that the Land's End Theme Park has become, Wolf Rock sits a treacherous two or three feet above the surface of the water. Some of the time. At others it is covered with a few feet of it, depending on the state of the tide and the swell. Speaking of which, I realized that day that, along with surfers and shore-based fishermen, there is a further point of view when it comes to swell size. Had I been surveying the sea that day with my surfboard tucked under my arm I would probably have dismissed the sea state as barely a foot and stashed the board back on the roof rack. Had I been carrying my fishing rod, and been contemplating casting over the waves, it might just have stretched to a couple of feet. As it was, I was gimballing around in a glorified bathtub, feeling definitely and categorically queasy and surrounded by billions upon billions of gallons of water, all of which were conspiring to amount to a range of what surely must have been eight-foot mountain peaks. On the way to the rock, and to take my mind off the state of my belly, I struck up with Tim again.

'What's that, then?' I pointed to a lighthouse a mile or two distant that looked as if it was miraculously floating on the surface of the sea. Tim nodded towards it.

'That?'

'Yeah.'

'That's Wolf Rock.'

'Oh, right. Why's it called Wolf Rock?'

'There's a big crack through the middle of it.' He laid his left hand out flat and scythed across it with the edge of his right to demonstrate. 'In the centre of the rock,' a poke into his palm with his forefinger, 'there's a hole.' He nodded, as if to check I was still with him.

'Uh-huh.' Don't be sick, belch. Don't be sick, belch. Don't be sick, belch.

'When a swell's runnin', th'water pushes into the crack, forcin' air outta the hole. Makes a noise like you never heard before.'

'Wow – what sort of noise?'

'Well, like a wolf, see.'

'Aaah, right. Cool – that must be really spooky. Especially at night.'

'Not 'ny more t'ain't.'

'Why's that?'

''Cos someone went an' built a fuckin' great light'ouse on it, dint they!'

Indeed they did. We spent at least an hour circling this grey-beige monolith, and I spent most of that time wondering how the hell they actually built it there. It must have been eighty feet tall if it was ten, and each radiused block surely had to weigh in at a couple of tons minimum. This human outpost, this abstract connection with the land, reminded me of the strangeness of the situation I was in compared with my everyday existence. The way that the emerald swell (realistically about three feet) sucked and tugged at its chewing-gum-grey and olive drab base in cold, thick, striated sheets of startling turquoise and blinding white froth disturbed me for some reason. It was a feeling similar to that engendered in me by a waterwheel, a dam or a canal – unnatural, brooding, jarring. To add to my creeps, Terry added that he had seen photographs of swell well over halfway up its solid column and whitewater beading ferociously over the top of its helipad. Because I was suddenly unnerved in a way similar to that which haunts you the day after an unremembered bad dream, I suddenly felt much more ill.

We fished at various points around Wolf Rock. I caught another, smaller pollack, shortly followed by Tim breaking his duck by heaving up a ling about three feet in length. I had never seen a ling before – an odd-looking beast that looked as if it was halfway along the evolutionary slope from cod to conger.

'That'll do even a fat bastard like you for your supper, eh, Simps?' Mike laughed kindly at Tim, who barely raised a grunt and an eyebrow in reply. It was becoming apparent that this trip, for these hardened folk, was a bit crap. Then something tremendously exciting happened. Geoff levered over a pouting not much larger than that first pollack I had caught in Scotland. Everyone (except me) dropped their rods and clamoured around Geoff's fish. At first, I thought that they were taking the mickey out of him and his diminutive appetizer, but when Terry retrieved his scales from his tackle box and weighed it at just under two pounds, it became apparent that this, in pouting terms, was pretty bloody extraordinary. Between us we had enough fish to feed us all for a few days, but this seemed to rapidly pale into insignificance next to a couple of fillets that I could probably have scoffed on my own and still been in need of a peanut butter sandwich afterwards.

'What's specimen for these, Tez?' Geoff enquired, squinting.

'About three, I think.'

Geoff made a 'ho-hum' face by pulling down the corners of his mouth and raising his eyebrows

'Still – good fish, eh?' reassured Terry.

'Oh aye. I'm 'appy wi' that.' Geoff was beaming.

In retrospect, Terry's encouragement was really quite magnanimous in view of the fact that, at that point, he was the only one of us not to have caught anything. I had bagged two, as had Mike and Charlie. Geoff had one and a half as far as I could see, and Tim was the distinctly indifferent owner of what looked to me like a fine ling. Terry stayed calm and quite ambivalent about his 'blanker' status, however, and on the way to our final destination, actually revealed himself to be relatively sane. We talked about the idea of 'specimen' weights, and I began a conversation about the culture of the 'geek' in fishing terms. I suggested that he, along with most other fishermen – indeed most other men – might be considered a geek of some sort. Most of us like counting, measuring, arranging, listing and comparing 'stuff' of one kind or another, and a good number of us spend quite some time congregating and comparing with others who count, measure, arrange or list similar things to ourselves. Terry, along with most others, seemed to resent being labelled a 'geek', however kindly I had meant it. He agreed somewhat grudgingly.

'Yeah, I s'pose so.'

'I mean, it's not a bad thing. I think it's something to be celebrated, you know. It's a passion thing – you weigh fish, right?'

'Yeah.'

'And you write stuff down about the fish you catch, and you look at catalogues for gear you want, and . . .'

'Yeah.' He was beginning to look genuinely interested.

'And you sit on the bog and make lists of stuff and . . .' a wry smile from us both, 'and you buy the mags and read about places you want to go fishing and the stuff that you would use there if only you had the money?'

'Er, yeah. I guess.' He took half a step back.

'It's the same with cameras! And stamps! And camping and, er . . . what else? Butterflies! And trains! And . . . and . . . I used to smoke, right?'

'Er, right.'

'Roll-ups, yeah? And you know, each Rizla packet has a little number printed on the inside flap. I collected those numbers for two and a half years. One to forty-two in all the different colours. I got all the greens, all but seven of the reds and all but six of the blues before I quit smoking. Oh, and a complete mixed set. Had them all framed up – like little card butterflies. Called them 'The Day Smoking Gave Up On Me'. So you see! It doesn't matter what it is you collect, what it is you hanker for or what it is that you spend way too much money on – you always want more of it. We're all chasing butterflies of one sort or another, and what you chase goes some way to defining who you are. YOU ARE A GEEK, TERRY! I AM A GEEK! WE ARE ALL GEEKS!'

I was a little breathless, and checked the corners of my mouth for foamy saliva with my tongue. I had certainly got Terry's attention now. I had also, unwittingly, got that of everyone else, slack-jawed, on board. There was the briefest of pauses, but after what felt like a month, Mike spoke.

'Bloody hell, boy,' he moved his head to the same side as his raised eyebrow in mild surprise, 'and there was us thinkin' it was Terry who was ga-ga.'

I felt, in a very isolated kind of way, and for the first time that day, a strange belonging. It was also now obvious to me just why I did so – I was in the company of five other people who also did not feel that they quite fitted in on dry land and perhaps left it behind on a regular basis so that they could stop worrying about whether they 'belonged' or not. Perhaps these people did not leave land to catch fish, but simply so that they could catch sight of who they were. I realized then that, thankfully, not one of these men had shown the slightest interest in 'what I do' on dry land. I have always struggled to find an answer to the question, 'What do you do?' I want to say, facetiously, 'When?'* On that boat, on that day, everyone would have given the same answer – 'Right now, I'm fishing.' The land, its complications, its relationships, its money, its taxes and possibly even their even more inevitable cousin, death, were irrelevant. My sense of time that day grew as distended and warped as a reflection in a fairground mirror. I was glad I had forgotten my watch – if fishing is all about living in, and concentrating on, the moment, what better way to focus on

---

* My brother-in-law Jon has gone one better by answering, 'What do you mean?'

and extend those moments than by losing grip of the means by which they are measured.

After our unspecified amount of time at Wolf Rock, we began to make our way back to Thirteens. Charlie reckoned that we may have more joy there on the ebb tide. On the way, I saw two seagulls gliding over the open water. On land, gulls are a squawky, gawky, greedy and somewhat seedy pain in the backside. They caw and cackle, bicker and bother and crap on you and steal your pasties when you so much as glance away. They look a bit shifty to me and are always an awful lot bigger and much more menacing than I think they should be and should be shot and put in big pies with equal quantities of cat. Over water, however, they made perfect sense. Using the updraft from the surface, I watched them swoop their way along, expending as much energy as most folk do snoozing in front of the telly on a Sunday afternoon. The occasional tilt of the wings to keep a constant height above the rolled and crepuscular, pinking, steel-grey sea was all that they seemed to need. Streamlined, graceful, efficient and surprisingly beautiful in their economy. I wondered, as Terry inexplicably threw his crisp packet into the sea, if we looked as belligerent, arrogant and opportunistic in their environment as they do in ours.

There was a cry of excitement from Mike. 'Porpoises, look!' He pointed to a blank sea while shading his eyes from a lowering, partially cloud-obscured sun. Then out they wheeled again, as if connected to some subaquatic hub, playing. Although it was a lovely sight, I still preferred my seagulls – even if, and perhaps especially because, I wasn't about to counter Mike with 'Hey guys, look – seagulls!'. Somehow though, the surprise of their gracefulness at sea and its contrast with their lack of decorum on land seemed to make them that much more appealing. The beauty of dolphins and porpoises just seemed like a bit of a cliché in comparison. The seagulls struck a similar chord to that strummed by the surprise poetry of a pinned collection of torn numbers. I would far rather have my preconceptions challenged than confirmed – that porpoises are graceful and elegant is no surprise. That gulls can be is an uplifting one. Besides, I bet people wouldn't be so keen on dolphins if they nicked their lunch and shat on their head.

When we arrived back at Thirteens, I think Terry felt that he had a couple of points to prove. Not only had I unwittingly out-fished him so far that day, but I had also equally unintentionally out-looned him (I thought everyone collected fag-packet numbers). I think he now realized that on the latter score he had some way to go, but obviously reckoned that he could redeem himself on the fish front. Once again he, along with everyone else, switched lures, and once again I persevered with the same one that I had started with. The sea air had an unfamiliar but certain staleness about it – we all felt, I think, that we had been out for just a little too long. I had caught fish that I could take home for my woman (ugg), and my nausea (glug), which had abated a little while we were motoring, had returned with a vengeance as we rolled about the boat like the dregs in the bottom of a swilled teacup. Everyone else, especially Terry, just seemed a little dejected due to the fact that they had not killed enough things that day. We fished for a while, though, and I landed my third of the day. Nobody else caught so much as a cold. Except Terry. On what was literally his last drop (everyone else had agreed to wind in and go home), his rod bent violently and in a tighter arc than anyone's that day. When the fish came up, we saw why – a truly impressive pollack with decompressed eyes as large as golf balls, which weighed in later at a fin over ten pounds. Terry was, predictably, wild-eyed with delight.

As we skirted the coastline on the way back, the proximity of land made my stomach feel as if it once again wanted to be a part of me, and Terry pointed out a dozen or so secret rock-fishing 'hot spots', which I thought was very kind and trusting until I realized that he knew very well that I wouldn't have a clue how to subsequently find them from land – not least because I was still trying to keep an eye on 'my' fish for when we got off the boat. For some reason it seemed important that the fish that we ate later was going to be the very one that I had caught earlier. Eating another man's catch just didn't seem like the right thing to do. This might not have bothered me a few years previously, but I guess as you get older you realize that you need a bit of moral fibre with your omega-3s.

Tim dangled his rubber lure just below the surface of the water as the boat sped shorewards and watched it as it wriggled along. I glanced down at it, and smiled at the efficiency of its design – the way that its tail flipped from side to side in imitation through some complex laws of hydrodynamics. As I looked up, Tim caught my gaze and smiled ruefully.

'How can a fish resist that?' he asked genuinely.

It *was* very lifelike and, well, alluring, I suppose. If you were a fish. I thought that Tim had perhaps been thinking like one for so long that he had also developed a reasonably strong desire to actually be one.

As Charlie nudged *Take* snugly against the harbour wall and tied her tight, I edged nearer to the fish box and unravelled my two plastic bags.

'Okay to grab my fish?'

Charlie turned and gesticulated that I should carry on. Nobody else seemed to be in a hurry to retrieve theirs, so I lifted my meals for three, five and seven into the bags where they sat, bent and heavy like a slumbering fat man in a hammock. I motioned to the others that I'd finished and that they could help themselves. Terry stepped up and lifted out his Fish of the Day, and Geoff eagerly rummaged around in the mass of slimy flesh to rescue his whitebait, spawning a new version of that well-worn saying involving needles and haystacks. 'Like looking for a pouting in a pollack box' rings well, I reckon. And that was it. Tim, Mike and Charlie stood about, hands in pockets and muttered, 'I don't bloody want it,' and 'No effin' use to me,' as if I had offered them a bag of dog shit.

'Terry?' offered Charlie.

'Nah. Got enough here, ta.'

'Tim – you want yer ling?'

'Not really.'

'Sure?' asked Geoff.

'What the bloody hell do I want that thing for?'

'All right, then, I'll take it.'

I was appalled. 'So what's going to happen to these, then?' I motioned towards the remainder of the lifeless, rigid pollack that they had dragged, eyes popping, to the surface.

'Dunno. Throw 'em in th' 'arbour, I s'pose. Gulls'll 'ave 'em.'

No they bloody won't. 'Anyone mind if I take them, then?'

'Help yerself.'

I unburdened myself of thirty-eight pounds by means of two twenty-pound notes, and accepted Charlie's two pounds in change with far fewer regrets than I had taken Brian Perks's three. I then picked up at least ten times that in weight of dead fish and stumbled back to the car. It had taken me eight hours to find my sea legs, but I was buggered if I could remember where I'd left the ones I was going to be needing on dry land.

On the way home, after deciding that I was absolutely ravenous, and had crammed two packets of fruit pastilles down my throat, I thought about the attitude that most of the people on board that day had displayed towards their catches. I was saddened by their indifference to their fish once they had been caught and killed – like the whole mice left to stiffen and rot after the bloody cats have had their fun. I wondered whether there was some connection between the way these men treated their fish – as trophies to be weighed, measured, photographed, recorded but ultimately not deemed to have any real use – and the attitudes that some of them displayed towards women on the boat that day. Possibly their approach towards life in general. Their continual switching of lures, their disappointment at such a 'meagre' haul, their assessment of 'a crap day's fishing' when in fact what we had all enjoyed was the luxury of a day's pleasure with no real cares or worries, made me wonder what would actually have made them all content with their day, apart from a slithery glut of dead creatures to feed to the seagulls. I wondered whether some blokes allow the actual meaning of what they are doing to become lost in the very process of doing it – ends are not merely justified by the means, but comprehensively overshadowed by them. I think that we diminish the fruits of our endeavours by the glorification of their swelling at our peril – despite his grinning, it didn't look to me as if *Tim* Simpson? was all that happy.

Pollack Fillet with Tarragon and Bacon

You will need (per person)

2 pollack fillets, big and recently deceased

3–4 slices organic, thick-cut smoked bacon

a good fistful of fresh tarragon leaves

1 plump clove of garlic

sea salt and freshly ground black pepper

1 lemon

a good glug of olive oil and a roughly similar quantity of butter

Heat the butter and olive oil in a heavy-bottomed frying pan over a gas hob loud enough to hear as you would a polite conversation from the other side of a largish room. Grind some sea salt onto the naked garlic clove to stop it from slipping about when you crush it with the side of an eight-inch cook's knife. Then, using the same knife, chop it roughly. Not only is this a more satisfying method of crushing garlic, it's also a damn site less fiddly than poking around in a garlic press to get all the bits out. It's also a handy trick to know when you are staying in a holi-day flat whose utensil drawer doesn't extend much further than a wooden spoon. Maul the tarragon about in your hands to release the flavour, then shred it with your fingers. Add this, the garlic mush and a few grinds of pepper to the pan and let it sing while you cut the bacon into roughly one-inch squares. Fry these for a further couple of minutes, turning occasionally. If the bacon is of decent quality (i.e. does not have too much water added to it) it shouldn't sweat too much, but if it does, drain the pan a little so that it fries and tans, not braises and blanches.

Turn the heat down to an even more polite whisper, push the bacon to the sides of the pan and lay the pollack fillets in it skin side up. Cover with the bacon to aid heat transference and leave it to go 'poff' and 'pock' for a while as the air escapes from underneath it. Five minutes should do, depending on the thickness of the fillets – if you are not cap-able of judging when a bit of fish is very nearly cooked through then you shouldn't be near sharp or hot things. Take the bacon off, flip the fish, whose flesh should be firm, white and separating chunkily, and sizzle for a couple more minutes on a heat just above muttering, while throwing the juice of the lemon over the flesh. If you fancy a drop of wine in there as well, it won't hurt but don't drown it. Remove the fish to a couple of warm plates while you crank the heat right up to a fairly raucous hullabaloo in order to crisp up the bacon and to goo up (reduce down) the juices.

Scatter the bacon and scrape all the bits of garlic and herbs onto the fish, and place in front of anyone who may have over-estimated just how much wine they should have drunk. If you also mound a good quantity of rocket on the plate and cram on a couple of good hunks of crusty granary bread and real butter, they will be your friend forever. I speak from experience.

5 A Clipped-down Rig

Of one fact about professed atheists I am convinced; they may be – they usually are – fools, void of subtlety, revilers of holy institutions, brutal speakers and mischievous knaves, but they lie with difficulty.

H. G. Wells, *A Slip Under the Microscope*

Sometimes it's not so easy being an atheist. True, you don't have to go through the interminable misery that is Sunday Mass, there is no need for wailing and bowing at a very old wall and, perhaps most importantly of all, the obligation to be pleasant to complete and obnoxious strangers when all you really want to do is be gratuitously rude to them is all but obviated. The downside, though, is the entire lack of security that stems from the 'everything's gonna be kind of okay because God, or god, says it's going to be' school of thought. In a godless world, there are no 'mysterious ways' to comfort when the 'why do utterly shit things happen in a world governed by a benevolent being?' question rears its inevitable head; when I lie awake at night, trying to work out a *point* to *it all*, let alone a *point* to fishing, I am bound to come to the ineluctable conclusion that, in actual fact, there is none – that any good deeds here on earth will stay right there, and will not allow me access to some higher or better place in the hereafter because, well, there isn't one.

I switched on my Internet connection one day – maybe I was looking for a new spinning reel, or possibly I just wanted to ogle at one of the Shimano beachcasting rods I had seen. Hilariously expensive but of high-enough quality to pass on to your grand-children only to hear them say, 'What's this piece of shit, Grandad, I wanted the new PlayGameBox 15.' Whatever my purpose, before I started to porn myself to overload, I checked my email. Almost always, my inbox is empty. Occasionally I will receive a mail from my agent telling me that she has just brokered a film rights deal for my first book for a sum so large she isn't even going to disclose it to me, but then I will either wake up and turn over or I will carry on dreaming about something equally unlikely such as our next-door neighbour, to whom I rarely speak, telling me she has just managed to get three swan's breasts for the price of two at the local supermarket and would I like one?

This time I did have one mail, though. I am still sufficiently childish and/or technologically challenged to always believe that this could, like the traditional post, possibly lead to something exciting. This one was from someone at my publishers, Macmillan. At last, Hollywood! It began:

> Here are the details of an old school friend who has got in touch with us.

At that point I knew that this was nothing more than a cruel hoax – I hadn't had any friends at school. The mail went on to list the address and telephone number of a guy called Mark Stephens – a good friend from jewellery-making days and fellow conspirator on many a raid on the student union bar. I hadn't seen him or spoken to him since just before I had left Loughborough (our college town) for Cornwall, a week shy of ten years prior to receiving this email. For some reason lost to both of us, we had had a minor falling out by proxy just after I'd gone, and had lost touch. I'd intermittently tried to keep tabs on him, but I think he'd been just as nomadic as I had in the intervening decade and I had eventually kind of given up hope. Then, he'd noticed a book in his local WHSmith's about an allotment written by some bloke who'd got his picture on the cover and thought 'I know that twat!'

Going back to this atheist schtick – well, in the absence of any real meaning or point to anything, there is a tendency to make one up. Martin Heidegger said that 'things gather worlds' – possibly his only saving grace considering he made Nietzsche look like a benevolent happy-clappy Christian and thought that Hitler was a damn fine chap – but in the absence of any kind of belief system we (I, at least) attach our own significance to perhaps the most mundane of objects, events or occurrences. And so it was with Mark and, more specifically, precisely when he had made contact. A decade always feels like some kind of milestone. Considering how much Mark used to drink, it seemed to me like some kind of miracle. I had also recently been experimenting with the manufacture of my own rigs for beachcasting, a type of angling that I had still not entirely come to grips with. Or, more accurately, a type of angling that I had not actually done yet. Furthermore, I was all overcome with faux mysticism when I noticed where he'd made contact from. The village with perhaps the silliest name in the entire country is called Praze-an-Beeble in Cornwall. It is also about five miles from where I had moved to the very day after I had last spoken to Mark. Spooky, huh? Well, no – I know, not really. But that didn't stop me from getting goose bumps, thinking that some things are just, well, 'meant to be', lighting a few patchouli-scented magnetic crystals and taking the rug from over the pentangle on my studio floor and dancing round it clad only in a cloak of virgin goatskin a few times before arranging to go and see him the following weekend for a spot of wicker man igniting and crying in the forest.

Considering the fact that he lived pretty near the coast, and considering this felt like a man's (as opposed to a boy's) trip, it seemed a bit silly not to take some or all of my tackle with me. Especially so as Mark was going to be at work for one of the days I was going to be down there. I reasoned that I should just chuck everything into Horace's boot so as to be prepared for every eventuality. The truth is that by this point I had managed to amass so much gear that to try to make any semblance of order out of it seemed a bit silly. I did make sure, however, that my newly purchased twelve-foot, twin-tip flatfish/bass beach-casting rod and pebble-smooth, ratchety-sweet multiplier reel were included.

As the day drew near, I pumped this reconciliation up into grotesque proportions, and truly started to believe that I would come home a New Man. I suspected that, considering my some-what changeable personality at the time, Jackie may have had her fingers crossed for a similar outcome. Maybe Mark, with his warmth, humour, compassion and 'what the hell' attitude was just what I needed and had been missing for so long. He was a large piece of my history, and maybe a missing mirror.

Beachcasting had, in my mind, come to be as near to impos-sible as 'Oh blow' is to swearing. I was convinced that I couldn't cast, and was equally unswervingly assured that my £25 fixed-spool reel and rod combo purchased before I went to Scotland were as good as uncastable anyway – hence the new, flash gear that would add inches to my cast. And here I think it is worth digressing slightly to consider the thorny notion (male obsession) of adding length. When I was at primary school, I shared a classroom – and, more importantly, occasionally a urinal – with a lad called Richard Smith. Smithy was the sort of kid who probably developed into a man with his own highly successful building or related industry business. Either that or he has become highly successful through selling snout in prison. Whichever, the important thing about Rich at the urinal was that he could pee higher than any other kid in our class. It was patent to everyone in that last year of primary school that Richard Smith was *the* man because he could pee much higher than everyone else. We could *see* that, so our roles were clearly defined and assured. Stay with me – I'm getting to the point shortly. Now, my brother-in-law has a theory with which I have yet to find fault which states that the fundamental difference between men and women is what happens when they urinate – men see it, women feel it. What's more, women, when they were little girls, were denied this opportunity to have 'how high can you pee' contests, so they learned to establish a pecking order by more circuitous means – talking, comparing clothes, body shapes, hairstyles, opinions and the list goes on. Boys just said, 'I'll piss you for it.' Through a decade, on and off, of counselling, one fundamental truth I have learned is that what is ingrained during childhood is carried through to being an adult – it is a sad fact that men are no longer allowed to sort out their problems by peeing contests, and I can't help thinking that Gerry Adams and Ian Paisley's lives would be so much simpler were it so (devolved government by shower pairing, perhaps?), but what we *are* permitted to do is go to a beach and wang out a load of lead as far as we possibly can in an attempt to prove our dominant status. Interestingly, there is a further parallel – when two blokes are fishing on the same beach, you never see them standing too close to each other.

Bearing this in mind, it was quite obvious to me, if not to Jackie, that I needed that new rod and reel – distance does, after all, depend largely on tackle. I also reckoned that I might be more successful than I had been of late if I took some of my own, hand-tied rigs. Maybe the fish can tell the difference after all. Or if not, perhaps I would fish 'better' if I had a more holistic understanding of the devices involved. So far I had tied a few fairly straightforward two-hook flapper affairs, which didn't do any more than those I had received with my first batch of gear. I wanted to make something that not only represented more of a challenge to fashion, but which would further enhance my chances of casting the furthest distance possible. I remembered that some back issues of *FiShingTOTALAngler* contained a series of two-page spreads detailing how to make a myriad of different rigs, and I wanted to find one that was going to to justice to this trip, which was, in my mind, rapidly turning into a homecoming of sorts, as well as being some kind of catharsis, to be a primal, chest-beating, rebirthing, Iron John-type journey of inner discovery. I also wanted to catch some bloody fish for a change to bring home to WOMAN, who really was starting to wonder quite why I needed seven fishing rods in order to catch, since the boat trip, four mackerel. I felt perhaps that I would improve the odds, as well as derive more pleasure from the experience, if I understood its business end a little better. I opened my most recent copy of *TotaLSeA*, and there it was. A three-hooked, clipped-down rig.

Now, a three-hooked, clipped-down rig is remarkably similar to the three-hooked flapper rig I employed to catch those Lazarus dogfish the previous November, with one vital difference. Yes – one flaps and the other is clipped down. On the flapper, attached to the main trace body are three lines, or snoods, fastened to it at regular intervals via swivels and knots. At the end of each snood is lashed a hook and that, apart from a swivel at the top to attach the main line and a clip at the bottom to snap a lead on, is it. The hooks, and consequently the bait, flap about as if the 1920s never went out of fashion. No bad thing underwater – essential, in fact – but less than helpful if you want to prove just how big and tough a man you are by casting huge distances. Often past where the fish are actually feeding, but no matter – if fishing were more about catching fish and less about proving just how capable men are of reproducing it would attract an awful lot more women than it does, and most tackle manufacturers would go out of business. So, when it comes to distance, the flapper will not do at all. Not only does a quarter pound of dead squid and lugworm flapping about play havoc with the aerodynamic efficiency of your rig, it will almost certainly fly off as soon as the G forces necessary for vast casts come into play. The simple answer is to clip them down. The means of doing this, however, and, moreover, the means of making sure that they become *un*clipped and *do* flap about as soon as they hit the water, has been thought out by someone who was anything but simple. In fact, it is such a beautiful and elegant piece of thinking that I think I would like to marry it.

On a clipped-down rig, each snood is cut to exactly match the distance between where it is tied to the rig body and the next swivel down. The top snood is attached to a standard swivel, but the middle and bottom swivels are different – they have a bent piece of free-moving wire attached above their barrels. This enables the snood above them to be attached via the baited hooks. At the bottom end is hung an 'impact lead' – all the features of the breakaway lead, but with an extra open steel loop at the top, to which is attached the hook of the bottom snood. To provide a little extra tension, the top snood is threaded to the rig body just above a slim, long spring, which in turn is held fast by a crimp and a bead. This ensures that all hooks remain in place during the cast.

AH! All well and good, we all cry – but what about when the rig hits the water? How do the hooks begin to flap? Why don't they just stay clipped down in a decidedly-unattractive-to-fish kind of way? What about that, smartarse? Well, this is the bit that had me hanging this rig up on my doorframe and playing with it like a special child for hours. On the impact lead, there is a bit of plastic – special, magic, slidey plastic – that, when it hits the water, is forced up the central shaft that it reciprocates on by the pressure, and pushes the baited hook from its clip. This releases all the tension in the rig, and the other two snoods follow suit in a sort of dominoes-type way, and I have just remembered that, and why, these particular swivels are called 'cascade' swivels.

When I had finished, I began to get some real primal urges – I guess it was a combination of the coincidence with Mark and subsequent dwelling on the last ten years of my life, the consideration of fatherhood and how it had changed me, the fact that I was returning to a location that contained more than its fair share of baggage for me that had me pondering on the Portent of It All a little more than I might have done. 'This', I told myself, 'is it. I am going to be *the* hunter-gatherer. All the stars are aligned, the tide is going to be right, the weather is going to be warm, slightly overcast and a little breezy – perfect for catching what I have been setting my sights on since first buying two rods and two reels for fifty quid. I am going to catch a bloody great bass.'

I continued in my ever so slightly pompous and a little bit gruff inner voice, 'What's more, I am going to catch it on a rig that I made.'

And then I realized.

The further I have gone – and got – into the world of angling, the more I have become, and felt comfortable with being, a 'geek'. Yes, fishing has its own peculiar dialect full of snoods, traces, cascade swivels and priests, just as much as surfing has rails, floaters and cutbacks and line dancing has, er . . . well, hats and stuff. Anyway, the point is made. The overwhelming majority of geeks are men, and I think I know why. Feminism was, as I've mentioned before, right and good, certainly, in that it emancipated women from what was tantamount to slavery at the whim of their male 'masters'. Feminism may have dragged the pendulum in the right direction, but an awful lot of men feel it has gone too far, too violently, and clouted them squarely in the balls. So, small wonder, then, that many of us take refuge in our gear – in our sheds, our tackle, our surfboards or our stetsons. The atavistic desire to brawl, piss our names in the snow, spit, sleep around and even to shoot furry things has already been frowned upon by the moral majority (in all but one, maybe two, of these cases, I feel, rightly so), but what has not been taken away is the vital and deep-rooted urge to ensure that our gadgets are fit for their purpose. It may well be that the last vestige of a 'real' man is his right to fettle – his right to be a geek.

Atheism (indeed, atheists themselves) may not be immediately and easily comforting – our answer to 'why do bad things happen?' may not get a lot more detailed or soothing than 'because they do – live with it or deselect yourself'. However, it is immensely rewarding to have taken the trouble to think about a riddle ('why am I such a great big geek?') for quite some time and actually figuring it out rather than giving up and coming out with some glib nonsense along the lines of God wanting me to be that way. I am that way because I have the honesty to be so. It's quite simple – before the twentieth century, in fact before things like clothes and houses and, indeed, for quite some millennia before Christ, men sharpened stuff. They sharpened stuff like arrows and spears and flints. They did this for two reasons – firstly for killing animals for food and warmth and secondly for killing each other when someone else threatened their young or any other aspect of their way of life. The more effective their weapons were at either providing meat or skin or for seeing off their enemies, the more likely they were to pass on their genes. The more they fettled, the more chance they had of their bloodline, their DNA, surviving. Now, as this last paragraph may have elucidated, I'm no Richard Dawkins, but I have yet to come across any phenomenon at first hand that cannot be explained, if not entirely then at least better, by means of simple natural selection than by any religion. The reason that so many people, so many men, feel so passionately about their chosen pursuit is that it is, quite literally, in their blood and their bones to do so.

I remembered Mark as a man whose chosen pursuit was a damn good fire. He wasn't, as I recall, particularly fussy as to whether it was indoors or outdoors, functional, safe or sanctioned. He just liked to hit wooden things very hard and then set fire to them. I recall a party at his house once where, at about 3.30 in the morning, most of the interior furniture was reduced to not much more than kindling and we watched it spit until we could see each other in the daylight. This is perhaps a little one-sided when it comes to this big bear of a bloke – he was also one of the kindest, gentlest and most sensitive men I've met. A bit screwed up, then

– like many post-feminist men, part Iron John, part Ironing Joan. I do remember sitting one day with Phil, our jewellery technician, having a blissfully geeky discussion about the melting points of various grades of solder, when Mark approached us. One of the knuckle-bones of his right hand had essentially been exposed and was dripping blood opulently. Polite as ever, he waited for a break in the conversation when most people would have been swooning or gibbering.

'Er, sorry to interrupt.' Mark hails from Middlesborough and is not, I repeat not, a fookin' Geordie. When I really wanted to wind him up, I'd remind him that he sure as fookin' hell soonded like one. Phil, nonchalant, looked up.

'What you done?'

'Was filin', an' ah hit me fookin' 'and on the vice. What d'you think I should do?'

To this day, I'm not sure whether Phil was joking when he replied, 'Is the vice okay?'

Mark is made of iron and I reckon he could pee twice as high as I can, but he's also very much in touch with his emotions, which makes for an interesting hug when you haven't seen him for ten years.

'It's been a while since I was picked up by a Geordie in a pub,' I wheezed after he'd let go.

'I am not a fookin' Geordie!'

The same kind, wry smile, the same questioning, could-be-construed-as-intimidating raised eyebrow. I had indeed, and without knowing quite how much, missed this man in my life. I had been a little worried that there might be something of an anti-climax in seeing him again, that maybe he had nothing to reveal or reflect. As it was, Mark was blissful confirmation that it is indeed possible to not see or speak to a *friend* for a decade, then sit down over a pint, ask 'What's new?' and be assured that there is plenty of time to find out.

It was an hour until low tide. By the time I had rigged up, figured out which way round my tripod went and convinced Charlie that seven hours really wasn't that long to sit around on a beach, it would be slack water. I had promised myself (and Charlie, lucky pooch) that I would fish the tide up until it was high, no matter what. Unless I caught a seven-poond bass in the first twenty minutes or so, of course. Then it would be the pub for both of us. I had dropped Mark at work pretty much on time, dreckly after we'd had breakfast, then headed to St Ives to buy myself a knife and to once again try to figure out whether the light really is different there or whether it just feels like it is because we'd been told it is by a bunch of absinthe-swilling and pretentious arty tosspots. I left with a rather smart folding pocket knife, a pasty and a bag of fudge for later. The light? Couldn't care less – it was about right for bass, and I'm not sure that they have any more of an opinion on Ben Nicholson than I do.

As well as the sun playing peek-a-boo behind the clouds, there was a stiffish southerly wind whipping sand across the beach from above the high-tide mark smack into the back of Charlie's north-facing head. From where I was fishing (somewhere to the west or east of the mouth of the Hayle estuary) this placed the wind firmly offshore, while what there was of the sun winked at me from behind my shoulder blades. Doubtless the wind, along with my super-streamlined clipped-down rig and my ancestor-trained strength and technique, would propel my terminal tackle among the fish feeding well over 100 yards from the shore. I wedged the three legs of the tripod into the wet, undulating sand, attached the multiplier reel to the assembled beachcaster and leaned it against the rod rest before threading the shock leader through the diminishing rings. Using a half-tucked blood knot, I attached the top of my rig to the main line, and clipped the five-ounce impact lead onto the bottom to stop it from billowing out like a pair of old woman's knickers on a washing line. Before turning to my bait box, I stood with my head into the wind and held my face up to the sky slightly to allow the breeze to fill my nostrils and swirl around my head as I inhaled deeply. I swivelled on my heel to face the sea, and exhaled towards it. If had known any t'ai chi I would have performed some, but as it was all I proceeded to do was go through 'reach down for lugworm, turn and impale messily on sharp hook'. I tipped all three worms with a small amount of squid (an extra means of securing them as well as adding a little more irresistible scent to the mix) and clipped each hook in turn. It may not involve kissing the bishop's ring or bashing yourself over the head with rocks until you bleed, but there is ritual and ceremony to be found in everything if you really want to find it.

I had deliberately positioned the tripod fifty yards or so from where the dregs of the small, rooster-tailed waves were soaking, spent, into the sand in order that I would have a chance of being able to place the rod on the tripod before one, two or all of three things happened. Namely, I caught the fish I was destined to do battle with that day, I opened the bottle of Stella I had thought-fully added to the bait box in order to keep the lugs cool and thirdly before my feet got wetted by the oncoming tide, an eventuality that seemed all too likely in my experience. I know very well what a daft cnut I can be sometimes.

Having lashed everything down that was not already stuck in the sand for fear of it blowing away, I strode down to the water's edge with what may as well (for all the portent and meaning I had imbued in this gleaming, whippy and really rather natty red and grey rod) have been a spear and prepared for casting. Just enough line out to suspend the weight a few inches off the sand; click the anti-reverse off and cinch the spool with my right thumb; bring the butt end of the rod forwards; pause; concentrate all the energy in my body towards punching this weight out; explode in a smooth, whipping motion, pushing with my right arm, pulling with my left; release the trapped line at a moment that no one can define but everyone can feel and watch as my clipped-down rig soars in a beautiful arc on and on and on towards the sea. It may well have been with the wind behind, but I swear I watched (a still twitching spring) my clipped-down rig sail to the part of the map which used to say '*Here be Dragons*'. It took forever to land (or 'sea', I suppose), and when it did, I'm sure I just heard the 'ping, ping, ping' of three hooks unclipping, deadly and enticing. Having checked the spool with my thumb once more upon impact, there was no bird's nest. I let line pay out as I walked back to my gear and my dog, who was sat in exactly the same place, squinting and resolute, as he had been as I'd been baiting up. Not only was I his master, I was master of the beach, of the sea and of the whole goddamn world. Homo erectus. As I approached Charlie with my rod in one hand I beat my chest with the other.

'Man back. Dog good. Man catch fish. Man beat dog in pissing contest.'

'Dog cold. Man bad. Man put dog back in car or dog piss over man's coolbox.'

I leaned the rod into the rest on the tripod and wound in a little line in order to fully employ those wires on the lead in their task of holding bottom. Back in the car? It wasn't that bloody cold and besides, I still hadn't quite forgotten his petty sniggering the previous summer when I had cast about two yards with a spinner in Scotland. I would wait until the tide came in around our ankles, move up the beach and take him back to Horace then. I put one hand around a cold bottle and the other inside a warm pocket, and waited.

'Dog really very cold. Dog now shivering. Dog quite adamant that he wants to go back in car and will keep looking at you like this until he does.'

It was a good thirty-minute walk back to Horace, and I could not say with any certainty that by the time I returned I would not only be dogless but also *sans* means of providing a reunion dinner for my long-lost chum and me.

'Oh, all right. Just let me wind in and we'll get you back.'

I picked up the rod and heaved lugubriously to release the breakaway lead. Only it didn't break away. Something else did, though. My main line snapped and fluttered pathetically in the offshore breeze in the direction of the rig, pathetically echoing my desire to find it and become reconnected with it again.

'Come on then, Charlie.' Even though this snag had patently been his fault entirely (what else are dogs for if not to take the heat in a blameless situation?), for some reason I couldn't bring myself to be cross with him. A turn of events that should have been irksome, irritating and deflating only served to mildly amuse me. I had not only built this trip up into some kind of culmination of my prior angling learning, but had also come to see it as an exposition of my opinions on natural selection, atheism, feminism and the cyclic nature of our entire existence. All I had, though, was a detached rig 120 yards offshore of a low spring tide, a bruised ego and a cold dog.

I let an eager Charlie clamber up onto the back seat of the car before returning to my gear in order to fish the bloody tide up, and for the rest of the afternoon I involved myself in what I imagined to look like 'Thelwell' fishing. Knots and hooks where they shouldn't be (mid line and in the fleshier parts of my hands respectively), lines becoming entangled around reels, rods, each other and my feet and ankles. Everything that had even the slightest capacity to go wrong did so and, despite using virtually every piece of tackle I had (at mid tide I gave up on beachcasting and got the spinning rod out with similar success), did not even get so much as a bite. On that particular day, in the words of Groucho Marx, I started at the bottom and worked my way steadily downwards.

Later that evening, while sitting in what is almost certainly the best pub in the known universe (The Ship in Porthleven) while Mark was retrieving another pint, I made a few notes in my journal. I wrote that I had had 'Quite possibly – in fact almost certainly – the worst day's fishing' I'd ever had, and went on to detail just why it had been so appalling. By this time, however, the fishing had paled into insignificance due to the fact that I had managed, through an altercation with a granite mooring bollard in reverse gear, to render Horace useful only as a rather extravagant and poorly designed dog-kennel. He's now as dead as Rocinante. The only possible reason I had to sit, and sup, and smile and say 'Cheers, mate,' then, was because of the realization that, of course, there was to be no 'culmination' of anything when it comes to fishing. All anglers are nympholepts at heart. What's more, all angles are necessarily incomplete, and all are defined by virtue of their missing degrees.

6 Incongruous Eels – A Fish Out of Water

Never forget that only dead fish swim with the stream.

Malcolm Muggeridge (attr.)

So far, all my excursions had been to – and ever-so-slightly beyond – the crumbling edges of Britain. Revisitations to places familiar from increasingly recent periods in my life. From this point of view, these forays had been fascinating in terms of regression therapy, but I still felt a vague sense of unease as to exactly what form of fishing was really going to 'grab' me, as opposed to something that was merely an entertaining means of taking me to some distant times and places. True enough that my rebirth into fishing had been nothing but enjoyable, but I also felt that my gear-bought to fish-caught ratio was still lacking somewhat, even if I had redressed the balance a little by landing my heaviest haul so far using borrowed tackle on *Bite*.

In 1998 I found myself (by virtue of wanting to watch my recently estranged children grow up) in Winchester. Having, for as long as I can remember, felt an urge to be near the sea I touched down in a place with which I had no connection, and which did not smell of crisp damp salt, hot sand and suncream. It's true that Winchester is not far from Southampton but to me, having recently moved from wildest Atlantic Cornwall, the English Channel, and certainly the Solent, amounted to no more than a large, dirty and salty river. Real Sea has rugged boulders and granite cliffs and sand that blows into your teeth and waves that could claw your car off the road just because they felt like it. John Fowles once described a boiling sea as 'consolingly disastrous' – if ever anything could be disastrously consoling, then to me it was the relatively benign and emasculated South Coast. Somehow, then, I could not bring myself to visit what I came to see as pastiches of the sea – Lee on Solent, Titchfield Haven, Calshot – and the gurglings of the local rivers only came to represent tributaries to my disappointment and echo my abiding indifference to my location. Bloody kids. Are they grateful? Are they bollocks.

People (my mother predominantly) would visit me, and I would take them for travels with Charlie through my secret and unquestionably 'pretty' landscapes, and tell me just how beautiful it was. Through frosted glass I could see they were right, but there is an agonizing difference between knowing beauty and feeling it.

Eventually, it took a mate, a dog and an allotment garden to fully ease me into my new skin, but reservations about freshwater fishing remained. These probably stemmed from childhood, when being taken to the local pond on a Sunday afternoon at the age of eight and being left in the company of a bunch of men with nothing better to do than sit about in rubber in the company of eight-year-old boys did not really appeal. Also, it *just wasn't the sea*. As an adult, my feelings had not really changed. As I drove home from Cornwall after my Worst Day's Fishing, knowing that my next angle was to be acutely brackish, I was, to be candid, less than enthusiastic. However, I wanted to at least try to understand the mindset of freshwater fishermen. I thought that perhaps doing so might even enable me to find something out about my own. If I could forget my prejudice, then pursuing inland fish would also widen my angling opportunities.

With this imperative in mind, there was only one choice to be made: 'game' or 'coarse'. Although I knew that the chance of me doing anything coarse was slim indeed, I did at least pick up *The Complete Encyclopedia of Fishing* to see if it could do anything to persuade me otherwise. It said this:

Coarse Fishing Many people have a problem with the term 'coarse fishing'. It implies that there is something rather uncouth or unsophisticated about the pastime or even the anglers who pursue it. People have claimed that the term came about because trout and salmon, the main game fish, were delicacies on the table, while freshwater fish such as roach, bream and chub are coarse tasting and unpleasant to eat.

Didn't do it for me – in fact, positively reinforced what I already suspected. I turned to the game fishing section, which told me that:

In fishing parlance, game fishing means fishing for members of the salmonidae family: salmon, sea trout, brown trout, rainbow trout and grayling, and it is difficult to say precisely why these fish have such a fascination for anglers. Other fish, notably the big sea fish such as sharks and tope, fight harder. Some coarse fish are more difficult to outwit and capture, and a number of coarse fish, such as carp and barbel, are renowned for their strength and guile when they have been hooked.

It is true that game fish, particularly salmon and sea trout, make a notable contribution to the table, but many would prefer to eat Dover sole or turbot, and some trout caught in reservoirs can taste rather indifferent.

So, that was that cleared up then. Also involved in the decision-making process (what little there was of one) was Jackie, who very kindly offered to buy me a day's fly fishing tuition at a local fishery as a birthday present. I couldn't help wondering whether anyone had ever bought for their beloved a day's piking on the local canal, and if they had, had they had the good sense to keep the receipt? This gift came with the small proviso on my part that I could contribute to the cost, and one on her part that we pay an extra thirty quid so that she could come along too. Unfortunately she accepted my offer of financial assistance, and I was hardly in a position to turn down her request.

We arrived for our lesson at the trout fishery that, in a quirky parallel with Garlieston's secret war, claims to be 'Hampshire's best-kept secret'. I would hate to disappoint the folks there by stating its name, so won't. On getting out of the car, I still had very little idea of how you go – sorry, 'one goes' – about fly fishing. Luckily, we were greeted by a man who looked as if he had dealt with my type before. Roughly my height, a beige waistcoat hanging loosely over a pressed olive shirt and a felt trilby-style hat held in place by a thick sweep of hair as silver-white and lustrous as a trout's belly. With kindly, lapis-blue eyes and a liver-spotted outstretched hand he welcomed us.

'Good morning. You must be Robin and Jackie?'

'Yes, good morning. Peter, I assume.' His name had appeared on the pre-trip paperwork.

'That's it. Peter Knauss. You're stuck with me all day, I'm afraid.'

Did he say *nous*? We all shook hands, after which Peter gave an expansive sweep of his left hand towards the office – a log cabin with a veranda. I had supposed Peter to be of Germanic extraction, but although his tones were clipped, it sounded as if the shears were sharpened in Hampshire, not Hamburg.

We entered the cabin, where we were introduced to Tim, the fishery manager. A stocky man a few years younger than me with ginger-blonde hair, amused blue eyes and a seemingly indefatigable smile stretched across a freckled face that appeared to think that life was, in general, pretty damn good. He welcomed us as we made a fuss of his black Labrador, Parker.

Peter then led us, via the pathway that bisected two of the four lakes, to the 'fishing barn' at the top of a small rise that overlooked the whole site – a total of around six acres of water fed by a nearby tributary of the River Test. On the way, he pointed out a wild brown trout in one of the air-clear streams. He explained that the trout will invariably face upstream in order to keep a constant supply of both oxygenated water and food entering its system. I noticed that it did so by means of the minutest flexings of its body and the merest shimmerings of its tail. No more than it needed. He elaborated that it followed, quite logically, that river trout should always be approached from downstream. Peter also drew our attention to a couple of varieties of insects on the wing: a hawthorn fly (abstractly recognized but previously unnamed from walks with Charlie), as black and heavy looking as July thunder, with its sagging, pendulous rear legs lending it an almost deformed appearance, or as if it were carrying young or prey. We also strolled past a small flurry of early midges, hurtling busily and apparently aimlessly like electrons around a mislaid nucleus. I instinctively waved a shooing arm at them as we walked past.

'Don't worry about those – not the biting kind,' assured Peter.

'Really? I thought they all nipped.'

Peter stuck out his lower lip and shook his head. 'Mostly buzzers round here, and we like buzzers.'

'We do? Why's that?'

'Because so do trout! Also because they don't bite.' He raised and wagged an emphatic forefinger and smiled.

'Of course.' I realized then that Peter's knowledge, and his dissemination of it, was not simply a sackfull of nebulous nuggets of spurious self-aggrandizement. The fact that he obviously had more than a fundamental grasp of entomology made it quite obvious that fishing for trout required an approach more holistic than that of any other form of angling I had thus far encountered. Whereas plucking out a pollack didn't require much more finesse or understanding than waggling something that looked a bit (but not much) like a small fish in front of it, teasing a trout out of the water involved a good understanding of its seasonal and mercurial epicurean habits.

'There are quite a few non-biting species of midge – or Chironomids, as the genus is known,' continued Peter, 'mostly around from March to September.'

'Uh-huh.'

'Have you heard of bloodworms?'

'Vaguely, I think so. Jax, you?'

'Erm, sort of.'

'Bloodworms are the aquatic larvae of non-biting midges, yes?'

This occasional interrogative at the end of Peter's sentences was merely a way of checking that we were following his train of thought. From a self-important mouth it might have become irritating or patronizing, but Peter's voice was unhindered by either plums or silver spoons. His tones were more mellifluous – honey blended with the merest soupçon of English mustard.

'Er, right, yes – so where does the "buzzer" thing come in?

'Well,' Peter smiled kindly at me as we strolled two abreast, 'did you hear them as you walked past, or were you too busy trying to shoo them away?'

We sat ourselves around the large table inside the barn with a mug of tea each, and Peter presented Jackie and me with a hand-out as a means of backing up what we were to learn during the rest of the day. Interestingly, on the cover page, along with a title and Peter's details, appeared a line drawing of a mayfly *Ephemera danica* – not, as might be expected, a depiction of a trout. The means, at this point, seemed complementary to, and balanced with, the ends. I flicked through the pages of the handout while Peter gathered his thoughts and some equipment, but it all looked extremely complicated – full of technical drawings, Latin names and insect life cycles. Luckily, Peter seemed like the patient type.

'Right then. Where do we start?'

I correctly assumed this to be a rhetorical question, as opposed to an echo of my own thoughts. I would have inserted 'the hell' between the 'where' and the 'do', though. Peter, however, had done this a few times before.

'I always think that, with fly fishing, the further you come away from the water, the less important your equipment really is.'

I smiled and nodded enthusiastically to this echo of my own beliefs.

'So, we start with the least important tool – the reel.'

In front of us was a black spool of around four inches diam-eter and an inch and a half wide. Its sides were drilled with a multitude of holes, presumably to save materials and weight.

'The fly reel is basically nothing more than a means of storing your line when you are not fishing. When you are fishing, the line is either on the floor or in the water. It has a one-way ratchet system that provides adjustable resistance – or "drag", yes? – when playing a fish.'

The least important bits also seemed to be, logically enough, the least complicated. At this point it occurred to me that it might be construed as inattentive or rude if I did not occasionally also say 'yes'.

'Yes.'

'Speaking of line,' Peter wrenched a good length of thick, bright-green plastic yarn from the spool with a whirr of the ratchet, 'this is called a "weight forward", or "WF" line, which means that it has a taper to it, thickening at the fly end. Either of you know why?'

Jackie and I looked at each other as if to suggest that it should be obvious enough, but that we hadn't got a clue.

'Er, no. No idea whatsoever.'

'Well, a fly has very little weight, agreed?'

'Certainly.'

'Agreed.'

'So, when you cast a fly, you need some momentum – some impetus to cast the required distance, yes?'

'Ye-es.'

'Uh-huh.'

'This line is fatter and therefore heavier towards the fly end to give that impetus.'

So it really was that obvious. Funny how, if you know someone has the answer, you are less likely to bother to find it for yourself. Peter went on to explain that other lines were available: a 'shooting head', which was trickier to use but capable of being cast extremely long distances, and a 'double taper', which is essentially two short 'weight forward' lines joined at the middle. These do a similar job to a 'WF', but have the advantage of being reversible so that when one end wears out, the opposite end can be used.

We were then shown how the as-yet hypothetical fly is joined to the thick fly line by means of a 'tapered leader', of which Peter showed us a range, sitting sheaved inside a wallet that he produced from one of the chest pockets of his waistcoat. I was nowhere near halfway through counting how many compartments this garment had when Peter explained the leader's purpose to us.

'The thick end of this is attached to the fly line,' he held it between thumb and forefinger, 'the thin end,' waggling in the opposite hand, 'to the fly. This provides a smooth transition from one to the other via a further, very thin length of line called a "tippet".'

He gave us a brief explanation of how these connections were made by means of loops and knots and glue, and that was it. No weights, no swivels, no rigs, no booms and no fuss. This was not much more than a bamboo cane, some string and a bent pin – for grown-ups.

We were taken outside the hut into the warm haze of the mid-spring mid-morning, where Peter assembled one of his own three-piece rods for us to look at. Like the reel, it was a thing of the most simple beauty, and when he passed it to me I was staggered at its lightness and balance – as if I was holding something that had corporeal form, but was not actually there.

'How much does this weigh, Peter?'

'Just a shade under three ounces, I believe.' His answer was rapid and accurate enough to make me believe that, even if he had not been asked before, he had made it his business to know.

'*Three ounces?!*'

'Yee-es.' His answer was calm and, this time, there was no question.

'Wow! That's amazing! Feel that, Jax.' I passed it to Jackie, who had been, I realized, eyeing me with the understandable mix of amusement and concern of someone who had seen my burgeoning collection of fishing rods and credit-card statements. Her smile changed to one of amazement, though, when she grasped the cork handle of the rod and did that strangest of things. It has no name that I know of, but it can most accurately be described as 'doing the opposite of dropping something that is much heavier than you thought it was'. Gravity caught napping.

'Bloody hell!'

The rod I had used to somewhat ungraciously heave a six-pound pollack onto a boat had felt, in comparison with this gossamer toothpick, like nothing as much as a telegraph pole. It had been, essentially, a dull, dumb stick, whereas this whipping, twitching and elegantly tapered length of carbon really did feel as if it could become that ultimate cliché when it comes to describing all the very best tools – an extension of your own arm. Peter gently placed it on the picnic table and gummed a cigarette paper at each end to stop it from floating off before we headed back to reboil the kettle and, finally, look at the really important bits.

We reconvened around the table with a fresh brew each. From another (the fourteenth?) pocket of that splendid waistcoat, Peter produced a small tin. Its enamel paint was so scraped and smoothed by the fabric of both waistcoat and time that its original purpose had become obscured. The only boxes of flies that I had seen before had been the stereotypically arranged, ranked and immaculate (probably unused) collections glanced at unseeingly in advertisements or shop windows, but as he opened its hinged lid it became apparent that Peter's flies were for fishing with, rather than mere ornament or ostentation. Pricking a hand-cut rectangle of foam inside the tin were around forty different flies, some no more than tiny sharp fluffs of black with a gold bead at the head end. Others were obviously very creditable attempts to emulate actual insects, and a few were simply astonishing and exquisite pieces of the most delicate and minute form of suggestive but functional sculpture. When I had stopped making jewellery some seven years previously, I had done so because I eventually struggled to find any good or worthwhile reason for continuing – I didn't really see the point of it. But in that moment, in this tiny tin, swathed in the heady, medicinal, faintly addictive whiff of preservative naphthaline, I immediately saw the opportunity to invest whatever craft skills and urges I had left in objects that were at once both beautiful and purposeful. That had a point, in both senses. My mind wandered – what was it like to catch a fish on a fly that you had made yourself? Could I finally learn to shoot straight with my air rifle, bag myself a rabbit or a pigeon and make a fly from its fur and/or feathers with which to catch a fish? My head felt lightened by the ether of possibilities that seemed to be expanding in front of me. Or maybe that was just the smell of mothballs.

'Now, of course, the subject of flies is one about which we could happily spend a day discussing in its own right.'

'I don't doubt it!' I enthused, possibly a little too rapidly. What I did have reservations about, though, was my own sanity, as I could think of few better ways of spending the next few hours. For some it is slippers; for others, caravans. For yet more unfortunates it is vegetable gardening. For me, middle age had come knocking at my door – unexpected and totally uninvited – wearing a multi-pocketed waistcoat and carrying a box of fishing flies.

'Suffice to say for now, though, that there are two main types of fly: the wet fly, and the dry fly. I won't patronize you by telling you where in or on the water they both are fished, yes?' This time, the question was accompanied by a raised eyebrow and the finest trace of a smile.

'What's that one?' I pointed to an especially elegant and beautifully coloured fly wedged somewhat unceremoniously between a couple of other, much more dowdy and bedraggled-looking specimens.

'Ah. Glad you spotted him. The Invicta – absolute mustard in the summer when the sedges are hatching.'

'Really – why's that?' I thought it was a reasonable question.

'Because it looks remarkably like a hatching sedge,' said Peter benignly and with no hint of sarcasm. As such, it was an even more reasonable answer.

'These little flies', he continued as he closed the patinated box, 'are all the fish, ultimately, care about. But not,' he slid the tin back into the left lower front pocket, secret and dark, before zipping it up reliably and patting it gently at the same time as tapping the side of his nose, 'but not all *you* should care about.'

I knew what he was implying and, moreover, his pat, his tap and his sneaked glance towards me suggested that he was very well aware that I knew this. Geeks. It takes one to spot one.

'How many pockets has that waistcoat got, Peter?'

'I'm sorry?'

'Your waistcoat – just out of interest – how many pockets has it got?'

'Er, I don't know. Erm, I've never coun—'

'No, no – it's okay. I was just curious.' I caught the gaze of Jackie's eyes, and they were glazed with the effort of restraining what looked like a life-threatening fit of the giggles.

'What!'

'You!'

'I just quite fancy a waistcoat, that's all! What's wrong with that?'

All the day consisted of after that, then, was grabbing a rod, a reel, and a few flies to dangle in the water, which we trotted on down to and proceeded to heave a few trout onto the bank.

Er, no. Not exactly.

The truth is that any silly bugger who is patient enough and is capable of tying any more than a granny knot that won't come undone under load (i.e. a double granny knot) can, fairly easily, lob a bit of bait or a lure over the side of a boat/pier/rocky outcrop and pull out their dinner. Even I'd managed it. This is good, as it means that not only had my interest in fishing thus far been kindled, but also that there are branches of fishing that are quite egalitarian in terms of the number of people that can participate. There are, myself included, an awful lot of silly buggers out there, after all. In the hour or so during which Peter spent patiently imparting the rudiments of the overhead cast to Jackie and me on the lawned area in front of the fishing hut, I learned that a multiplier reel is not necessary to create a 'bird's nest'. I also figured out that any assumed snobbery that existed within fly fishing was based not on money, class, occupation or even on what colour your school tie was. It was, if there were any at all, founded in skill levels. If you can't cast a fly the required distance or direction, you can't fish with it with any degree of success.

Peter started by showing us the theory of casting, and I smiled inwardly at how I had previously been intimidated by the notion of beach fishing. I had fooled myself into believing that this was due to all sorts of things – inexperience, the weather, tide times, illumination problems, etc. – but in truth all I had really been concerned with was how far I was able to cast. Everything I have read in countless sea-fishing magazines on the subject of beach-casting has been about distance – about length – and frankly I have felt less than adequate in that respect. I'm not really sure that I see the point of casting long distances – if you want to target fish 200 yards out, wouldn't it be quite a bit easier to find a friend with a boat? I have also read a similar number of articles suggesting that fish can be caught less than forty yards from the shore, which on some beaches is within wading depth, so I'm not sure I understand why it is that I should risk putting my back out to achieve something I could manage just as effectively by going paddling.

Casting a fly, I could see instantly, was different. As Peter talked us through the theory, he recapped his point about using the weight of the line to achieve the necessary distance – not 'as far as possible', but 'to where the fish are'. He stressed that the 'presentation' of the line, and consequently the fly, was far more crucial in this context than how far you could cast. He also pointed out something quite delightful to a mind such as mine, which likes to suck allegory from life like a constricting snake squeezing life from a young animal. This was the fairly-obvious-when-you-think-about-it concept of it being just as important when casting a fly to look behind you as it is to focus on what you are aiming at. As far as the line is hurtling towards your target, it is reciprocally being flicked behind you as you build up the distance by 'false casting' – a series of casts that do not touch down, but that release more line each time.

'If you don't pay attention to what's going on behind you, you can't expect to have much success in front of you.'

Quite, Peter.

Prior to this trip, it will be no surprise that I had buried myself in a good deal of related literature (more 'erotica' than 'porn') in an attempt to at least familiarize myself with some of the required terms and equipment. I didn't get that far, largely because I spent too long looking at the pictures and couldn't understand the text anyway, but did notice one trend. I had tried specifically to find some information on casting, as I had already sensed that this may be in some way pivotal for the day's proceedings. However, with the exception of some illustrated suggestions of how to perform some obviously very advanced techniques like the single-handed, double-throw, triple-pole whiplash cast, I couldn't find a word on how to perform a bog-standard, back-to-basics numpty cast. The only exception was an answer to a similar question in a letters page, which said something along the lines of 'we're not going to tell you – go and get some professional help'. Or perhaps that was the response to the letter from someone asking about the quantity of pockets on waistcoats.

Casting a fly is one of those activities that really, truly requires the help of not just someone who knows what they are doing, but of someone who knows how to tell someone else when – and crucially why – they are doing it wrong. The two are remarkably different, as anyone who has ever had a drunken but well-intentioned neighbour inspect their DIY skills will testify to. In an obscure kind of way, what separates an effective teacher from a poor one is what he or she chooses *not* to impart. There is also a wide, but to the ineffectual teacher invisible, chasm between 'learning' and 'being taught'. This is especially so in the case of intuitive skills like fly casting – sure, there are certain impartable technicalities that make life easier, such as how much line to strip off the reel before you start, that the back-cast should be swift and should stop just behind your ear at the 'one o'clock' position and that the forward cast must be crisp and precise and should release the line at 'ten o'clock' in front of you. But nothing can tell you in anything but the most rigid of terms what casting a fly will feel like when you get it right. When you can *feel* the weight of the line as it whips through the top guide ring on your first few false casts; you can eventually *gauge* the exact time that the fly has reached the most straining, strangling extent of the back-cast and you can only *sense* what it's like to convert all that potential energy and make it delicately, accurately, kinetic. When you *know* before it lands that your fly line will sit, straight as a well-pressed trouser crease in front of you, with the leader unfolding, billowing in a perfect and silent arc and again landing perfectly straight, deadly and undeviating from the course of the fly line. These are all things that can be *taught* in words, but must be *learned* through experience. As must the sagging, exquisite disappointment that inevitably follows the realization that this perfect cast was performed on an area of decidedly fishless grass and you will never, ever, be able to do it again when it matters.

Over lunch, and in order that Peter did not think me completely uninformed, I mentioned a phrase that I had read in *Today's Flyfisher* (correctly spaced with the requisite capital letters in all the right places).

'What's this I hear about "Duffer's Fortnight"?'

Peter smiled and shook his head slightly while exhaling nasally, noisily, as if in a hurry to reply. He craned forward to awkwardly swallow his mouthful of ham sandwich and ran his tongue over his obscured teeth a couple of times before he answered.

'Towards the end of May, dear boy. You're a little early.'

'But what exactly is it?'

'Well, it's "like it says on the tin", I suppose. A couple of weeks or so where pretty much any damn fool can catch a fish.'

'Why the end of May, though?'

'Mayflies, mostly. Mayflies hatch, mayflies are a bit soft and giddy, trout go all silly. They've been known to go for bare hooks sometimes.'

'So is there a mayfly hatch here?'

Again, he waited until he had polished off a crust, and wiped some butter that wasn't there from the corners of his mouth.

'Not a significant one. Not for some time, anyway. A few years ago a friend of mine and I did try to establish a population – to introduce them – but they're finicky. No real rhyme or reason to them.'

'Environmental factors?'

'Oh, almost entirely. It's just that we don't really know what they are. Not in conjunction with all the others, anyway. They're all intertwined: temperature, humidity, minuscule pollutant factors, human activity. The very fact of them being studied may even have its part to play.'

'It sounds like you've tried to find out.'

'Well, for a time it was in my best interests to know.'

'How come?'

'This pal of mine and I tried to set up a business – introducing mayfly populations to waters and fisheries where there was none. The more mayflies there are, the more fish will be feeding. The more the fish are feeding . . .'

'The more fish that get caught?' interjected Jackie. Peter turned to her and smiled again.

'Precisely.'

'And the more fish that get caught . . .' I unravelled the thread further.

'The more people want to go fishing. Simple, really.'

'Big money?'

Peter assessed the remains of his sandwich intently while drawing his head to one side and raising an eyebrow, simultaneously using one corner of his mouth to smile wryly and suck air through his teeth with the other.

'Potentially.'

'So, if it's not a rude question, how come you are teaching us about fishing today rather than breeding mayflies and becoming very wealthy?'

'Not rude at all. No, not in the slightest. Good point, in fact. I wish I knew exactly. Obviously. We did everything we could. We did all kinds of research – environmental, financial, market, scientific, atmospheric, you name it – but,' he stuck his bottom lip out and shook his head in defeat, 'I suppose, ultimately, nature just doesn't like being told what to do. She doesn't like to be bullied.'

'And mayflies aren't called *Ephemera* for nothing.'

'I think that Linnaeus got that about right, yes.'

Peter seemed remarkably philosophical about his aborted venture. Perhaps what he was doing for a living right then wasn't too much of a hardship.

'Do either of you know much about the life cycle of the mayfly?' He looked at us both in turn. Jackie politely said that no, she did not, and I replied similarly with an enthusiasm that, three hours previously, might have given me grounds for concern.

'The mayfly spends the first year or two of its life under the water, as a nymph buried in the mud. Most of those that are taken by trout are somewhere between this stage and the next – "emergers", as they are called.'

'For obvious reasons?'

'Indeed. This is when they are most vulnerable, as they hang partially submerged as they shed their final skin. The adult mayfly – the dun – then emerges from the water, and the bugs will often seek refuge on a nearby tree or rock while they wait for their genitalia to develop.'

As well as being scientific, there was a wholesome enjoyment of Peter's use of the word 'genitalia' – not lascivious, but as if he merely liked the shape of the word.

'How long does that take?'

'Oh, well. A few hours or so, I suppose.'

'So, then what?'

'Well, when they are sexually mature, most will mate . . .'

'Most?'

'Oh, yes. Not all are successful. Then, after mating, the female will lay her eggs, then both male and female will weaken and die. This is when they become known as "spinners", for equally obvious reasons.' Peter nodded towards me and smiled as he finished the crusts of his sandwich.

I found this genuinely fascinating. That a species deems spending between one and two years in the mud only to emerge for less than a handful of days with no guarantee of getting laid before they croak a sensible way to go about things seems to contradict my belief in natural selection. 'Born, flap about for a bit in what must be blinding sunshine, shag if you're lucky, die shortly afterwards then get eaten by a trout' just doesn't seem to compensate for the dark, silty years, somehow. I also recently found out that they are so short-lived that nature didn't even bother giving them a stomach. My opinion of Darwin may have been given the once-over, but at least this backs up my refusal to believe in such a thing as karma. I mean, what did the mayfly do to deserve that?

'But now,' Peter nimbly raised himself to his feet, brushed imaginary crumbs from his trousers and scrunched up the paper bag that had contained his sandwiches, 'now we fish!' He raised a triumphal finger in the air before striding towards the cabin and aiming his paper bag squarely into the middle of a bin that was just a little further away than I would have been confident of hitting.

'Back in a mo. Nature calls.'

I dare say that he hears it when it does.

The theory behind fly fishing is that it is sufficiently difficult to do well to give the quarry a sporting chance of getting away if you get it wrong. To catch a trout you must out-stalk it, outwit it and out-think it. True, it is only a gormless trout, but it has spent an awful lot more time thinking like a fish than I have. It can also swim in its sleep. Because of the differing refractive indices of water and air, when we look at a solid three-pound trout below the surface, we see what looks like a herring. Conversely, when a trout looks at a 180-pound human wearing all that *gear,* it sees Godzilla. With big guns. Not surprisingly, they tend to swim away as soon as you get near, and will certainly be hot-finning it as soon as you make an indelicate cast. Wild brown trout are apparently very skittish indeed, but Peter told me as we approached the water that 'stockies' – stocked, as opposed to indigenous, fish – were a little less wary.

This pleased me immeasurably – most of my casting on grass would almost certainly have given the local mole population a fright, so what effect my clumsy lobbings were going to have on the fish I had no idea.

'No excuse for sloppy casting, though,' admonished Peter. For a moment I was concerned that I may have lapsed into one of my episodes of saying what I thought I was only thinking.

'No, no! Of course not!'

'Right, you stand here and cast out to, well, see that moorhen there?' He clasped a paternal hand lightly on my shoulder as I stared down his arm towards a rather confused-looking bird swimming in triangulated circles in an area a distance away that I might have struggled to throw the rod to, let alone delicately present a small fly in. 'Don't worry, you won't hit him, but that's the general direction you're aiming for.'

'Okay, will do.'

Peter moved off towards Jackie, who was already pulling line off her reel in readiness to cast. I did the same, and proceeded to whip the rod back and forth in an attempt to emulate some of the more successful casts of the morning. My first effort wasn't bad – the fly hit the water, as did the leader. Even a good length of the fly line itself wetted my fingers as I stripped it, utterly fishless, back in again. The line didn't exactly lie straight ahead of me as much as sit in floppy coils heavy on the surface of the water, but still, I felt that I had started to fly-fish.

There are only a limited number of ways of describing the experience of fishing for seemingly interminable hours and not getting so much as a lick, let alone a bite. It is no different whether you are wallowing around in a boat, tottering atop a slimy, isolated rock or sitting squarely on a jetty with a bottle of wine. Wherever you fish, it is only a matter of time before the same thought pops into your head.

'What the fuck am I doing this for?'

Just as soon as I'd come up with some possible answers – 'because the countryside is beautiful', 'because I am spending a rare day almost alone with my woman', 'I'm sure there was something else' and 'nope, that's all I can think of right now' – Tim came bouncing past, grinning and mounted on his grumbling quad bike, complete with what looked like an enormous washing-up bowl on the back. As he approached he stopped the engine and pulled silently to a halt just behind me.

'How's it going with you?' Not, I noticed, 'Any luck?'

'Well, I'm trying for that one out there – see, near the middle?' I had moved around the lake a few degrees, and pointed towards a great, fat fish near the small island in the middle. Peter had issued us each with a pair of 'polarizing' sunglasses. These are fabulous bits of kit, firstly because they're not bad at keeping barbed hooks from pulling your eyeballs out while you're casting, and secondly because their polarizing nature allows you to see below the surface of the water. For reasons that I really don't care about, they cut out the reflected light bouncing off the water. Previously I might have deemed being able to see what you catch a little unsporting, but after fishing for what seemed to be an unstocked pond for what felt like days, I needed all the help I could get. Tim followed my arm while he flipped down his own polarizers.

'Which one?'

'That big one, see – looks like he's near the bottom.'

'Oh yeah, I see him.' Tim stood up straight and folded his thick arms.

'I think my casting's okay,' (it had got much straighter and more accurate after I had discovered not only that the rod would do the work but also exactly what its job description was) 'but it just doesn't seem to want to know.' I turned to Tim, who was rocking slightly on his heels and had an even larger, friendlier grin stretched across his face.

'Well, no. It wouldn't.'

'Sorry?'

'Erm, that's not a trout.' He rubbed his chin.

'Oh?'

'This used to be an ornamental pond, see. That one kind of got left in there, and no one's been able to get the bugger out since.'

'So what is it?'

'It's a golden orfe.'

'And they don't like flies, then?'

Tim stuck out his bottom lip and shook his head. 'No idea what they like. More chance of catching the clap in a convent that getting yer hands on that thing.'

He restarted the engine. 'Just gonna go get some more.'

'More what?'

'More trout. Out of the stew ponds.' He nodded towards around one o'clock on his clockface.

'Stew ponds?'

'Yeah – where we keep the stockies.'

'Oh, right.'

'Back in a sec – give you a few more to aim at.' He trundled over to a narrow channel, filled the washing-up bowl on the back of his bike using the bucket that had been stashed inside it, and unceremoniously hauled four or five fish from the 'stew' to the bowl. As he drove back to the corner of the lake, water splooshing out of the bowl and fish no doubt gripping the sides in a desperate bid to stay sub-aqua, I wondered whether *It's a Knockout* should make a welcome and overdue return.

As he heaved the fish one by one into the lake, each of them wriggled and squirmed in the air, as though they were attempting to fly rather than swim. Then, with a clapping splash and a dart for the weed beds, they were gone. I was to see one of them again later. It did, of course, cross my mind to ask Tim whether he would object strongly to my borrowing his quad bike, his bucket and his washing-up bowl – it did seem like an awful lot less trouble than wafting about like I was. Not, however, fish or no fish, anywhere near as much fun. More than any other angling I had ever experienced, the definition of success or otherwise of the day became wider and wider the longer it went on.

I thought I might try the next lake down. I had no idea whatever whether this made good fishing sense or not, but I had probably scared all the fish in the first pool senseless with my witless thrashing, so thought it only fair to go and inflict myself on some others for a while. My casting had, in truth, improved steadily to the point where I knew when I'd got it at least half right. As Peter said in passing once, when casting a fly you only need to mistime one back-cast or one false cast and the whole thing goes, as Peter did not say, tits up.

After about a quarter of an hour, and having settled into my rhythm of 'ten o'clock, one o'clock, ten o'clock, one o'clock, ten o'clock, oh bollocks five to two' while sporting an inane grin at just how *pleasant* this all was, I heard a splash and a faintly surprised yell from where Jackie had been fishing. My initial reaction was, of course to half drop, half place my rod on the bank and do my version of running (half walk, half mince) to where I naturally assumed she had fallen in. However, as I rounded the willows that semi-screened her lake from mine, she was still on the bank, dry as a July wind and giving an excellent demonstration of just how bendy these rods are. Assisting her, of course, was a trout doing its absolute utmost to go in whatever direction she did not want it to. Peter knelt beside her, landing net in hand, giving tips on when to let line out, when to pull it in and when to say 'way-hey!' when the fish jumped out of the water, tail flapping, in an attempt to free itself. I had never seen a fish fight like this before – mainly because the jousting lances and tow ropes I had been using had never given them a chance to. At that point, I began to wonder whether my previous insistence on fairly prosaically heaving fish to land as shortly as possible after hooking them constituted missing the point a little. Perhaps by using these tiny hooks, this lightweight tackle and a more thoughtful approach, these fish really do stand more of a 'fighting chance' against us.

Eventually, after a few runs, a few triple salkos and the occasional and obdurate refusal to go anywhere at all, the trout tired. As instructed, Jackie stripped in sufficient line and raised the rod tip high enough to bring the fish to the net.

'Sometimes,' said Peter, 'the fish will look tired, but as soon as it sees the ne—'

With a twitch and a flash, it dove for cover once more, and again Jackie let out taut line to accommodate its frenzy. She gently coaxed it back towards the net, and as it approached it floated limply on its side, as if it somehow knew that any further resistance was futile. This time Peter slipped the wooden frame of his net under its body and pulled its sagging form onto the grass. He unclipped his priest (tapered mahogany handle, heavy, bulbous brass head) from inside his waistcoat and handed it to Jackie.

'I insist that everyone kills their own fish.'

'Absolutely,' replied Jackie, possibly a little to quickly, 'Where do I hit it?' Definitely too enthusiastically.

Jackie was already grasping the slimy, tensing form just behind the gills. Peter pointed to the spot just behind the eyes at the top of the fish's head.

'Just about there.'

She brought down the priest with an authoritative thud, just once. It was enough, and the rainbow trout, later weighed at 2 lb 9 oz, lay flaccid and iridescent in the hazy sun. When it's you doing the killing you seem to focus on the job in hand. This is possibly because if you deliberated over the moral and ethical issues, you almost certainly would not do it very effectively. There has to be no doubt in your mind that you want this creature dead as quickly as is humanly – and humanely – possible. Watching someone else issue a *coup de grâce*, however, is a little like being a passenger in a car – it allows you to take your eyes off the road and instead lets you look at the wider picture. I wondered why there was a difference between wringing a rabbit's or a chicken's neck and killing a fish. I could only deduce that it is easier to club a fish with a clear conscience than something furry because:

1. Fish do not look particularly cute before you start chasing them.
2. Fish do not have expressive faces, therefore they do not have the capacity to register anything that we might recognize as fear just before we kill them.
3. Fish do look remarkably and recognizably like a foodstuff just after we have killed them. Fluffy things still look cute and frightened until we make them into unrecognizable meat.

It turned out that this was, in fact, not only the first fish that Jackie had ever caught, but also the first fish caught on the lakes that day. Tim came out with his camera to record the occasion, and as I beamed at Jackie, then at the camera, I realized that I was doing so with not the merest hint of envy. It wasn't that I didn't *want* to catch a fish, but simply because I had already reached the conclusion that it did not matter in the slightest whether I did or not. Nor did I feel any hint of having had my 'male pride' dented – mainly because fifty-odd years of the more radical aspects of feminism has all but beaten the pride out of most men of my generation, but also because this turn of events meant that Jackie could now go and do something useful (it had been ages since the last cuppa) while the boys got on with catching some real fish. Two pounds nine ounces? Crabsticks.

Which is what, as it transpired, I might as well have used as bait that day. Yes, I blanked. In fact, I did worse than blank.

I landed another man's fish. I did even worse than that, come to think of it, as even doing that took me two attempts. After Jackie's success, we all took a stroll to survey the remaining lakes for promising signs (such as those pointing to the 'Convention of Hungry and Suicidal Fish'). After a few speculative casts into Meadow Lake, Peter took us to Ash Tree Lake, the most remote pool of them all. He stationed Jackie on one side, while we stalked round to the other. We cast long, short, floating, sinking and on our bloody heads, but still nothing happened until, finally, Peter had one hooked.

'D'you want to land this one?'

'Er, yeah, okay.' I put my rod down and Peter handed me his. Instantaneously, I forgot everything I had been thinking about delicacy and timing and 'playing' the fish and letting it fight, and shut my ears to everything that Peter was trying to tell me. I clamped my fingers knuckle-white tight around the line and the rod handle and yanked.

'Let it run! Let it run!' implored Peter.

The fish sliced an arc through the air before belly-flopping in again. I tugged on the line like a bell-rope, at which the fish dug its metaphorical fins in and pulled resolutely against me. In an instant, the hook broke free and the fly, the line and the leader whipped just past my left cheek to land in an inelegant scribble on the grass behind me. Peter was reeling in my line for me.

'Hold on too tight, old chap, and you will inevitably lose them.' He smiled at me sagely.

'Yeah. I know.'

'Not to worry. Let's try over there.' He strolled back towards Meadow Lake while I retrieved my fishless line.

The next time Peter got into a fish, and handed me the rod, I remembered – keep the tip high, and keep the line tight. Don't give the fish any slack, but don't try to tug it to the shore either. Let it fight, and let it tire itself out, then it will come to you. This time, it did. All 2 lb 9 oz of it. I found that it was difficult to get too excited, though. Despite the fact that landing a trout is obviously an enthralling art in itself, having someone else hook it in the first place just seemed a little like getting your best mate in school to ask a girl out for you. Still, it did mean that we got to take two trout home instead of one, and we had had such a memorable and relaxing day that it really didn't seem to matter.

Before we left, we sat in the lodge with a mug of tea while we filled out the catch record book for the day. Peter magnanimously reported that I had caught his fish, and truthfully remarked that Jackie had done it all by herself. Duty done, Jackie spoke first.

'I didn't see many women here today. Is that normal?'

'I'm afraid so. I wish it weren't, but the overwhelming majority of the people we see here are men.'

'Why is that, d'you think?'

'I don't know really. There's no reason why women can't fly-fish just as well as men. If not better.'

I decided not to take this too personally.

'Better?' I asked him.

Jackie stared at me, smiling defiantly. She obviously thought that I should.

'Well, yes, in some ways.'

'How d'you mean?'

'Well, women do as they are told.'

At this point I should possibly point out that Jackie has one foot placed solidly on 'Aaampsheer soil and the other quite comfortably poised in Hampshah. She is therefore at once enormously polite as well as being one of the least easily offended or flustered people I have thus far encountered, which possibly explains why she puts up with me. She laughed, but Peter, obviously concerned that we might think him misogynistic, still felt a need to elaborate.

'For instance, if I take a woman stalking with me, and I advise her to 'squeeze' the trigger, she will do just that. Men tend to be much more aggressive. They will try to "pull" the trigger because, well, I'm not sure why really.' He shrugged, took a mouthful of tea and redirected his look benignly towards me. 'Maybe they think they've got something to prove. I don't know.'

Once again, Peter looked as if he was quite aware of my eagerness to decipher his sometimes somewhat cryptic tropes.

'Almost certainly true!' I attempted to return the warmth of his expression. He spread his hands and leant back in his chair with an expression that suggested that it was not for him to judge before flashing me another knowing look and picking up his tea mug. As he lifted it towards his mouth, he quickly replaced it on the table, nearly spilling some of its sloshing contents, and raised his opposite forefinger in the air.

'Ah! Yes. Now – nearly forgot!'

'What's that?'

'Nineteen.'

'Nineteen?'

'Nineteen, yes. Pockets. Counted them earlier.'

Baked Trout with all the bits and Dauphinois Potatoes

You will need (for two)

1 trout. As a rough guide, approximately 2½ lb of fish (after gutting) fed Jackie and me with not a great deal left over for sandwiches, children or dogs. Mind you, we had spent a full day in pursuit of the little sod and can both eat like horses. That would have fed my sparrow-like mother for weeks before she made soup out of the bones, so use your common sense.

as for the rest of it, well, take your pick from the following: parsley, dill, bay leaves, white wine, lemon juice, bottled green peppercorns, tarragon, lemon grass, salt, pepper, lemon juice, white wine

For the dauphinois

two good-sized potatoes. I've tried a few varieties and to be honest the best I've come across are some cute, sweet little new spuds whose name escapes me

about 200 ml each of double cream and milk

a clove of garlic or three

salt and pepper

'Dauph' needs a bit of experimentation to get it right. For some reason, I've found that a lot depends on the tin. I use the one whose sole other purpose in life is Yorkshire pudding. It's about 8 x 10 inches and is solid enough to really bloody hurt if you dropped it edge-ways onto your bare foot. It's probably to do with heat transference, but a skimpy affair that looks as if it came from the pound shop in a set of three doesn't quite do it. Smear the tin (sides and bottom) with butter.

Preheat the oven to no more than 150°C and mix the milk, cream and crushed garlic in a measuring jug. Some folk (Nigel Slater included) will tell you to smear the tin with the garlic, but I like the texture and pungency of little crisp shards of the stuff to cut the cream along with the pepper. Besides, what the bloody hell does Nigel Slater know about cooking? Slice the spuds into thin discs – Nige reckons the thickness of a pound coin. I reckon that if you can get them a bit thinner you'll be doing yourself a favour. Place a layer of these onto the bottom of the tin and dribble over enough of the milk and cream to just cover them. Stir the mixture while you are pouring, otherwise all the garlic will sink to the bottom and come out in one big plop at the end.

Carry on layering the potatoes and the dairy stuff until everything's in the tin. If you fancy, a few blobs of soft cheese – goat's is my favourite – will sit and gurgle nicely on top while it cooks. Put this in the bottom of the oven.

Check out a proper cookery book to find out the cooking time for your fish. Two and a half pounds shouldn't need much more than 40 minutes (or doesn't in my oven, which has a bloody great fan inside it), so bearing in mind that the potatoes will pock away quite happily for a good hour or so before they are done, you should have plenty of time in which to stuff your trout with any or all the ingredients listed above. Slice the skin both sides before you do, and get to it. It doesn't have to be pretty – the trout sure as hell won't be when it's cooked, with its white puffy eyes and gawping gills, so just bung it into the belly. It's a good idea to molest all the herbs a bit before you put them in to let the flavours out. Don't skimp, but don't forget that you are dealing with a really delicately flavoured and tasty fish (unless it's come out of a reservoir, apparently) so make sure that whatever you put in isn't going to overpower it.

Wrap the trout loosely but securely in foil and place it in the oven in a baking tin just above the potatoes. Tidy up, grab a beer and regale your riveted girlfriend with tales of how many people you could have fed if only . . .

Serve with some good, fiery watercress and the remains of the bottle of wine you used for cooking with.

7 The Adipose Fin Thing

Organic life, we are told, has developed gradually from the protozoon to the philosopher, and this development, we are assured, is indubitably an advance. Unfortunately, it is the philosopher, not the protozoon, who gives us this assurance.

Bertrand Russell, *Mysticism and Logic*

Shortly after he had levered the hook from Jackie's fish at the lakes that day, and replaced his grass-wiped forceps in one of his manifold pockets, Peter gave us a brief anatomy lesson.

'Now, I'm sure you are familiar with this, but this band of pinkish colouring here,' he traced his first two fingers (in approximation of the stripe's width) delicately from just in front of the gill cover and stopped, with a punctuating prod, just short of the tail, 'is what gives the rainbow trout its name.' He continued by telling us that, in true mullet fashion, some rainbow trout are in fact uniformly silver just to confuse us, others are blue and some are golden. He continued by pointing out each of the fins, moving clockwise from the apex of its back.

'Dorsal, yes?' He checked for a nod from each of us.

'Adipose, caudal – or "tail", as it is commonly called – anal, pelvic and pectoral.'

'Adipose?' The others were familiar names, but I pointed to the small, fleshy, fin-like protrusion on the fish's back, above and just behind the anal fin.

'Adipose, yes,' affirmed Peter. 'All members of the Salmonid family have them – rainbow, brown and sea trout, Atlantic salmon and grayling.'

'Oh, right. And wha—'

'We don't really know what it does,' he said quickly, pre-emptively, almost apologetically, 'but, well, there it is. The adipose fin.' He looked at us both in turn, as if we had somehow caught him out, and perhaps was hoping that one of us might be able to provide an answer to this conundrum – as if to say 'please' rather than 'yes'.

'Right,' was all I could manage, though.

'Cool!' enthused Jackie

When Peter had said '*we* don't really know what it does', I got the impression that he was not simply referring to a gap in his and Tim's knowledge. I assumed that the wider angling, environmental and biological research bodies also had no clue whatever when it came to what the adipose fin actually did. Surely they would not have all been churlish enough to withhold this information just from these two. Indeed, when I next sat in front of my computer, I typed 'adipose fin' into my search engine and got a return of 73,500 entries in an astonishing 0.02 seconds. Astonishing, that is, until you discover that it only takes that length of time for all the relevant sites (about six of them) to do the same thing – give one of those quasi-gallic shrugs that translates roughly as 'I do not know, and I do not care enough to guess.'

It would seem that the adipose fin, like some external piscine appendix, is a bit pointless. At the time, this tickled me like an itch on the inside, and it wasn't until I was out on a 'Golf Course Junior' walk with Charlie a couple of days later that I managed to have a good old scratch. Just as we were passing one of the tees at the very moment that someone was making a 'thwack-ping' kind of a noise with what looked like a driver, I smiled to myself while I asked Charlie just what the *point* of golf was. With something resembling disbelief that I was still asking him stuff like this when I knew very well that if the answer did not involve Gravy Bones then he had no idea whatsoever, he reciprocated my inquisitive glare.

'Hell,' he protested, 'I don't even know what the point of chasing rabbits is – I just do it 'cos it's fun.'

I thought then, as I had done more times than I understood the meaning of, of the adipose fin, and proceeded to spend a good length of the wooded path alongside the fifteenth fairway pondering on just how much research has been carried out on the Salmonid fish in the last couple of hundred years or so. They have been caught by every method known to humankind, from crude nets to the most exquisite of hand-made feather trinkets. They are sometimes 'spooned' post-mortem by anglers to examine the contents of their stomach in order to find out what they have been feeding on. We have given them sumptuous Linnaean names such as *Thymallus thymallus* because the flesh of the grayling tastes so similar to that particular herb that they named it twice. We have concocted many ways of eating them, from raw with sticky rice to mashed up with binders as a sicky paste in sandwiches. We have dissected them and farmed them, stuffed them and framed them. Good lord, we don't even have to call the tail a tail any more because we can call it the caudal fin, but there is still one small, obstinate nobble of these fish that gets the entire angling and scientific communities scratching their heads, pincering their clipboard-full hands skyward and saying, 'We don't know what it does, but, well, there it is.'

After half a mile or so of the bracken-lined footpath which led away from the fifteenth green and into a small copse, I realized that, since becoming a born-again fisherman, I have been subconsciously searching for 'a point' for being one – for some kind of justification for what I am doing. Moral justification for taking an animal's life, financial justification for buying all the gear that I need. Actually, buying all the gear I need does not pose a problem – it's buying all that stuff that I probably don't need that I lose sleep over. Justification in terms of the time it takes to go fishing, and in terms of all the other things, 'pointless' or otherwise, that I could or should be doing instead.

Most of our lives are spent making these decisions and explaining these rationales, either to ourselves or to those around us, and I realized, as Charlie was inevitably outwitted by another bunny, that perhaps we all need our own adipose fin. That we should all be allowed a part of our selves and a proportion of our time to not need any justification, any explanation, or any real 'point'. As I have always suspected, the only 'point' in fishing that truly matters to the fish is the barbed one lurking under whatever it is you are trying to deceive it with. Everything else is merely down to hoarding instinct.

Now, towards the tail end of this book, I am not convinced that I am an awful lot wiser as to my true motivation for going fishing – or anyone else's for playing golf, surfing or indeed partaking in line dancing. However, it's with an enormous sense of relief that I now realize that my not knowing any of this is utterly irrelevant. We – Peter, Tim and probably everyone else in the angling fraternity – may not know exactly *why* we are standing waist-deep in water with a stick, a bit of string and a bent pin in our hands, but, well, there we are.

8 Invicta

Perhaps delicate, seductive wings can even make fish rise through dust and rock in an ancient streambed. Dreams are part of fishing, and daydreams surely are part of fly tying.

Darrel Martin, *The Fly-fisher's Craft*

There must be countless others out there like me. People who are convinced that purchasing that one more piece of gear will make them a better fisherman. Or surfer. Or line dancer. That that rod will reach those fish just yards further out than my current one will; if I buy that leash I'll surf with that much more confidence; I bet those jeans make slapping my thigh so much more/less painful – delete as appropriate according to predilection. As I sat, browsing The Lakeland Fly-tying Company's online catalogue and trying to figure out whether buying a certain type or colour of feather really would make my patterns irresistible, I wondered whether there was some kind of help I could get. For, sure as the pull of any whisky, I was lured. It was never meant to be me that got hooked. And if there were some kind of Shopaholics Anonymous, what would I say when I got there?

*

'It all started harmlessly enough.' I glanced uneasily around the circle of the dozen or so men who were to be my companions for the evening, all sat on stackable orange plastic chairs while I stood, sweating, cold. At my opening gambit, some stared at the floor, while others caught my eye and gave me a knowing smirk and raised eyebrow. It always starts harmlessly enough.

'I just wanted to get myself some gear so I could have a good time. Y'know, forget about the real world for a bit?' I wanted reassurance. This was a less than easy thing to do. Admitting that there was a problem in the first place had taken far longer than it should – confronting it in this way was tougher still. A couple of nods and ironic, assenting grunts and snorts told me that I was free to continue. These guys had all been there. Most of us were probably never going to leave entirely.

'Just a couple of rods, I thought. Won't do any harm. A bargain, too! Reels, line, the whole lot – and all for less than fifty quid.' I didn't quite catch where it came from, but under his breath, one of the guys muttered 'bastard pushers'. The man sitting to my left spoke next, quavering and on the brink of shouting.

'They know bloody well what they're doing. They sell you cheap gear, and 'cos you ain't done it before it's okay for a bit, but then, bastards – they fuckin' know – you need more. And then more ain't enough. Three hundred quid on a fuckin' beach-caster last week . . .' He pinched the bridge of his nose to stem the swelling of tears that had started even before his outburst. I held his shoulder in sympathy as he took a deep breath.

'No, no. Sorry mate. You carry on. Your story.'

'Ta. Well, I guess you guys know the rest, huh? You read the mags, you see the gear and you think that if only you could have that rod, that reel, that lure, that set of waders, that landing net, well, you think you'll be a better fisherman, yeah?'

Shakes of heads – part dry amusement, part wry agreement.

'And how is it that, even though we know that simply isn't true, we still keep on doing it?' Coming to the most thorny confessions of all, I paused, and breathed as if I was about to go underwater.

'A few months ago,' I exhaled, 'someone introduced me to fly fishing.' There were a couple of shocked but supportive gasps. I could sense that some of these men had never sunk this far – that this was too hard core even for them. A few looked round furtively – perhaps they just hadn't waded out of this particular closet just yet. Emboldened by the sense that I was therefore perhaps not alone, I ventured further.

'And since then, I've done it half a dozen times, maybe more. I know the harm it's doing to my credit card, but I just can't stop myself and,' deep breath, 'I've got heavily into fly-tying – furs, feathers, tinsels, wires. Two trays of hooks, all labelled, two cases of threads and flosses, vices, tools – the whole damn lot.' My voice had started to quaver and my palms felt as if they were dripping sweat.

A couple of men burst into tears, a few more folded their arms in either disgust or denial, three ran from the room in terror and one fainted. The group leader called what was left of the room to order, fixed me with a nervous gaze and said,

'What do you want to do about this, Robin?'

'Do about it? What d'you mean "do about it"? I'm going home to roll myself a size 12 Black Pennell – that's what I'm going to do about it!'

Like I've said before, we don't go fishing in order to get all wound up about real life, and when those cares are forgotten in the boot of the car along with our Environment Agency rod licences and a our carefully prepared flasks of tea, currents of fantasy ebb and swirl inside our heads instead. Well, they do in mine, anyway, or is that the Acid and Special Brew habit talking? Without wishing to belittle the stigma, hardship and sheer bloody hard work that drug and alcohol addicts have to endure (some research is harder won than others), I do think it it is interesting that there are so many parallels between addictions. A junkie of any description will pursue his or her favoured substance or passion to the exclusion and indeed to the detriment of their friends and family, they will venture out in the most horrific weather at the most absurd times of the day to feed their cravings, they will lose sight of the financial cost to the point where it becomes irrelevant, and to top it all they will become crashing bores at parties where no one else happens to share their predilection. Now, I wonder how many long-suffering partners of fishermen are smiling and nodding in rueful recognition of these symptoms. We are, in short, hopelessly lost causes, and my descent into the bowels of angling addiction truly reached its apotheosis in that most arcane of crafts – fly-tying.

That an ex-jeweller came to find pleasure and solace in the whipping together of tiny snippets of treasure may be no surprise. However, that someone whose working life has predominantly come to consist of documenting what happens when he is supposedly not working has actually discovered that – to me – most elusive of things, namely a hobby, is remarkable indeed. To write about that hobby, then, surely is a contradiction? True, but then so is the purchase of a golden pheasant skin with which to make fishing lures when all I could bang on about in my introduction to this book was animal welfare, and that didn't stop me.

When I spotted the Invicta in Peter's fly box that day at the lakes, he told me that he was 'glad' that I'd singled it out. He didn't expand at the time – Peter is not, I have since learned, given to an awful lot of expansion. If ever a man spoke in haikus then it is him. Small nuggets of wisdom handed down to polish. I sensed, though, that there was more to the Invicta than was immediately apparent, and this was reinforced over the following few months. Invictas come into their own during the summer, when the sedges begin to emerge, and continue to be useful into the autumn, when they decide that everything begins to look just a bit shabby and die. When I walked out of Smith's in mid May with the latest copy of one of my erotic periodicals, I did what I usually do – find the nearest bench, caress its neatly creased sheaves and pretend to be not the least bit aroused. As usual, there were a couple of mail-order catalogues inside, which I removed carefully for a more private moment later. Sure enough, right there on the left-hand page was a photograph of, oh yes, an Invicta. Odd how the finger you hit with the hammer is the same one that you sliced open with a shard of glass the day before, and equally strange how the new word that you have never heard uttered before suddenly passes everyone's lips and is in every book you scan. This fly, or possibly Peter's somewhat cryptic reaction to it, had somehow lodged in my psyche like a spinner in seaweed, and there it was again, just where the magazine had been ordained to fall open. It got weirder.

When we get really, really bored the boys and I will play the Argos catalogue game. The rules are simple: one person holds the catalogue while someone else shouts out a number between one and three billion (or however many pages the latest edition contains). Then we all laugh/groan/make envious noises about the items on that page. That's about it, really. I did say that it was for when we are really, really bored.

'Gimme a number between 1 and 239, Dyl!'

Dylan looked up from his extraordinarily detailed drawing of a man being killed in nine different ways.

'Huh?'

'Page number.'

'Oh. Hundred and seventy-two.'

'Ta.'

'That's him being stabbed in the foot.'

'Cool.'

If I'd been reading the Argos catalogue, page 172 would, no doubt, detail a whole bunch of Invicta variations. As it was, I wasn't – I was browsing *The Fly-tying Bible* by Peter Gathercole. Page 172? Uh-huh. The Invicta.

As a final kick up the backside from fate's more credible cousin coincidence, a month or so later I found myself in a pub in Kent. Sandwich, to be more precise. I had been asked to give a talk about my first book and to generally piffle on about weeding and writing. I have a morbid fear of being late for pretty much anything, so consequently I have a tendency to turn up anywhere between three hours and three days early for most engagements. Having ascertained the location of the bookshop for whom I was talking, the location of where people were going to be listening, the local cinema, swimming baths, library, council offices, police station and the piece of sculpture that every town seems to have but no one seems to like, I decided to locate the nearest bar. When I visit different pubs around the country, I like to savour the indigenous brew that is served there, and I am happy to report that the The Cow Inn in Sandwich serves as damn fine a pint of Stella as you'll find pretty much anywhere up and down the land. It also insists on playing the local radio station ('all the tunes from yesterday and today you hoped to god you'd never hear again') at a volume that is impossible to justify complaining about but is equally difficult to think over the top of. As I got halfway down my pint and realized, at the tail end of the song, that Huey Lewis never actually does seem to specify exactly what constitutes the power of love, the all-too-enthusiastic DJ informed me that I was engaged in the pleasure of listening to none other than Invicta FM. Bugger me. I leant across to the barmaid.

'Did he say *Invicta* FM?'

'Y'what?'

'The DJ. The Radio. Invicta.'

'Oh, yeah. Thassit. Invicta FM. Huey Lewis, eh!'

'I'm sorry?'

'Huey Lewis. Nice arse.'

'Erm. Yes. Thank you.'

I felt compelled to find out more. It has been a long time since I believed in anything even resembling fate, and instead choose to acknowledge that, on a daily basis, an awful lot of 'things' happen. Most of these things are ordinary and completely unrelated, but sometimes extraordinary and seemingly connected instances occur. Some put this down to the existence of a supernatural being. I put it down to the law of averages. However, what we choose to do with these events, and how we choose to interpret them, can surely lead to extraordinary goings-on. It was mid June, and the sedges would be making an appearance – what's more, I had yet to catch a fish on a fly of my own making. It was time I tied an Invicta.

The Fly-tyers Bible incorporates, along with clear, illustrated instructions, a difficulty grading system. This is denoted next to each pattern by means of a number of small 'hourglass' icons presumably informing the tyer of how many small glass objects he would like to throw at the wall while tying. One hourglass means that all that is required is to stick something shiny or feathery to the hook with some PVA glue, whereas five obviously means that the pattern should only be attempted by those with masochistic tendencies or a first-class honours degree in a craft discipline such as jewellery. The Invicta bears four hourglasses – I figured that, despite the warning that the Invicta is 'a complex pattern and involves tricky procedures', I was well qualified. Besides, the book goes on to say that 'once all the techniques used to tie the Invicta have been mastered, most other patterns can be tackled with confidence'. No problem.

I have another book entitled *Practical Fly Tying*, first published in 1950 and written by a chap named T. R. Henn. In this volume, Mr Henn advocates that the newcomer to fly-tying should begin tying without a vice. No doubt, if he were around today (he probably died of septicaemia after impaling the fleshy pad of his palm an a size 6 streamer hook), he would be hard at work penning a follow-up to *Practical Fly Tying* about camping and suggesting that a mallet was entirely unnecessary when it comes to the erection of a tent. It never had, and never will, cross my mind to make a fly without first wedging the hook into a decent vice, which is exactly what I did with this particular size 12 (Kamasan B170 medium-weight traditional trout, down-eyed, chemically sharpened, 12.5 mm long by 5 mm gape – point to shank).

I selected a rust-brown thread (Uni-Thread size 6/0), which I snapped into my Griffin stainless steel and brass bobbin holder. This bit of kit, consisting of two spring-loaded arms and a central tube through which the thread passes, holds the thread under tension, allowing you to let the spool dangle from the hook while you find materials or throw another hourglass at the wall. The thread is passed through the tube by means of a bobbin threader (a loop of fine wire on a metal rod), and my bobbin holder has a ceramic insert at its tip end to prevent thread breakage.

A prerequisite of all fly patterns is to attach the tying thread to the hook – a process that I'm not even going to attempt to explain. Suffice to say that it is one of those many techniques associated with fly fishing that is far easier done than said and involves the tucking of one bit of thread under another and, the first few times you attempt it, the sticking of the point of your tongue out of the corner of your mouth. Most patterns also require a layer of thread from the eye to a point along the hook shank. The reason for this is that steel hooks tend to be a bit on the slippy side – if they're covered with a slightly more grippy substance such as tying thread there is more chance that they will stay roughly where you want them to be when the rotational force of the thread takes effect when you are tying them on. This point varies according to the pattern, but for the Invicta the thread is wound down to a point opposite the hook barb (the nasty, spiteful little protuberance that helps keep the fish on the hook, or the hook in your trouser leg).

Next, I slipped my golden pheasant skin (found in a fishing tackle shop in West Bay, near Bridport), which I had placed conveniently and slightly uneasily to hand, out of its polythene bag and snipped off a pinch of its sulphur-yellow crest feather and caught it in as a 'tail'. On top of this I added a three inch gold strand of Lagartun varnished French oval tinsel. Not the cheapest at £2.70 for 20 yards, but super-strong for its tiny diameter and, I'm assured, the best there is. I left this to kind of dangle around brightly while I got on with the black art of fly-tying, which is known as 'dubbing'. I haven't even the foggiest idea why this process is so named, as it has nothing whatsoever to do with any branch of sound mixing, but it is quite plausible that 'dubbing' is much easier to say than 'a bit like gluing furry blancmange to a ceiling coated in Vaseline'. This would, however, sum up its achievability much more accurately. Dubbing, in this context, is the technique of applying fur to the tying thread, then wrapping the whole lot around the hook. My initial attempts at this ended up looking much less like the cigar-shaped underbody that it is supposed to and more closely resembled the kind of matted hair usually located around a tramp's dog's backside. The theory is that a small amount of beeswax or similar is applied to the thread and the fur applied along this length by means of subtle twisting, pressing and repeatedly imploring the bloody stuff to please, please sit where it is while sobbing ever so slightly hysterically. For some reason – I suspect because I was actually taking my time for once – the dubbing went onto the Invicta surprisingly well. I had also taken heed of another fragment of advice from an unremembered source: take the amount of fur you think you need, then halve it. The book said to use yellow seal's fur, but to me that is a cruelty too far – I could not maintain a clear conscience using a material when I knew that its source had undergone the unspeakable ignominy of being dyed yellow, so I used a mixture of around two-thirds Wapsi golden tan Antron with the remainder being Hareline hot yellow Ice Dub to add a little extra sparkle.

An important part of many flies is the hackle, a collar of feather fibres wound around part of the hook shank. This is included for a variety of reasons. Some hackles are intended to represent legs or wings, some to assist the flotation of a dry fly – the feathers from around the preening glands of ducks are especially good for this purpose as they are extremely waterproof. However, the Invicta is a wet fly, and as such requires a hackle to fulfil a further purpose – to provide movement or 'life' in the water. Fish sense this movement in large part by using their lateral line. I often wonder whether (as much as our coccyx is the stump of what used to be our tail) we still somehow retain this feature from our piscine ancestors. Where else does that sense of being watched, of there being another physical presence other than ourselves present, come from? In Japanese martial arts it is called *zanshin,* and I like to think we all have it to an extent. Especially when I'm singing 'I am what I am' in the bedroom while wearing Jackie's underwear. The hackle on the Invicta is what is known as 'palmered', which essentially means that it is much more difficult than it probably needs to be. It consists of a whole feather (a brown cock cape hackle, if you must know) that is caught in at the eye end of the hook with the bobbin and thread held in the right hand, then wound down in open turns to the other end of the dubbing with the left. Then, with the other hand, grasp the gold tinsel and wind it towards the hook eye to fasten the hackle . . . er. Oh. Hang on. I've run out of hands. Erm. Let me just put this thing here for a mo— oh bugger, that's come off. Right, if I just grab this and hold . . . er, that can go there a sec and then if that goes over this . . . oh shit, that brown thing's just gone twang. No – there is no easy way to do this, but somehow I managed it by a combination of dexterity, luck and holding my breath for what was obviously longer than I thought. When everything was held fast, I exhaled expansively, blowing all the remaining materials and feathers off the tying bench and onto the floor. As I stooped down to retrieve them I did what I often do in just such circumstances and impaled my forehead on the tying vice. Not hard enough for lasting damage, but with sufficient force to shout 'You bastard' probably a little louder than necessary.

Not to worry – only a couple of stages to go now. To recap, so far I had wound the thread onto the hook, put on a yellow tail, made a synthetic fur underbody over which I had crissed a brown palmered hackle and crossed that with the fine gold tinsel to hold it in place. Next up was the beard – or throat – hackle.

This is made of blue-jay fibres. Now, jays are pretty little birds with their unmistakable electric-blue-barred wings. What is less common knowledge is that they are a member of the magpie family and are therefore thieving little shitbags that deserve to be shot. Luckily, the powers that be agree, and jays are on the list of legal airgun vermin quarry species. It is therefore with some glee that I ripped a few fibres from one of the pair of wings (even I would think it cruel to just take one) I had purchased for this very purpose. I offered these up to the underside of the fly and with a little prodding, poking, fettling and sweating managed to cinch them in place with the thread, making sure I left enough room for the last stage.

The instructions called for a 'hen pheasant centre tail feather'. Now I might be wrong, but I find it unlikely that a conversation between two trout might go anything like the following;

'Oi! Burt – swim over 'ere a mo, will you?'

Swish, glide, a quick beat of the tail and a thoroughly gratuitous twitch of the adipose fin.

'Whassup, mate?'

'See that thing over there what looks a bit like an 'atching sedge?'

'Which one?'

A gestural pectoral.

'Oh, yeah, I gotcha. What about it?'

'Well, is it just me, or do them wings look a bit like a pheasant's tail?'

'Dunno mate – cock or hen?'

I had the odd cock pheasant tail knocking about, and reckoned I could probably get away with it, but somehow it just didn't seem *right*. I had tried to spot some suitable roadkill, but despite the fact that there is an awful lot of dead pheasant next to the road in Hampshah (not so much in 'Aaampsheer, funnily enough), the overwhelming majority of it is male, which leads me to believe that there are a good many hen pheasant out there clucking at the stupidity of their menfolk playing chicken with the traffic. Eventually I relented, and ordered a handful of hen pheasant tail feathers and sure enough, they did look markedly different from the cock variety in a not massively different kind of way. Still, there they were, and there they sat for a while until I'd plucked (no, not intentional and yes, I know, not funny either) up the courage to do what I was about to do. To explain this trepidation, a little anatomy might help. Feathers are made up of a central rib, or rachis, either side of which is a vane. The vanes are made up of miniature versions of the rachis, called barbs. These barbs are held together by, on one side, barbules, and on the other hamuli. The effect is a bit like Velcro, and without it the wind would whistle through the bird's wings like a hurricane through a string vest, the bird would plummet to the ground in a quite amusing fashion and, in the case of pheasants, a huge swathe of our rural economy would go to hell in a handcart. Now, when the feather is in one piece all is well with the fly-tyer's world (if not the pheasant's, admittedly); however, when the barbs become detached from the rachis things begin to get decidedly iffy. When *The Fly-tying Bible* suggested that I take a 'slip' of hen pheasant tail feathers three times the width of the intended wing and 'fold one edge of the slip to its centre, then fold the slip in half' I began to wonder a) what this means, b) why I was doing it, c) wouldn't it be much easier to buy an Invicta from Fishtec for 50p and d) haven't I already got one somewhere among those bulk sets that I got free with one of those rods? 'I have come this far,' I told myself. 'For what? To give up now?' I asked rhetorically.

Two mutilated entire hen pheasant centre tails later I had my answer, all clinched tight – perky and pretty and pointless as a girl band. A couple of coats of cement on its rusty brown head made it shine and blink at me, full of some kind of undeciphered meaning.

A few days later the Invicta was still in the drying vice, and I was pondering a silver variation, or perhaps a green with a white hackle. While I decided, I thought I might try to find out why the Invicta was so called, and what the word actually meant. Typing the word 'Invicta' into a search engine provided around 2,800,000 listings. The majority of the first ten were company names, including double glazing, taxi firms, sports equipment manufacturers and, obviously, Invicta FM. As I scrolled through the list, though, the entries became inevitably more obscure. One fishing-related site told me not a great deal more than *The Fly-tying Bible* – that the fly was invented by a James Ogden in the late nineteenth century, is fished wet and must, under every conceivable circumstance, have a wing of hen pheasant centre tail feather. Then I spotted a site relating to the county of Kent, which has been put together by a man going by the implausible name of Jim Riddell, who is bursting to tell us that:

> The long-serving motto [Invicta] is an allusion to the belief that Kent has kept its boundaries intact since pre-Roman times and that its people had 'reserved to themselves and their posterity their ancient customs and liberties' (Richard Kilburn, 1659).

Up until that point, I hadn't had any concrete idea of what had drawn me to this fly in particular. Maybe it represented some kind of culmination – an answer to what it was about fishing, all fishing, that kept on drawing me, despite its frustrations, its seeming futility, its expense, its drain on every resource I have, its days when all you have to show is some empty space in the tackle box and a bruised ego. For a hobby, this sometimes sure as hell felt like hard work, like some kind of battle.

Then I proceeded to read about why the county of Kent had chosen this as their watchword – 'Invicta', roughly translated, gives us 'undefeated' or 'unconquered'. Maybe I had begun to think a little bit like a fish after all.

9 Old Man

What does fathering mean? Listen to the language we use every day and it will tell you a lot. If we talk of 'mothering' children, we get a picture of caring, nurturing and spending long hours in close, sensitive contact. The word 'fathering' means something quite different. You can father a child in two minutes. At its most extreme, a father is just a sperm donor.

Steve Biddulph, *Manhood*

'I've never spent a night here on my own.'

This was neither a complaint, nor an expression of fear – merely an observation. I had been living with Jackie for a few months and, true enough, I never had managed to wangle the opportunity to get thoroughly hammered while listening to Sonic Youth as loud as I liked and proceed to fart beerily in a bed all to myself so much that not even I could stand the stench. I didn't actually want to – what I'd actually meant to say was, 'I've never spent a night here without you and with my brother-in-law and two kids throwing lager down our throats and having peanut fights.' It was time for a boys' night.

Jackie and I discussed this at some length (a conversation that consisted of her saying, 'Sounds good, I'll call Sue') and a few

Fridays later Jon, Gabe, Dyl and myself were alone, in the sitting room, with no girls to tell us how much beer we had drunk/ should not have drunk and how many bones/items of furniture we might break if we carried on wrestling like that. Now, there are a few vital skills that I think should be passed on to the next generation of boys. Firstly, there is wrestling. The author of the quote at the head of this chapter makes a compelling argument for this in his book *Manhood*. Boys, on the whole, tend to be more physically aggressive than girls – the trouble is that many lads are not taught what is and what is not acceptable in this department. 'Not knowing your own strength' is as much of a failing as not knowing your own weaknesses. Boys who are taught how to fight without hurting and without malice, but who are brought up to know that, within strictly controlled boundaries, it is OK to test himself and an adversary to prearranged limits will, it is my belief, grow to become men who have no desire or need to prove themselves. Furthermore, having perhaps had some controlled experience of what it is like to hurt another and to be hurt themselves, these men will have much more respect for their physical capabilities as well as those of others. Having said that, my own dad was so arthritic that he couldn't wrestle his way out of his chair, which probably explains why I'm so screwed up. Much easier to blame him; it's not as if he can answer back.

The second life skill that I feel I should pass on to my off-spring is that of drinking. Once again, in this department, my own parents didn't have a clue. I remember one Christmas when my dad took me to a party somewhere near Bromsgrove (where I was born). I would have been around eight years old, and on the way my old man dropped into an off-licence to get whatever he deemed appropriate to ingratiate himself. Considering the fact that he had not drunk since he was in his late teens, this was a

little like a parish priest shopping speculatively for a visit to an
S & M swingers party. He re-emerged from the dimly lit cavern
with, probably, a bottle of Liebfraumilch and a four-pack of
Skol. Oh, and something to keep the lad happy – in this instance
four bottles of Babycham. Initially I was delighted, as my dear
old daddy had bought me some bottles with pictures of Bambi on
them, but as the evening wore on I became happier and happier,
but had not the foggiest idea why absolutely everyone was my best
friend and why I was utterly convinced that I could dance.

My mother compounded this ignorance by being convinced
that the way to defuse and control my preternatural curiosity
about alcohol was to be permissive. In essence, I would, in part,
now agree with her, and certainly agreed with her when, at the
age of twelve, she bought me a home-brew kit sufficient to make
forty pints of bitter of indeterminate strength just in time for
Christmas. I think she thought that this might lead me down the
'kill or cure' way of thinking in terms of my fixation with booze.
That Christmas Eve, just after my best mate Paul had really very
narrowly avoided being sick in my dad's car on his way home (but
not, as it happened, in any sense avoided being sick over his mum
Eileen's hall carpet just after she had opened the front door) my
fixation with booze had, if anything, been intensified. I just had
to carry out more research into how one substance can make you
wish so vehemently for death and can taste so very different on
the way back up.

Mum had the best of intentions, I'm sure, but I can't remember the last time she opened a bottle of wine and drank it before
it became unfit even for cooking. Not unless I'm at her place, at
least – then it won't last until the morning, but that's because
she never buys me beer. Can't imagine why. Since my early
teens, then, I have had the devil in me when it comes to booze. I

hesitate to define myself as an 'alcoholic', as I think that this is a relative term, but I am writing this at 10.30 in the morning and am seriously considering nipping over the road to the offie . . .

I see this same gremlin in Gabriel, who has already expressed curious interest in the spirit selection. Okay, he downed a tumbler full of varying quantities of absinthe, brandy and amontillado recently and proceeded to spend the following few hours thinking he was hilarious. Actually, there isn't much funnier in this world than a thirteen-year-old boy staggering towards you, wrapping his arms around your waist in half affection, half support, telling you he loves you and then saying,

'To be brutally honesht with ya, dad, I'm toadally pished.'

The fact that he was pissed wasn't that funny, but the fact that he thought I wasn't aware of the fact was side-splitting. I therefore think that it is my duty as a dad to try to tread a line between permission and restriction. Quite how I think I'm going to do this when I keep veering off that line myself is a mystery, but I feel that complete prohibition is as much of a mistake as allowing the boys to drink as much as they want, whenever they want and wherever they want.

Therefore, that Friday night, the boys and I wrestled until we got carpet burns on our foreheads and sweated in most other places. Jon sat and watched as any sensible man in his mid fifties who had seen his brother-in-law laid up in bed for ten days due to this very activity might. Instead he gave the boys, as he has given me for the last quarter of a century, an object lesson in drinking beer. My parents may not have known about booze, or boozing, but from that vulnerable age of thirteen Jon has guided me through more (and paid for the vast majority of) tins of Stella Artois than I would ever dare count. The evening ended with all of us having drunk an appropriate amount of beer – from half a glass to half a barrel depending on age and experience, bearing a good amount of scrapes and bruises, and with all of us looking forward to the following day, and with me especially relishing the prospect of being able to pass on some of the finer points of skill number three that I think my boys can't live without. We had already, with the allotment, done a wee bit of gathering. It was time, in my own quite literally inimitable way, to show them how to hunt. With some sticks, string and bent pins.

We had already been fishing together before, but with not a great deal of success. In fact, had we been dependent on our 'hunts' for any kind of sustenance, as was our atavistic imperative, we would, by now, have deselected ourselves. Thank Darwin for Sainsbury's. If ever I needed to demonstrate to the boys the philosophy that it is the taking part that counts, then my fishing forays with them thus far were as succinct and eloquent a lesson as they were likely to get. However, Jon and I felt that it was time to introduce them to the slightly less subtle and more tangible arts of actually catching prey and, if we were lucky enough to land one large enough, clocking it sharply over the head and cooking it.

Having stood in an unfeasibly long queue in the local post office in order to purchase rod licences for Jon and Gabe (Dyl, being under twelve, did not require one and I was in possession of a full year's fish-taunting ticket), we made our way to Compton Lock, a truly idyllic spot on the Itchen Navigation complete with whispering willows and a pool fed by a weir over which water bound for old age and Southampton Water cascades and gurgles. This river begins – or continues, depending on which way you look at it – its endless cycle as a mere trickling youth near Cheriton. Between this callowness and dotage lies every river's stage of maturity, and as I helped the boys with their fiddly knots and inevitable hook-pricked finger tips, I checked myself and made sure that I knew exactly where along this particular river-bank I stood – it can become frighteningly easy to lose yourself while fishing sometimes. Childhoods can be both regained and prematurely discovered all in the space of an afternoon.

As I rigged up rods for everyone, Jon wandered up and down the bank, cursing that he had not brought his painting kit with him. A sculptor of some talent and repute for as long as I have known him and for some years prior to that, he has recently turned his beautifully co-ordinated eyes and hands towards water-based paint and away from his previously preferred tools, namely a bloody great chainsaw and a good selection of dangerously blunt chisels. An understandable move – he is much nearer to the sea than I am, and the nearer you get to the brine the more painfully aware you become of your own mortality.

Everyone was ready to fish. Except me. I had set Gabe and Dyl up with a size 8 hook on the end of their line, baited with a small section of worm. I hate using live bait, especially when it is live bait that is so good for the soil, but this method is virtually guaranteed to catch on water like this, and I wanted the boys to feel that tug, that twitch and that take. In addition to this, I added a small sphere of split lead shot – just enough to pull the bait under the water, but not so much that the fishing became literally leaden. This simplest of tackle was connected to their telescopic rods, purchased for them by their grandma a year or so before, and I'd rigged up a similar set-up for Jon as he'd pranced around the river-bank reciting poetry, picking flowers and wittering on about how glorious the light was. I lent him the eight-foot spinning rod that I had bought before going to Scotland what seemed like years ago. Possibly because it was. As I removed it from its cloth bag, I momentarily cursed, as I thought I had brought the wrong one.

In inverse proportion to those monuments that become less monumental when viewed through adult eyes, this rod had grown relatively thicker, chunkier, sturdier in the intervening time between last using it and that day on the river-bank as I eyed up my three-ounce fly rod. Once everyone was comfortably ensconced in their worm-drowning activities, I set about assembling its three sections. There is a good deal of pleasure to be had in this – unzipping the stout, protective tube, sliding out the flocked cloth bag and releasing the bows allowing it to unfurl always brings a half-mouthed smile of anticipation. Dare I say it is something akin to the anticipation of undressing a woman? No, thought not.

'Dad! Dad! Dad!'

This was what I was there for that day. Not the weather, not the pleasure of my own fishing and not even the company of the most trusted, loyal and long-standing friend I have. I was there primarily to demonstrate first-hand to my boys just why I have nearly crashed the car at least four times because I am too intent staring at a nearby body of potentially fish-holding water. It might, I thought, also benefit our relationship if they understood why my porn collection was so large. It was Dyl who'd been calling me.

'You got one, mate?'

'Yeah, I think so.'

I stepped over to him. The tip of his rod was bent moderately, but quivering with the unmistakable motion caused by a fish. I encouraged him to reel in – this was not by any means a large beast, and needed to be unhooked and released as soon as possible. Dylan lifted the tip of his rod as instructed and reeled the shimmering flash to my waiting and wetted hand. Approximately eight inches long, still thrashing and perfectly pretty, I held a gorgeous little wild brown trout while I eased the hook from its mouth. I called everyone over to look at its foil-bright skin and remarkable red and black spots while I cradled it gently, allowing it to recover. When I felt its flanks begin to once more pulse with life, I let it swim away. Perhaps a little further downstream, wary. Maybe even a little wiser. At that moment I realized that I was not engaged in something primal after all – what I was trying to instil in these small men was the notion of civilization. In a way that was so similar to wrestling with each other or battling with an addiction, this was nothing more than confronting nature and allowing it to win. The weekend, it turned out, was essentially about learning some respect. For all of us.

I baited up again for Dyl, and very nearly managed to strip some line off my reel in preparation for my first cast of a fly onto a river, when Gabe – thirteen and smiles only when paid to – began to forget himself and got all excited. He brought his own fish to hand, which I helped him unhook. I remember thirteen being a tough age – you have just left that steep, brookish stage of child-hood where everything is new, bright and simple and entered a strange kind of water – deep, boilish and treacherous. You can see the calmer, broader flows of adulthood, but sometimes feel as if you will never gain sufficient strength to swim to them. What's more, the main male role model in your life, to whom for years you looked up to as faultless and demi-god-like has, almost overnight, turned into a tedious old tosser with cringeworthy dress sense. As a parent, similarly seismic changes are happening to your offspring. That angelic, white-blonde-haired boy who kept everybody in his thrall simply by being alive has just as instan-taneously transformed into a gobby little smartarse whose sole means of communication seems to be txt msgs. Written or spoken. That apart, Gabe and I seem to get on pretty well, and never more so than when we are in situations that do not demand our normal masks to be worn. Fishing is one of the greatest of levellers and, after I had released his fish, I patted his still slight shoulders and said 'Alright, mate?' upon which he tried, and failed, to hide his pleasure by nodding and smiling.

'I think I get why you're such a bloody great geek now, Dad.'

I smiled and winked a pricking eye as he cast out again.

The afternoon continued in a similar vein. Jon caught trout, and Dyl and Gabe got on like brothers as they formulated their own good-natured fish-catching competition. Eventually, they lost count and called it a draw. I'd like to say that Gabe was magnanimous enough to tell Dyl that he'd won, but Dyl is not keen on being patronized and not even I am about to start claiming that fishing makes anyone – especially not a thirteen-year-old – feel that selfless.

Me? Oh, got a line wet, eventually. Did I use my Invicta? Not likely – it's still in the drying vice, which is probably where it's going to stay.

On the way back to the car, Jon asked me, with his knowing eyebrow raised, whether I preferred to fish alone or in company. I think he had rightly detected a little frustration on my behalf during the afternoon. When I see water now, I just want to fish. I paused as I watched the river run past our feet and wondered, not for the first time, whether any of the molecules I could see had ever touched me. Whether one had glanced off me as rain, had ever crashed over my head as I ducked under another wave, caught me as spray from the bow of a planing boat or been thrown kindly and playfully over me by my sister on a burning childhood holiday. The chance is infinitesimal, but there is still a chance that it may have happened. After all, none are created or destroyed. Merely transformed. It is this same reasoning, this optimism, that keeps us all fishing – it's just that the odds are slightly shorter. Having said this, I have had days when it has seemed far more likely that I've been touched by the same drop of water twice than that I will ever catch a fish.

'To be honest, I really don't know. It depends, I guess.'

'On what?'

'I s'pose it depends on what my intentions are when I set off.'

'How d'you mean?'

'Well, depends on whether I'm going fishing, or if I fancy doing a bit of fathering. Not sure if it's possible to do both at the same time.'

10 Caudality

And all I ask is a merry yarn from a laughing fellow-rover
And quiet sleep and a sweet dream when the long trick's over.

John Masefield, *Sea-Fever*

Like the graceful surprise of a pair of seagulls maintaining constant velocity and distance over the reticulated grey of a rough inshore chop, it is often those experiences of which least is expected that are the most enjoyable. When I visited the 'secret' lakes for a day's fly fishing, what I was anticipating to be an interesting and informative exercise in thoroughness transformed into something of a Road to Damascus experience. An epiphany of sorts. However averse I may be to the religious overtones of such expressions, it is difficult to find any secular alternatives that say quite the same thing, with quite the same impact. It wasn't just my prejudices towards fresh water that were challenged that day – I was also forced to think about my attitudes not only towards how I went fishing, but also to those who stood on the the bank or beach next to me.

There are many aspects of fly fishing that seemed to immediately make perfect sense and, in a clichéd kind of way, provide me with something I did not even know I had been looking for.

Something that, when I found it, felt as if I had 'not been look-ing for' for quite some time. Naturally, the equipment was a big draw for me – gear that really did seem necessary as opposed to that which was collected merely for collecting's sake. And all those (often wearable) methods of storage . . .

Then there was the fineness – the finesse – of that equipment. Its seeming 'no more than you need, no less than you want' design ethos; the apparent joy of the manufacturer making a reel (the least important bit, remember) so achingly beautiful and equally painfully expensive *simply because they can* is testament to the level of care demonstrated by both manufacturer and consumer. So far, I had acquired – for far less money than might be expected – three fly rods (and could easily justify at least two more), a couple of reels, somewhere around three hundred flies, enough fly-tying tools and materials to have a set for tying at home and one for taking with me whenever I go away, waders, wading boots, vari-ous storage devices and, yes, obviously, a waistcoat with nineteen pockets. The exclusively fly-fishing selection of erotic literature on my side of the bed is approaching twenty inches tall, and I am now on first-name terms with at least three members of staff of my chosen mail-order tackle company.

However – and it would be a big 'but' had my old English teacher not drummed it into me so hard that I should never start a sentence with 'but' – much as I had begun to enjoy my fly fish-ing, having returned to Hampshire's Best-kept Secret and some other still-water locations – it still felt as if there was something 'missing' from fly fishing. I loved its subtlety and refinement, had been amazed at how you could almost feel the teeth of the trout that had fallen for your lure, and had marvelled at the way in which they had fought – at how I had been forced, through the fragility of my gear, to allow them to fight, but a few things snagged at me like a snippet of fishbone stuck between two teeth. Firstly, fishery fishing just seemed a bit, well, contrived to me – there is an expression involving shotguns, fish and barrels when it comes to how easy something is, and I didn't ever get the sense that catching 'stockies' fundamentally involved an awful lot more than one of those fairground games involving plastic ducks and sticks with hooks on. Fun, certainly, but hardly hunter-gatherer time.

Secondly, all stocked fisheries operate a policy of limiting the quantity of fish taken in one visit. In principle, I can see the logic in this – if not necessarily from an environmental or moral stand-point then certainly from a business one. A roughly handled fish or one that has been made to fight a little too long or hard will, if returned, either die or become diseased, with obvious conse-quences for the remaining inhabitants. In practice, though, this is an unmitigated pain in the arse – when you have bagged your limit, you have to go home. I guess I just don't like being told when to stop fishing: how enjoyable a day on the water has been can be fairly accurately quantified by counting how many times 'one last cast – you never know' silently and shapelessly passes your lips, and my day's fishing is not remembered in quite the same way when someone metaphorically taps me on the shoulder and, loudly and pointedly, says, 'Well, you know now, so you can bugger off.' Part of the fun of coming home late from fishing (or surfing, or perhaps even line dancing) is in not knowing whether you are going to be in trouble for doing so.

Thirdly, and bluntly, fly fishing is expensive. It's true that, in terms of the *necessary* gear, fly fishing need not be any more costly than any other branch of the sport. However, there are two further stumbling blocks here. Firstly, when you go fly fishing you generally have to pay to do so – the only additional expense when you lob a spinner in the sea is your pint and pasty at the end of the day. Secondly, I have discovered to my literal cost that there are so many more *unnecessary* things that you need for fly fishing than for any other branch of the sport. A waistcoat with nineteen pockets? Of course! Something called a 'zinger', which attaches your quite indispensable de-barbing tool to your nineteen-pocketed waistcoat via a retractable lanyard that makes a 'zing' kind of noise when it retrieves your tool? You mean you haven't already got one? It is my true belief that the list is – potentially and literally – endless. There is the possibility for some river fishing in various parts of the country (at the time of writing, Devon, South Wales and the Borders region) that, by virtue of government schemes and the goodwill of an awful lot of farmers, can be had for not much more than the price of a pint and a pasty, and the larger reservoirs (Bewl, Rutland, Kielder Water, etc.) can be accessed quite inexpensively. Firstly, though, if all you've got in your pocket is twelve quid, you're going to be really hungry after a day's river fishing; secondly, reservoirs are unnatural and dams just give me the big heebie-jeebies; and thirdly, well. Erm, thirdly . . . Aaah-hem, I mean, well, thirdly, erm . . .

It's just not the sea, is it? I mean, yes, true, most fly-fishing locations are idyllic little spots in which it would be nothing short of churlish to do anything but have a blissful and contemplative day. But I still needed a salt fix. I still craved to flare my nostrils into a stiff sea breeze and feel the ozone pervade the emptying spaces of my head. I still yearned for the relentless suck and surge of hundreds of tons of aerated brine on the clackety-smooth and rolling pebbles. I craved the sea, but my recent outings to the shore had been quite a lot less than productive. True, it is not strictly *necessary* to catch anything during a fishing session, but after a while not doing so does get exceedingly tedious and a sniff embarrassing. That day on the river with the boys might just have salvaged any last scrap of interest they may have had in fishing that had been almost completely stripped by a series of fruitless sea-fishing ventures previously. We had been to Warsash and Hamble-le-Rice – two local terribly-terribly super little marinas on the Hamble river, most definitely in Hampshah – half a dozen times or so. A couple of times with the boys, and once with a neighbour and his two boys just to increase the odds, but all we'd managed was a couple of ballan wrasse so small that putting them back was absolutely imperative – firstly because they were massively undersized and secondly because to have admitted to have caught anything that small was more ignominy than we could bear.

We also went beach fishing three or four times on various stretches of Chesil Beach in Dorset. From what I had read, to fish there and blank was regarded as virtually impossible. I must, then, contact the *Guinness Book of Records* forthwith, as out of these visits the boys and I managed to procure just one decidedly diminutive mackerel and a bird's nest of line wrapped around a breakaway lead belonging to someone else that had evidently not performed its eponymous task.

I toyed with the idea of coarse fishing, but my view of it had not really changed, and all it represented to me was the 'sport' end of angling – when you go sea or game fishing, you can reasonably expect to catch something that you can eat (as far as I could remember, anyway). From what I could see, when you catch something when you go coarse fishing, you are confronted with something either hideously ugly, viciously dangerous or wholly inedible. Or all three. A leaf through Hugh's *River Cottage Cookbook* told me that pike make extremely good eating, but doesn't mention anything about the fact that they have a similar opinion of us and have teeth sharp enough and plentiful enough to give all sane men the collywobbles. *New Fish Cookery* by Marika Hanbury-Tenison mentioned that perch and roach are perfectly edible. She goes on to say, however, that they 'do tend to have a slightly muddy flavour', 'are a bit on the bony side' and that you should 'remove the sharp spines along the back as soon as you start to work on the fish'. Considering their generally small size, all this fuss didn't really seem to warrant a) all that work and b) killing something in the first place. Nothing I could find persuaded me that coarse fishing was worth the bother.

I then remembered the success I'd had with boat fishing. Maybe I could call someone loc— er, glob. I could borrow a rod again and . . . ah, blug. Nope – even thinking about going out any distance on a boat again had my stomach contracting and the beginnings of retchings working their way up. I desperately wanted to carry on fishing, but was yet to discover which of its myriad branches was going to have me hook, line and, well, you know what I mean. It looked like I was going to have to persevere either with still-water fly fishing, which I was heartliy enjoying in a fishing-as-business-transaction, like-one-of-those-fairground-games-with-ducks, sticks, hooks-and-eyes kind of way, river fishing, which had proved itself to be terrific fun as long as you did not mind the weight of lost tackle during a session being greater than what you caught, or sea fishing from dry land, from which I continued to derive a good deal of pleasure simply because it meant I was at the edge of a continent even if what lay beyond it patently did not contain any fish.

I was reading through an old copy of *TotalSaltWaterfishingAngler-TotalFISHseA*. I think I was looking for an article on How Best to Kill Your Dogfish when my eye was drawn to an item entitled

'Learning to Fly' on the contents page. The blurb under this banner assured me that a chap called John Findlay would be spending a couple of pages 'exploring the ins and outs of tackle choice if you want to take up saltwater fly fishing'.

I can only assume that the reason this feature had escaped me until then was because, prior to that day, I had never picked up that particular magazine with any interest in any kind of fly fishing, let alone saltwater. I hurriedly flapped my way to the relevant page to find Mr Findlay doing pretty much what the contents page had promised. The text (whatever it said) was accompanied by a large photograph of him in a tackle shop and handing over what was presumably expense-account plastic for all the rods, reels, spools and lines specifically necessary to fly fish in salt water. It was all I could do to stop myself from getting onto the Internet and kitting myself up in a likewise fashion. However, I resisted for as long as it took to ascertain the best deals, which items would be best suited to my needs and which rods and reels would just look groovy sat next to each other. Eventually, I was in posession of a Grey's four-piece 8/9-weight rod, a Vision saltwater-proof reel complete with spare spool, onto which I lasciviously wound one floating and one fast-sinking cold saltwater line and tipped these with a pair of fairly chunky tapered leaders. The fly-tying bench gained some unusual additions such as a selection of bucktails, some heavier-gauge tying threads, synthetic 'flash' fibres and 'dumb-bell' eyes – all requisites for the Deceivers, Clouser minnows and Whistlers used around the coast. I set to work and tied myself a selection of each, along with the odd shrimp or two and a couple of home-grown designs that at times had me thinking like a fish until late in the evening.

The addition of a second-hand kayak and its associated propulsion and anchorage devices allowed me access to hundreds of places around the coast inaccessible any other way, and completed what, to me, has the potential to be the perfect way to fish – the delicacy of fly fishing, the ruggedness of the coastline, the isolation of boat fishing and the chance to catch any species available from the beach.

I juggled the names of a couple of locations in which to try out my new toys, my new weapons – the immediately accessible south coast tempted me with convenience, but still seemed a little too benign. At the other extreme, the open ocean seemed to be asking for trouble – gone were the days when I was untroubled by whirling currents and boiling, sucking swells. An estuary, with all its ambiguousness and sense of transition, of transformation, seemed perfect – halfway between river and ocean felt about right. Since childhood, it has become a habit for me to venture west – I have been to the east coast but once in my life, and could not quite understand what felt so very wrong about the sun setting behind me as I watched the sea shimmy. The further west I go, the easier life seems to get; I'll be on the Helford dreckly, I told myself as I headed for Cornwall – and for the lonely sea and sky – once more.

Acknowledgements

The following people are all, to one extent or another, for good or for ill, at least partly responsible for the existence and content of this book. In some instances it would not have happened at all were it not for my desire not to speak to them and to write instead. In the order in which they spring to mind when I think about gutting a fish, they are:

Gabriel and Dylan Shelton. Frankly, I would disown both of them did they not display a perfectly healthy desire to poke fish innards about. Jonathan Mulvaney – time was when this beast of a man would have eviscerated a decent sized fish with a chainsaw. He'd probably paint some namby pamby picture of it now. He rides a girl's motorbike too. Jacqueline Mulvaney, with whom I found out at an early age that it is in fact extremely difficult to remove the eyes from a dead mackerel. Elizabeth Shelton – I don't actually remember my mother gutting a fish, but she's my mum so I kind of feel she should come before Stevie and Lizzie Newcombe, neither of whom I associate with disembowelling haddock, but at least they both know the difference between a bass and a mackerel when it's served to them. Not many people would be as ambivalent about having their bathroom transformed into a film set somewhere halfway between *Psycho* and *Re-animator*. Nice one, Jax. Jeremy and Simon – the London boys – nothing to do with fish guts, but bloody nice blokes anyway and both of them would almost certainly not be able to draw a fish without their tongue poking from the corner of their mouth. Mark Stephens. Mark *bloody* Stephens. Geeza. Never seen him gut a fish but I have

Acknowledgements

seen him hit Jeremy's knee with a machete so I'm not going to mess with him.

I reckon that Ingrid Connell, my trusted editor, could – and would if she had to – deal with fish guts. She's an all-round good egg – and besides, I don't like arguing with her at the best of times. I'm sure she'd be just as incisive with a blade as with her pen.

I like to think that I have reasonable powers of description. However, there are simply no words to describe what contortions Mary Pachnos' – my agent's – face would screw itself into if asked to gut a fish. I don't think the countryside thing is really her bag. I asked her to come down to Twyford on a social once and she went a bit faint and unnecessary. Still, she – along with Ingrid and the London boys – gives me an excuse once in a while to visit the smoke in order that I can appreciate just how peaceful and unsmelly my life is.

There are many people that I've met during the course of writing this book who are deserving of mention. However, I've rarely learned their names so those in the text are often whatever seemed to fit. Those who deserve my thanks know who they are, as do those very few that don't deserve a mention. Some secrets are best kept that way for one reason or another. However, I would like to extend a special thanks to Brian Perks of Whithorn, Scotland. Not only for the priest, but also for reminding me of what a good hardware shop looks – and smells – like.

Robin Shelton
Twyford, September 2007